Orchids
& How
to Grow
Them

PRENTICE HALL PRESS

New York   London   Toronto   Sydney   Tokyo

GLORIA JEAN SESSLER

To my husband, with love

Published by Prentice Hall Press
A Division of Simon & Schuster, Inc.
Gulf + Western Building
One Gulf + Western Plaza
New York, NY 10023

Originally published by Prentice-Hall, Inc.

PRENTICE HALL PRESS is a trademark of Simon & Schuster, Inc.

Library of Congress Cataloging-in-Publication Data

SESSLER, GLORIA JEAN.

   Orchids & how to grow them.
   1. Orchid culture. 2. Orchids I. Title
SB409.S46   635.9′34′15   78-9684
ISBN 0-13-639617-8

Manufactured in the United States of America

10 9 8 7

GLORIA JEAN SESSLER is a long-time orchid grower with her own private greenhouse. She has contributed numerous articles on orchids to publications in this country and abroad.

HOME GARDENING HANDBOOKS
GENERAL EDITOR: Edwin F. Steffek • Editor Emeritus, *Horticulture*

CONTENTS

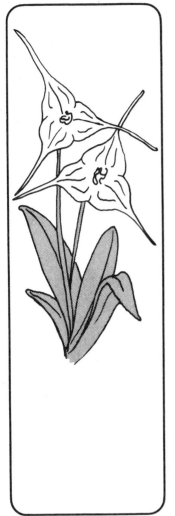

Care at Different Stages & Times 117

Increasing Your Collection 139

Growing under Special Conditions 153

Coping with Insects, Diseases, & Other Problems 187

Warm-Climate Orchids 217

Cool-Climate Orchids 257

FOREWORD

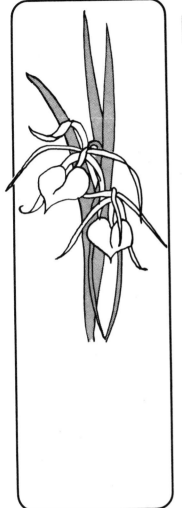

Orchids anticipated the green plant revolution of the 1970s by nearly two centuries. First appearing in European conservatories some time after 1800, orchids gained a real foothold in North America with the establishment of the first commercial orchid firm in 1895 in New Jersey. Today, orchid culture in the United States is probably the most highly developed aspect of modern amateur floriculture. Thousands of people, from preteenagers to retirees, grow anywhere from one to thousands of plants on windowsills, under fluorescent lights in the basement, or in large greenhouses. The orchid, once called the flower of kings in nineteenth-century England, is now truly a flower for everyone.

A body of literature surrounding this exotic family of plants has gradually developed. Books on culture have, unfortunately, been fewer in number than scientific works. Gloria Jean Sessler, whose excellent articles appeared for many years in the international orchid publication the *American Orchid Society Bulletin,* has created a well-researched book on orchid culture for both the novice grower and the person who has many years of experience behind him.

Major chapters discuss the five basic factors of successful orchid growing—light, air, water, temperature, and potting. Additional chapters explore cool-intermediate-, and warm-growing orchids, applying natural principles to indoor cultivation. Orchid pests and diseases are fully explained, while a brief history of orchid culture, plus notes on exhibition, orchid personalities of the past and present, and a most helpful and unique "Calendar of Seasonal Activities" provide excellent reference material. Numerous black-and-white and color illustrations enhance the text.

Interest in orchid culture shows no sign of waning. In fact, An Orchid in Every Home may one day be a new motto. Until then, readers will find the problems and pleasures of orchid culture set forth in a clear and comprehensive fashion in this appealing book.

RICHARD PETERSON
Editor, *American Orchid Society Bulletin*

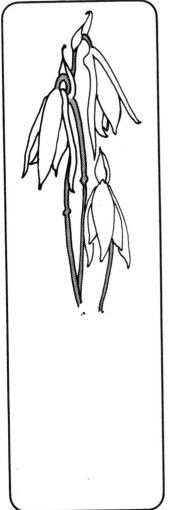

ACKNOWLEDGMENTS

John Donne once observed that "no man is an island," and nowhere is this observation more true than when embarking upon the task of writing a book. No writer has ever been blessed with kinder or more understanding friends than I have been. To each my heartfelt thanks.

Without the devoted assistance of my husband, who put up with an enormous amount of inconvenience while I was writing and who read every page, offering invaluable suggestions all along the way, this book could never have been written.

The idea for the book was suggested by an eminent horticultural editor, Edwin F. Steffek, for whose proofreading of the final manuscript I am deeply indebted.

ACKNOWLEDGMENTS

To the kindest and most understanding of editors, Marjorie Streeter, go my very warmest thanks not only for her skilled editing but for her never failing encouragement. Her line drawings have done much to enhance the chapters.

My great appreciation also goes to Raymond A. Perry, from whom we bought our first orchid many years ago and who has shared with us through the years the knowledge he has acquired through half a century as a commercial orchid grower.

I also wish to express my gratitude to the following:

To Gordon W. Dillon, the first executive director of the American Orchid Society, who has been an inspiration and who has broadened my interests in all facets and phases of orchid growing as no one else has ever done.

To Richard Peterson, Executive Director of the American Orchid Society and the editor of the *American Orchid Society Bulletin*, for his many kindnesses, not the least of which was spending so many hours with me in the selection of pictures from the society's files.

To Marguerite M. McDonald and Charlotte K. Hodsdon, who with great graciousness have always been willing to render assistance.

To Ralph Collins, an outstanding photographer whose detailed pictures of orchid culture have proved so helpful.

To Helena Baraya de Ospina, who graciously loaned the picture of Colombia's Joaquin Uribe Botanical Garden.

To Grayce Carney Gavin, who understood so well the difficulties in producing a book and who was always there to offer support, encouragement, and understanding.

To Mary W. Fidler, who took time out of a busy law practice when the deadline for the manuscript's completion drew near to spend many hours deciphering my handwriting and typing up several of the chapters.

To Elizabeth Steffek, who with unfailing good humor and perseverance typed the entire manuscript and without whose long hours of dedication it would have been impossible to complete the book.

Finally, to the commercial growers whose assistance, encouragement, and kindness in loaning pictures is so deeply appreciated: Raymond Burr and Michael Kirch of Sea God Nurseries; Gay Bonello of S&G Exotic Plant Co.; Frank E. Shride of The Beall Co.; Harold Larsen of Black River Orchids, Inc.; Ernest Hetherington of Fred A. Stewart Orchids, Inc.; Daniel F. McNamara of The Quiedan Co.; Syd A. Monkhouse

ACKNOWLEDGMENTS of Adelaide Orchids; Carlota M. Off of Brighton Farms; Wallace R. Wirths of Westinghouse Corp.; Claire Blake and Howard Cross of Lord and Burnham; Homasassa Springs Orchids; Gary C. Gallup of G&S Laboratories; Irving R. Versoy of Faire Harbour Boats; Chuck Herron and Ernest Lee of the U.S. Department of Agriculture, Animal and Plant Health Inspection Service; Leo Halquin of Armacost and Royston of Santa Barbara, Inc.; Robert R. Johnson of Rod McLellan Co.; G. Thomas of Automatic Sunblind Installations; Robert M. Scully, Jr., of Jones and Scully, Inc.; P. F. Vacherot of Vacherot and Lecoufle; J. P. Bourgin and François Muller of the Laboratoire de Biologie Cellulaire of the Ministere de L'Agriculture; Standard Engineering; Shaffer's Tropical Gardens, Inc.; and to all who gave of their time and effort and who only because of the limitations of space cannot be mentioned, many, many grateful thanks.

Line drawings at chapter openings are of the following orchids:

Contents: *Masdevallia amabilis.* Foreword: *Brassavola nodosa.*
Acknowledgments: *Lycaste gigantea.* Chapter 1: *Cattleya* Emma
Lou Stokes. Chapter 2: *Dendrochilum filiforme.*
Chapter 3: *Rhynchovanda* Wong Yoke Sim.
Chapter 4: *Renanthopsis* Yee Peng. Chapter 5: *Masdevallia
coccinea* 'Chester Hills.' Chapter 6: *Lycaste aromatica.*
Chapter 7: *Epidendrum atropurpureum* var. *album* 'Henrique.'
Chapter 8: *Anguloa cliftonii.* Chapter 9: *Eria fragrans.*
Chapter 10: *Calopogon pulchellus.* Chapter 11: *Paphiopedilum
philippinense.* Chapter 12: *Dendrobium* Circe 'Gail.'
Chapter 13: *Paphiopedilum* Transvaal 'Malvern.'
Chapter 14: *Cycnoches loddigesii.* Chapter 15: *Phalaenopsis*
Elisa 'Chang Lou.' Chapter 16: *Aeranthes grandiflorus.*
Appendix: *Miltonia flavescens.* Index: *Trichoceros parviflorus.*

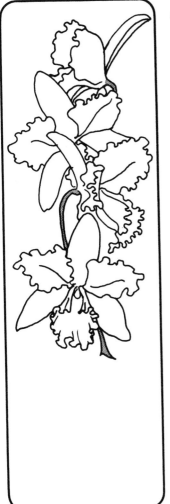

The Wonderful World of Orchids

CHAPTER 1

Welcome to the wonderful world of orchids, to one of the largest families of flowering plants in the world, comprising about 30,000 species and an untold number of hybrids of some 700 different genera.

If someone were to tell you that one family of plants could bear flowers resembling swans, moths, butterflies, nuns, pansies, scorpions, tigers, doves, dancing ladies, and lady's slippers and that they come in every conceivable color and combination of colors, some with stripes, others with polka dots and blotches, and whose flowers range in size from the smallest true miniature (*Pachyphyllum schultesii*), with flowers less than $\frac{1}{16}$ inch in diameter, to the *Sobralia macrantha*, with flowers 10 inches across, and

Figure 1-1. Cattleya orchids growing on a tree in a South American jungle.

flowers that vary from just one on a stem to hundreds on a single spray, you might find it difficult to believe. Yet this is what is meant when we speak of the wonderful world of orchids.

Orchids can be found all over the world, from the hot, low coastal regions of the tropics to the highest mountains in the Himalayas, from the equator to the near-Arctic, and in all the areas in between. Thus, there are cool-growing orchids, orchids that require warm temperatures, and those that need intermediate temperatures. They are found in bogs, along wet meadows, in swamps, on rocks, in sand dunes, high up in trees, in shady woods, and even underground. There are orchids that are less than 1 inch high, like the *Bulbophyllum minutissimum,* while others grow to 20 feet, like the *Gramatophyllum speciosum.*

Regardless of plant size or genus, all orchid flowers

have the same basic structure: three petals, three sepals, and a column that emerges from the center of the flower to contain the nectar that attracts the insects for pollination. The anther (male reproductive organ) and the stigma (female reproductive organ) are located within the column. The anther, which is located at the top of the column, holds the pollinia. Below this is the sticky surface of the stigma, upon which the pollinia from another flower are deposited at the time of pollination. There is also an ovary, which expands into a capsule that contains the seed—a single orchid seed pod can contain several million seeds.

The word *orchid* comes from the Greek *orchis*, meaning "testes," and was used by the ancient Greeks to describe the testicular-shaped bulbs of many of the orchids growing

Figure 1-2. Left: Parts of various orchid flowers—*p*, petal; *l*, labellum or lip; *ls*, lateral sepal, sometimes called the ventral sepal; *ds*, dorsal sepal; *t*, throat; *m*, mask or macule; *vs*, ventral sepal, the combined lateral sepals in cypripediums; *c*, column; *st*, staminode. Right: Structure of a cattleya, showing a plant in bud and a single, detached flower—*b*, bud; *c*, column; *ds*, dorsal sepal; *e*, eye; *l*, lip; *lf*, leaf; *ls*, lateral sepal; *p*, petal; *ps*, pseudobulb; *r*, root; *sb*, sheathing bracht; *sh*, sheath; *st*, stem.

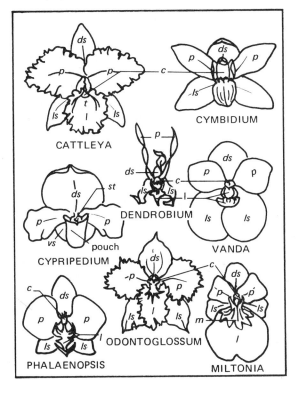

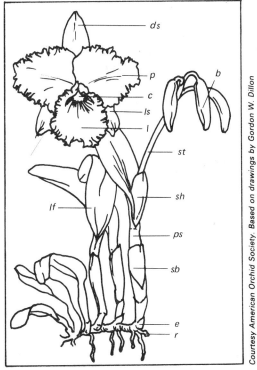

Courtesy American Orchid Society. Based on drawings by Gordon W. Dillon.

in that area of the world. This connotation gave rise to a school of herbalists who felt that the orchid was useful medicinally. At one time orchids were also used as aphrodisiacs, and at yet another time as contraceptives.

It comes as a surprise to many that so little is actually known of the orchid's true beginnings. Orchids are thought to have originated from the same stock as the lily family. That they have been in existence for thousands of years becomes apparent as we search through the literature of the various civilizations that have come and gone and find references made to members of the orchid family.

ORCHIDS IN HISTORY

Early History

In 2800 B.C. in ancient China the Emperor Sheng Nung gave some advice on the use of a dendrobium orchid for medicinal purposes. Furthermore, most people in the Orient were interested in orchids not just for their flowers as we are today, but also for their delightful delicate fragrance. There are many orchids whose fragrance rivals those of the finest perfumes. Anyone who has a *Cattleya walkeriana, Epidendrum fragrans, Rhynchostylis gigantea,* or *Brassavola nodosa* in his greenhouse can readily attest to this.

In that ancient and most revered of all Chinese books, the *I-Ching* (Book of Changes), which is thought to have had as one of its authors the great philosopher Confucius, the orchid is referred to as the "King of the fragrant plants." The Chinese word for *orchid* is *lan,* and the *I-Ching* contains these lines: "the words by friends with one and the same heart are just as sweet as the aroma of lan." It is believed that Confucius was here referring to a cymbidium whose small yellow flowers have a magnificent fragrance.

Throughout Japan, where the orchid was referred to as *ran* (the Japanese version of the Chinese lan), cymbidiums, dendrobiums, and the aerides orchids were frequently found. Just as later on in Europe, orchids were grown and enjoyed almost exclusively by the wealthy class.

Matsuoka wrote what is believed to be the first book on orchids in Japan, *Iganasai-Ranpin;* in it he gave his famous rules for the cultivation of cymbidiums:

> In spring don't put them out of doors
> In summer don't expose to too much sun
> In autumn don't keep too dry
> In winter don't keep too wet

4

The cymbidium was as much admired for its long and graceful foliage as it was for its lovely flowers and always has been a favorite subject of Oriental art.

During the seventeenth century the vanilla plant, the only member of the orchid family ever to achieve prominence economically, was used both as a flavoring and for healing. The history of the vanilla vine in the New World dates back to the days of the Spanish conqueror Cortez, who arrived in Mexico in 1519. The Aztec emperor of the time served him a delicious and highly perfumed drink. Cortez took some cuttings of the plant whose beans had been used to make the drink he had so enjoyed back with him to Europe. There the flavor became extremely popular.

Vanilla plants grow quite tall, like a vine, and have extremely thick leaves. Their flowers are rather small, greenish yellow, and resemble those of the cattleya. These flowers give off the lovely scent of vanilla perfume. They remain open only for 24 hours. The pistil and the anther on the flowers are separate, which means the vanilla flower cannot be self-pollinated. Even insects experience great difficulty in penetrating these flowers, which means that the flowers have to be hand-pollinated, a stupendous undertaking when numbers of the plants are grown commercially. It takes several months for the seed pods to become fully ripened, at which time they are harvested and shipped to manufacturers all over the world to be used in making flavorings.

It was also during this same seventeenth century that the epiphytic (tree-growing) orchids were first discovered in Jamaica. As the European countries sent out explorers and eventually traders to the so-called New World of the Spice Islands, to New Guinea, and to the Philippines, some of these men began to identify and collect orchid plants along with their other activities. The beautiful phalaenopsis, for one, was discovered by these explorers.

It was also at this time that the history of orchids commences to be filled with romance, danger, and adventure. In 1731 the first tropical orchid was introduced into England. It had been collected by Peter Collinson in the Bahamas, was named *Bletia verecunda,* and was successfully grown and flowered.

Beginning of the Orchid Adventure

In England The Royal Botanic Garden at Kew was founded in 1759 and from the beginning engaged in the cultivation of orchids, but it was not until the very early 1800s that the Europeans began to evidence a serious interest in growing orchids. At this time it first became fashionable to grow orchids as a hobby, largely as a result of the interest and support of the sixth duke of Devonshire, William George Spencer Cavendish. At his ancestral home, Chatsworth, conservatories were built to house what was to become one of the greatest collections of orchids in all of England.

The duke engaged the services of many collectors, whom he sent abroad in search of new species. It seems, too, that those who love, grow, and collect orchids have always had a great variety of other interests, many of them becoming quite famous and distinguished in other fields.

For instance, Captain Bligh of the infamous H.M.S. *Bounty* collected orchids and brought them back to England. Members of the staff of Kew Gardens accompanied Captain Cook on the H.M.S. *Endeavor* on one of his worldwide trips and collected many species of orchids in Australia.

Although we normally associate Charles Darwin with the theory of evolution, it is not so well known that it was his interest in the reproductive parts of an orchid that led to his revolutionary theory. Almost all that is known about the pollination of orchids by insects today is based upon the work of Darwin. His famous book *On The Fertilisation of Orchids by Insects* has remained the basic text on this extremely fascinating subject.

In 1818 a plant collector named Swainson collected in Brazil some exotic species, not of orchids but of other plants, which he shipped back to a William Cattley in England. It was this shipment that was to have long-lasting repercussions, for Swainson had wrapped his finds in some plants which in his estimation had little if any value. However, when Cattley unwrapped the shipment he became fascinated with the plants used as wrappings and somehow or other he was successful in getting one of the plants to flower. Never in his life had he seen a flower quite like it, and felt it to be one of the finest orchid flowers that he had ever seen. This plant was classified as a brand-new genus in Cattley's honor, and because of its distinct trumpet-shaped labellum it was given the name *Cattleya labiata*. To this day there are few people who do not consider a cattleya one of the most beautiful flowers in the world.

As might be expected, the flower caused a sensation among horticulturists, and from this time on the growing of orchids rapidly developed into a craze. Until then all orchids had been brought back from distant lands more as curiosity items; but from the time that that cattleya flowered, more and more collectors were sent out in search of orchids to be grown as exotic plants. Many collectors perished during their searches because of the dangers encountered in unfamiliar lands. Considering the jungles and forests in these out-of-the-way places, the primitive conditions they were forced to live under, scourges like malaria and yellow fever, dangers encountered not only from hostile environments but from hostile natives as well, it is amazing that so many returned home at all. Because the journeys they took were long, and few if any provisions could be made for adequate care of the orchids they collected, vast numbers of the plants perished en route. Others died because they arrived in such poor condition, and nothing was known at that time that could possibly have saved them.

The unfortunate decimation of entire forests and the

Figure 1-3. A native guide points out several different genera of orchid growing side by side in a tropical forest.

scooping up of such vast numbers of orchids still strikes an awesome note. Orchids were fast becoming a valuable commodity and increasingly in demand. It took ruthless men to hunt for them and equally ruthless men to preside over the firms that sent them out.

Even though the orchids were as securely packed as possible for the long journey home by sea, there was no certainty that a shipment would arrive at its destination. Many of these ships were sunk during fierce storms at sea or were destroyed by fire. The ocean floor became the final resting place of untold numbers of orchids. Yet the more orchids that died, the more orchids there were imported to replace them. Some areas were literally stripped of all orchids to satisfy this demand.

In London in 1842 a Dr. Ward developed a packing case that was thereafter to bear his name. The wardian case was an airtight box with a screw-on lid, made of glass. The theory behind the box was that after the plants had been thoroughly watered they would require no additional water until they arrived at their destination. Water would evaporate from the plants, condense on the underside of the lid, and then run back down on the plants to keep them moist.

This certainly was an improvement over the older method of having to open closed wooden cases during the heat of the day to water the plants and then cover the boxes with a tarpaulin to keep out the salt water during storms at sea.

The manner in which one firm spied upon another in their quests for orchids was like a modern-day James Bond thriller or some CIA feat of espionage. Cabled instructions were stolen or misdirected. Others fell into the hands of rival collectors. The whole object of these expeditions was to collect orchids—with no regard to the manner in which it was done. Natives were bribed for information not only about possible locations of orchids but also for information on the activities of other orchid hunters.

During the 1800s it was possible to sell a plant for as much as 1000 pounds sterling, at a time when the pound was equivalent to $5. The famous *Cattleya labiata* was for a good many years considered to be a lost orchid. The first plant shipped back to William Cattley had been an outstanding specimen, and scores of orchid hunters were sent out to collect more of these plants where it was believed the first one had been found. Swainson, who had found the original plant, was of no help—he had just grabbed it out of a pile of plants to wrap specimens he considered far more valuable. As a result, vast areas of the mountains and jungles of Brazil were scoured in trying to find another *Cattleya labiata* at vast expense in time, money, and manpower. It was the "Orchid King" himself, Frederick Sander, who, after having spent years in fruitless search of it, finally found it in a shipment of plants that had been sent to Paris from Brazil. Although Sander's men had been unsuccessful in locating the much sought *Cattleya labiata*, they were successful in finding *Cattleyas perciviliana* and *sanderana* which won numerous awards and were later used as the basis of much of the early hybridization by the Sander firm.

As the craze for growing orchids became more widespread, the prices paid for them continued to climb astronomically. Auctions were frequently held in various parts of England where collectors vehemently bid against one another in the hope of acquiring an outstanding plant that eventually would bear their names.

Commercial firms still sent out collectors by the hundreds, and the Sander firm became the foremost and largest grower of orchids in the world. David Sander, the illustrious grandson of the founder, recently made arrangements to publish a fascinating biography (*Frederick Sander, the Orchid King,* by A. S. Swinson) of his ancestor, who, among his many other achievements, began in 1856 *Sander's List of Orchid Hybrids,* where even today all new orchid hybrids are registered.

Without a doubt, England had become the foremost country in the world in the importation and growing of orchids. The names of such commercial firms as Conrad Loddiges and Sons and Charlesworth and Co. will always be remembered for the *loddgestii* and *charlesworthii* hybrids that bear their names.

During the nineteenth century, orchids were still considered solely the province of the wealthy, as they had been in ancient times. The Royal Botanic Garden at Kew was the first horticultural institution of note to embark upon a program of acquiring and fostering an interest in orchids. In 1859 the Royal Horticultural Society gave its very first award, a First Class Certificate, to an orchid plant, *Cattleya dormaniana,* which had been exhibited by the Veitch firm.

9   Up until this time all of the orchids that had been

grown and exhibited had come from collectors. In 1894 Joseph Charlesworth, whose name has been immortalized by the addition of the varietal name *charlesworthii* on so many outstanding orchids, was one of the first persons to succeed in raising orchids from seed.

Unfortunately, the growers of the first imported orchids felt that the junglelike conditions of a hot, humid, steamy atmosphere with no ventilation had to be duplicated to enable them to grow. Who knows how many thousands of plants perished in the nineteenth century under conditions

Figure 1-4. John Mutch, one of the first commercial orchid growers in America, in his Waban, Massachusetts cattleya greenhouse in 1930.

Courtesy Raymond A. Perry

that would strike horror into the heart of a modern-day orchidist? Luckily, John Lindley, who became known as the father of modern orchidology—because it was he who first developed a much-needed system for classifying orchids—realized that, if orchids survived the rigors of the journey from their homelands only to die in conservatories, it was high time some precise information was gathered from those in far-off lands who knew at first hand the conditions in which the orchids that were to be shipped out actually grew. Having assembled this information he then proceeded to disseminate it to his fellow growers through numerous books and lectures.

About this time, too, some of the collectors began to send back orchids from regions that were much cooler than those areas that had up to this time supplied most imported orchids. These newer regions had climates more like that of England, and consequently much greater success was achieved when growing these cooler-climate orchids than had been the case with their jungle counterparts.

Orchids in the United States

It was not long before the craze for growing orchids spread across the Atlantic to the United States, where Boston became the center of the American orchid world. Just as the Royal Horticultural Society had taken up the cultivation of orchids in England, in the United States a prestigious group of orchid growers banded together and, with Albert Burrage as its first president, founded the American Orchid Society. In 1940, a man who was to have a far-reaching influence upon the orchid world joined the society as the assistant editor of its publication, the *American Orchid Society Bulletin*. His name was Gordon Dillon. In later years, as the editor of the *Bulletin* and as the Society's executive director, it was he who first saw that growing orchids need not be a strictly regional affair but rather should be a worldwide endeavor where there would be an opportunity to unite people of all countries and all races in the sharing of their experiences in growing orchids.

In the pages of the *Bulletin*, Dillon himself wrote and had written by eminent growers some of the finest articles dealing with the culture of orchids that had been seen up to that time. Thus, through his endeavors the *Bulletin* became the Bible of the orchid world and the Society the foremost of its kind. It was in the pages of the *Bulletin* that the latest developments in culture and the names of places where orchids could be purchased were found. Heretofore, much of this information had been confined to scientific journals that were not readily available to the average grower.

With the benefit of Dillon's counsel and guidance, the American Orchid Society embarked upon a program of education for the orchid enthusiast and published many informative booklets—such as *The Handbook on Judging and Exhibition* (1949), *An Orchist's Glossary* (1974), *The Handbook on Orchid Culture* (1965), and *The Handbook on Orchid Pests, Diseases, and Ailments* (1967)—to help make every facet of orchid growing easier to understand.

Gordon Dillon encouraged orchid growers from all over the world to contribute their ideas and to share their experiences, whether in growing or in collecting orchids. He truly brought the past and present together.

Under his leadership the American Orchid Society also established a Fund for Education and Research; through grants the Fund enabled scholars to engage in research and to report on important facets of orchid culture. In education, the Fund has been used to help support much-needed conservation efforts such as the Lankester Garden in Costa Rica and to initiate short courses in orchid culture for everyone, whether members of the Society or not. A noted orchidist, Don Carlos Lankester, who had spent his entire life locating and collecting the native orchid species of Costa Rica, created one of the most beautiful and complete orchid gardens to be found anywhere at his home, near Cartago. In this garden can be found a remarkable representation of the flora and fauna of his country, for every attempt was made to naturalize the garden area with swamps and high-ground elevations so as to duplicate as nearly as possible the conditions in which the plants he had collected were found. Orchids comprised the largest part of this extensive garden, and it was not long before it became a mecca for researchers, scientists, and every orchid lover who visited Costa Rica.

Upon his death, to prevent this priceless garden from deteriorating, a local orchid society provided aid and assistance. The University of Costa Rica lent its aid in the identification and labeling of the orchids, which, although well known to Don Carlos, had never been properly labeled. It is the hope of this orchid group that they and the University will be able to open the garden to the public.

It was at this point that the indefatigable Rebecca T. Northen, one of the most admired and certainly one of the most knowledgable orchidists in the world, stepped forward and suggested that Don Carlos's garden be made a project of the American Orchid Society's Fund for Education and Research. It has been her hope, and one for which she has worked diligently, to have this garden supported by all orchid growers as a tangible means of conserving and preserving for all time one of the truly great orchid collections of the world.

Orchids Worldwide

From all these endeavors it was just a step for Gordon Dillon, a man of great vision, to initiate the idea of having World Orchid Conferences in different parts of the world every few years. The first conference was held in 1954 in, appropriately, the United States at the Botanical Garden in St. Louis. Other conferences followed in London, Singapore, California, Australia, Hawaii, Colombia, Germany, and Thailand.

It was at these conferences that the concept of the One World of Orchids was truly brought into being. From the four corners of the earth orchid growers, commercial as well as amateur, scientists, and educators gathered to see, hear, and share. Ideas and views were exchanged and lasting friendships made. It gave growers an opportunity to see at first hand many of the orchids they had hitherto only read about.

Gordon Dillon, through his vision and determination, has accomplished in the field of orchids what has not been possible in the everyday affairs of men—that is, to bring people from all nations together in one place where there is no dissension, no consciousness of any differences in nationality or origin, and to have them embark in a spirit of harmony upon a program of further development in the world of orchid culture. He has brought order out of chaos, correlating a vast collection of written material and making it available in one place for easy reference, the Society's headquarters at Harvard University's Botanical Museum in Cambridge, Massachusetts. To him, more than to any other person, is owed gratitude for fostering the feeling of brotherhood that all of us who grow orchids feel for one another.

Each World Orchid Conference has been noted for its *13* lasting achievements, and nowhere was this better exemplified than at the Seventh World Orchid Conference held in Medellin, Colombia in 1972. This Conference's executive director was Colombia's charming and famous first lady of orchids, Helena Baraya de Ospina. It was she who, as president of the Colombian Orchid Society, saw the appropriateness of having her country, one of the oldest centers of culture in the Western Hemisphere, as the setting for a World Orchid Conference. Some forty-five nations sent their foremost scholars, scientists, and orchid hobbyists as well as their choicest plants and flowers. Social events, tours of many orchid ranges, and visits to historical places all made the visitor's time both enjoyable and instructive.

Under the impetus and guidance of Señora Ospina the Conference was held at the vast Jardin Botanico Joaquin Antonio Uribe, which had been named in honor of one of Colombia's great scholars, botanists, and authors.

Appropriate trees were planted on which the native Colombian orchids could grow with the intent of preserving and displaying so far as possible all the existing indigenous species of orchids. It was also the aim of the congress to develop facilities for research and hybridization and to provide not only the citizens of Colombia but plant lovers the world over with a veritable paradise in which to browse and to learn.

The theme of this Conference was, appropriately, "Orchids and Ecology," as suggested by Senator Mariano Ospina H., and the discussions were global in scope.

Each of the World Orchid Conferences is held under the joint sponsorship of the American Orchid Society and the orchid society of the host country. In this case the Colombian Orchid Society, whose distinguished president was also the executive director of the Conference, was responsible for the vast organizational work. In years to come every visitor, student, and researcher will be grateful to this ardent orchid grower, who combined her love of her country, of orchids, and of the people of the world by creating a permanent setting where the plant treasures of Colombia can be preserved. For her achievement, the grateful President of Colombia presented to Helena Baraya de Ospina one of his country's highest honors, the Ordean de San Carlos.

In the 1920s, orchid growers in the United States, both commercial and amateur, began to import orchids not just from their native habitats but also from the old established

Figure 1-5. The Jardin Botanico Joaquin Antonio Uribe, in Medellín, Colombia, scene of the Seventh World Orchid Conference in 1972.

orchid firms and private collections in England and France. In some cases the sums paid were astronomical, but it brought to the United States the finest contributions of Europe's most famous orchidists. Included were both rare species and the finest new hybrids.

15   Orchids have played a significant role in botany, evolution, science, and medicine. They have been written about

in literature from the early *I Ching* to the medical treatises of the Middle Ages, have been referred to by Shakespeare in *Hamlet,* and have become synonomous with one of the most famous of all fictional detectives, Nero Wolfe.

Orchids even played a part in the most publicized romance of the century. The first gift given by King Edward VIII of England to the woman he loved, the woman for whom he later relinquished his throne, was an orchid plant from the royal greenhouses. It took a whole year for the plant to blossom again, and when it did the event was greeted with great delight by the two lovers as a sign of their enduring love, and Wallis Simpson had, indeed, shown her horticultural expertise when she succeeded in flowering it in her first attempt at growing orchids in her London flat.

In recent years, among those who have also gained fame in areas of activity far removed from the world of horticulture yet who have found the growing of orchids to be a rewarding and pleasurable respite from the pressures of their everyday work is the renowned American actor

Figure 1-6. Following a tradition set by his father, William Kirch, Sea God Nurseries general manager Michael Kirch (a) is doing extensive breeding with cattleyas in conjunction with renowned actor Raymond Burr (b), thereby becoming a second-generation nurseryman in breeding experience.

a   b

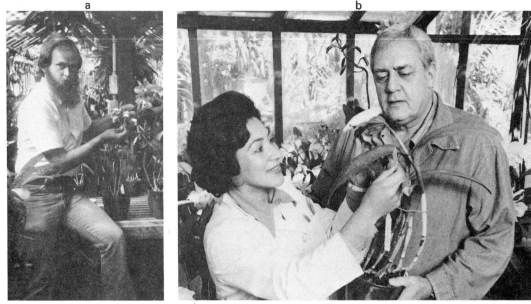

Raymond Burr, who expanded a personal collection of plants noted for their quality and diversification into the commercial firm of Sea God Nurseries, a firm specializing in plants of the cattleya–laelia alliance.

NATURAL HABITATS AND CULTURE

For all practical purposes orchids can be divided into two major groups: the terrestrial orchids and the epiphytic ones. Terrestrial orchids grow, as their name implies, on the ground, be it in the more open areas of a forest, alongside swamps, or in wet meadows where they receive dappled sunlight and the necessary amount of shade they require. These are the orchids that have no means of storing water and thus should never be allowed to become dry. Paphiopedilums, the slipper orchids (formerly known as cypripediums), are good examples of terrestrial orchids. The material in which they grow is composed of humus. In this there is rarely any danger of the plants becoming waterlogged, since humus is both light and porous and has excellent draining qualities, and it is these conditions that must be duplicated wherever terrestrial orchids are to be grown, whether in pots or in baskets.

Their native habitats also influence the culture of the epiphytes. *Epiphyte* means "on a plant," and these are the orchids that grow on the trunks of trees. Yet these orchids are not parasites. They derive no food from the tree itself. Its only use is to give them some place to which they can cling where the growing conditions are to their liking. Usually epiphytes can be found clustered together in the very tops of trees where there is plenty of air and light. Here the only moisture they receive is from the frequent rains and dews. Therefore, nature has provided them with thick leaves and pseudobulbs in which they can store water for use during the drier seasons. The roots of these plants are always exposed to the air. This creates a problem when an epiphyte such as a cattleya is grown in a pot, and to overcome the lack of air in the pot growers have found that the pot must be heavily crocked to insure good drainage. Secondly, since the roots must be able to breathe, materials such as bark or osmunda are used primarily to hold the plant steady in the container without blocking good air circulation. These materials provide no nourishment. Epiphyte orchids have fleshy roots that are covered with a white coating called velamen. These roots can very easily

Figure 1-7. Epiphytic orchids growing on an oak tree beside the picturesque shores of Lagos de Montebello, in northeast Chiapas, Mexico.

rot if the bark or osmunda is not allowed to dry out between waterings.

In the beginning, Europeans, and especially the English growers, found that orchids did not do well in the peat-moss-and-loam mixture in which they had first tried to grow them. They decided to try osmunda, which proved ideal. There is, however, a definite knack to potting in osmunda, and it is a time-consuming job, so as the commercial nurseries grew in size and osmunda became scarcer, a cheaper and more abundant material had to be found. In the early 1950s many materials were tried with varying degrees of success, materials such as buckwheat hulls and wood chips to name but a few. Finally, it was found that Douglas fir bark proved an excellent potting material if chopped into small pieces. Since then the use of fir bark has spread rapidly until today it is the most widely used potting material.

18

The first orchids imported into England had, of course, come from the tropics, and the growers provided them with what they considered to be a tropical atmosphere. As time went on and orchids from cooler areas of the world were sent back, they joined the tropical orchids in perishing in the stuffy, ovenlike atmosphere thought to be so necessary.

As more knowledge became available and the conditions under which orchids thrived were better understood, growers, thanks to the pioneering efforts of Joseph Cooper in 1830, began to open up their hothouses and to let in some much-needed fresh air. Temperatures were reduced, humidity was lowered, and the results were amazing. Plants that had been dying rejuvenated. These same basic conditions first recommended by Cooper are still followed in the growing of orchids.

Growers had also come to appreciate the many delightful orchids that come from regions other than the tropics, such as the odontoglossums, which because of their need for cooler growing conditions became great favorites with the English growers. In fact, the search for new orchids has by no means ended. It still continues as men find their way into previously unknown places or look more closely in those areas previously explored.

The twentieth century, for example, has seen the discovery of a new type of orchid. In 1928 in western Australia there was discovered a subterranean orchid, *Rhyanthella gardneri,* a small leafless plant that spends its entire life cycle underground. In 1931 another subterranean orchid was found in New South Wales. Although they have no commercial value, they serve to point up the extreme versatility of orchids, showing that they can be found anywhere on this planet.

As Africa has been visited by more and more orchidists in recent years, a whole new world of species has been opening up to the collectors. This time, however, there will be no destruction of whole areas such as took place during the orchid craze of the eighteenth and nineteenth centuries. The governments of Africa as well as of other regions have enacted strict laws to preserve those areas where orchids are found, to limit collection, and to supervise and regulate exportation. It is important not only that the exportation of these species continues to be regulated, but also that their habitats be preserved instead of falling prey to logging interests that could demolish the trees they grow upon.

THE CLASSIFICATION OF ORCHIDS

With all the thousands of orchid species becoming available in the early 1800s it soon became necessary to devise some method of classification. Taxonomists, those who determine the classification of living things, found through the years that the orchid family did not hold true to the previously conceived ideas concerning the relationship between species and genera.

The first attempt at classification was made by the renowned Swedish botanist Linnaeus. Then came Olaf Swartz, followed by John Lindley, who published a detailed enumeration of orchids in his *Genera and Species of Orchidaceous Plants* in the middle of the 1830s, which was the most important work of classification up to that time.

Then as orchids became available from countries that previously had not been known to have native orchids, the work of classification continually underwent revision. Richard Schlechter, a noted botanist and ardent orchidologist, amassed a collection of some 20,000 orchids as a result of two decades of traveling the world over in search of them. His observations on these various species and genera were made available in over 300 publications. Schlechter was finally able to resolve some of the difficulties previously encountered by showing the similarities of orchids' reproductive and vegetative growths, which could then be used in classifying them. It is this system that has been widely adopted to give us the present-day classification of orchids. Thanks to all this work, it is now possible to trace the ancestry of any present-day hybrid back through the various crosses to the species from which it came.

For a simplified explanation of how orchid (or any plant) classification works: the term *species* refers to a group of plants having in common one or more characteristics that separate it from any other group. It is a plant that is distinct from other kinds of plants. The term *genus* (plural genera) is a subdivision of a family consisting of one or more species that have similar characteristics and appear to have a common ancestry.

IMPORTANT SPECIES AND THEIR INFLUENCES

Whenever orchids are collected in their native habitats it is the pure species that are usually found, since nature permits very few natural hybrids. Otherwise, plants would cross indiscriminately and confusion would reign supreme.

Courtesy American Orchid Society

Figure 1-8. A jointed pole is used to remove some native orchid species in Mexico.

And in spite of all the species that have been discovered, the future still holds promise of the discovery of, perhaps, as many more species growing tucked away in untouched areas of the world as were found in the heyday of the orchid hunters.

In any case, as the number of orchids collected began to reach astronomical proportions, even the importers themselves realized that this collecting could not go on indefinitely. Therefore, efforts were made to propagate orchids by cross-pollinating existing ones, and thus were produced the first hybrids. Of all the orchids collected, a few proved to be outstandingly vigorous growers and prolific producers of flowers. It was from these that the original hybrids were made.

A brief rundown of the colors, growth habits, and flowering times of a few species in the better-known genera will give you some idea of why they were interbred to produce the lovely crosses we see today. Also, by knowing something of the localities in which they were found, one can have a better understanding of why orchids have different cultural requirements.

Specie orchids are sometimes more difficult to grow than are hybrids. Each has its own cycle of growth, which seldom varies, and there may be times when we are not able to duplicate the conditions to which they have been accustomed. Since the species are not grown as widely as are the hybrids and information on their culture is limited, it is often up to the grower to devise ways of meeting their needs.

NOTE: Once the orchid genus name is mentioned it may be abbreviated in technical names—as *Cattleya mossiae* becomes *C. mossiae.*

Cattleya

The following few are among the best known of the over fifty cattleya species and will serve to show how the combination of their characteristics, in crossing one species with another, have led to our modern superhybrids.

aurantiaca. A small, bifoliate (two leaves), from Mexico and Central America, it has small bright cinnabar flowers in clusters in spring and summer.

bowringiana. Another bifoliate first found in Belize (British Honduras) and Guatemala. It blooms in autumn with a cluster of a dozen or more small, rosy lavender flowers with distinctive maroon and purple flaring lips.

dowiana. A labiate species (it has only one leaf on each growth), it originated in Costa Rica. Its flowers are extremely large, some as much as 7 inches in diameter, and have a crimson-and-gold-streaked lip. The white, a variety of *C. dowiana alba,* found in Colombia, has been much used in hybridizing.

labiata. As its name implies, a one-leaf species that comes from Brazil. This is probably one of the most famous of all the cattleya species. It flowers freely and has rather large blossoms.

mossiae. A labiate species, it is vigorous and flowers

rather freely. Its blossoms are large and a heavenly shade of lavender. Because it flowers in spring it has become known as the "Easter orchid" and has been used extensively in hybridizing. Some *C. mossiaes* can still be seen in collections as magnificent specimen plants with literally hundreds of flowers.

perciviliana. A labiate from Venezuela, it is known as the "Christmas orchid," because it invariably produces a pink and lavender flower with a deep crimson and purple lip just in time for the holidays.

trianaei. Found in Colombia, its usual blooming period is during the Christmas holidays. It is easy to grow and flower and is still found in many collections. It, too, has been widely used in hybridizing.

Having gone this far, it becomes apparent how crosses can be made that will produce plants of differing heights, flowering seasons, and colors and sizes. It also helps explain why a cattleya that has always been labiate may suddenly revert to bifoliate like another ancestor.

Paphiopedilum (formerly Cypripedium)

Although the paphiopedilum hybrids are more popular and more easily grown than the species, still it is the species, such as the following, that have given us the lovely hybrid lady slippers we cherish today.

callosum. One of the largest paphiopedilum species. From Thailand, the flowers are a greenish white with markings of purple and brown.

fairieanum. A truly dwarf species found in Assam and Sikkim in Asia. Its flowers are a colorful blend of white, green, purple, and brown. Hybridizers used it in creating some of the smaller paphiopedilums.

insigne. One of the most famous of all paphiopedilums, it is a cool-growing sort found in Nepal, Assam, and northern Burma. It is probably the most important of the paphiopedilum species used in hybridizing and the most widely known species.

rothschildianum. Found in New Guinea, it has long, glossy leaves, requires warmer conditions, and is a vigorous grower producing many flowers.

villosum. A robust grower from Burma, with large flowers. It blooms during the winter and has been used extensively in hybridizing.

Cymbidium

The cymbidiums comprise about sixty species that furnish a wide variety of colors. Its flowers are exceptionally long-lasting. Most of the cymbidiums grown today are hybrids that can trace their ancestry back to at least one of these species:

ensifolium. A miniature from Assam in India. Its leaves are dark green and sword-shaped. Its spikes produce a dozen or more 2-inch yellow-green flowers spotted with brown and purple. It blooms in the fall and has played a large part in creating the miniatures so popular today.

erythrostylum. From Assam. With white flowers and a red column, another small species. Its most noteworthy characteristic is that it blooms from late autumn to early winter, making it invaluable for early-flowering hybrids.

giganteum. Found in Nepal, northern India, and Burma. Robust and one of the most fragrant of all orchids, it produces flowers that are yellowish green.

insigne. Found in Assam. A plant that appears in the ancestry of most of the best hybrids. Its tall, erect flower spikes carry about a dozen large, white flowers touched with rosy lavender in spring.

lowianum. From Burma, it usually produces more than two dozen 4-inch, gorgeous, bright yellowish green flowers veined in red with a yellow lip in late winter and early summer. A great favorite of the early hybridizers.

pumilum. A miniature species. Although it originated in China, it became very popular in Japan, where miniatures have always been admired. The stem is almost upright and carries two dozen small, reddish brown flowers with white lips marked with brown dots. Along with *Cym ensifolium*, it was used in creating the modern miniatures.

Phalaenopsis

There are over forty species of phalaenopsis.

amabilis. The first phalaenopsis to be discovered, it is a native of the Javanese jungles and islands of the Malayan

Archipelago. It produces more than a dozen snow-white 3- or 4-inch flowers on a stem.

aphrodite. From the Philippines. It is used extensively in the breeding of white hybrids.

lueddemanniana. By far the most popular of the Philippine species. Its many 2-inch flowers of white and yellow have brown spots and an overall lavender hue.

schilleriana. From the Philippines, it is a vigorous grower noted for its many large pink flowers in the spring.

Dendrobium

There are a tremendous number of dendrobium species, but these will give you some idea of what went into the hybrids.

aggregatum. An evergreen dwarf from northern India, Burma, and South China, it has drooping sprays of many yellow flowers and makes a handsome hanging plant.

anosmum. Deciduous; that is, it sheds its leaves at the end of the growing season. From the Philippines, it has 3-inch purple flowers in the spring.

dearei. Evergreen. Also from the Philippines, it blossoms in summer. It has 2-inch white flowers with green throats and was used extensively by hybridizers.

densifolium. An evergreen from Nepal and Assam, it needs cool winter nights to produce its yellow and orange flowers. One of the most popular of dendrobium species.

nobile. From India, it is the most popular of the dendrobium species and has been extensively used in hybridizing. Its flowers are a lovely rose lavender. It needs warmth and a period of cool nights to flower.

Vanda

There are more than seventy vanda species, but very few are cultivated today, having given way almost completely to the hybrids.

caerulea. A blue-flowering species from the hills of northern India and Burma, it has been widely used in hybridizing. It needs cooler conditions than most.

dearei. A warm-growing species from Indonesia. It has long-lasting, fragrant white flowers in summer.

sanderiana. From the Philippines, considered by many one of the finest orchids. It was the dominant species in vanda hybridizing. In fall it bears large, flat, white flowers with touches of rose, brown, and green.

spathulata. From India and Sri Lanka (Ceylon), it has been used to produce the yellow hybrids.

tricolor. Native to Java and Bali. Easily grown, it flowers profusely, bearing varicolored 3-inch blossoms any time of year.

Oncidium

In all there are more than 700 species of oncidium.

cheirophorum. A miniature from Colombia, it has short sprays of numerous small yellow flowers. It grows well indoors on windowsills.

lanceanum. From Trinidad, Guyana, and Surinam. This species has no pseudobulbs (which means it has no place in which to store water and will therefore need to be watered more frequently than do plants that do have pseudobulbs). It is warmth-loving and is much used in hybridizing. Its 2-inch flowers are greenish-yellow spotted with red and flat lavender tips.

leucochilum. From Mexico, it has no particular blooming season. Its flowers are yellowish green and brown with white lips.

ornithorhynchum. From Mexico, it has short clusters of rose, lavender, yellow, and white flowers. It is often grown in greenhouses for its spicy fragrance.

papilio. The original "butterfly orchid," from Trinidad and Venezuela. Its flowers are large and a combination of purple, green, brown, and yellow.

varicosum. From Brazil, it has large pseudobulbs and in the fall produces the many yellow flowers that gave the name of "dancing ladies" to oncidiums.

Miltonia

There are about twenty miltonia species and eight natural hybrids.

candida. From Brazil, a handsome plant with narrow, yellow-green leaves and, in autumn, 3-inch brown flowers spotted with yellow. The white lip has two distinct purple patches.

phalaenopsis. A Colombian, it blooms in early summer, bearing flat, white flowers with large, crimson-streaked lips.

spectabilis. From Brazil, it flowers in the fall, producing large, flat blooms of purple to white, lined with purple.

vexillaria. From Colombia, the finest of all the miltonia species, it is found in many hybrids. It is a vigorous grower with a large flat lip either white or colored.

Odontoglossum

These are but a handful of the over one hundred species.

bictoniense. From the highlands of Mexico and Guatemala, it has 2-inch flowers, green petals with brown markings, and heart-shaped lips that vary from white to dark rosy lavender. It blooms at various times.

crispum. From the high Colombian Andes, considered one of the most beautiful of orchids. It has two rows of 3-inch flowers with frilled sepals and petals and a lip crest of yellow.

grande. Blooming in the fall, this plant from Mexico and Guatemala has many large, yellow, brown, and white flowers with a varnished look. A sturdy grower, it is often grown in greenhouses.

pendulum. Also called *Odm. citrosum,* it comes from Mexico, which means it is warmer-growing than the others mentioned here. Its 3-inch flowers in early summer range from white to rose.

rossii. A dwarf, from Mexico and Central America, its 3-inch flowers have brown spots and marks. It also has an attractive wavy white lip and a yellow crest.

Epidendrum

There are over 1000 epidendrum species, divided into two groups, those with pseudobulbs and the so-called reed type.

Epidendrums with Pseudobulbs

atropurpureum. From Mexico and northern South America, it is small, with egg-shaped pseudobulbs and a height of 4 inches. Its 3-inch flowers are extremely fragrant and come in a wide range of colors, each with a white lip splashed with magenta.

frangrans. A favorite from Mexico, the West Indies, and northern South America, its pseudobulbs are flat, usually with one leaf. The 2-inch flowers are creamy with a purple-striped, shell-shaped lip.

vitellinum. From high altitudes in Mexico and Central America, it needs lower temperatures. The plant carries three sprays, each with a dozen or more small orange-red flowers.

Reed-Type Epidendrums

skinneri. From Guatemala, it has slender stems about a foot tall. Its flower spikes have one to three dozen 1-inch-deep rose flowers.

radicans (Epi. ibaguense). A terrestrial that grows in dense masses from Mexico to South America, it has 1-inch orange, yellow, or red flowers and can be used as a bedding plant where it is warm enough for outdoor culture.

Over and above their value in hybridization, some of these species we have just looked at make delightful plants for the enthusiast. Among them can be found a range from the tiniest of miniatures to the largest of plants. Some growers devote their entire lives to collecting species and have built up magnificent collections.

Still, no matter how ardent the desire, it is impossible for any one person to obtain a plant of every species of orchid known. Some are so rare they have been seen only once. Others cannot be taken from their native habitat lest they perish. Among those that add interest to collections are the "jewel orchids," the haemaria, and *Ophrys insectivera,* known as the "bee orchid." Then there is the "blue orchid," *Aganisia cyanea,* and one species that has no foliage at all, as well as no flowers: it is merely a mass of roots and has become appropriately known as the "ghost orchid," *Polyrrhiza lundeni.*

If, by chance, you come into possession of a species and cannot identify it, the Orchid Identification Center of the Marie Selby Botanical Gardens, 800 South Palm Avenue, Sarasota, Florida 33577 will do it for you. Any part of the plant, a leaf or a flower, for example, should be wrapped securely in a newspaper, placed in a carton, and mailed with a fee of $5.00. It will also facilitate matters if you can send along a picture of the plant. If not, be sure to enclose an accurate description of the plant and of its native habitat if known.

HYBRIDS

The great breakthrough in the growing of orchids came in 1852 when John Dominy, grower for the famous Veitch Royal Exotic Nursery in England, hand-pollinated an orchid for the first time. In 1854 he sowed the seed from this cross (*Calanthe furcata* and *Calanthe masuca*) and in 1856 flowered the first man-made orchid hybrid, named *Calanthe domini* in his honor.

One result of Dominy's efforts was to cause botanists and taxonomists to reevaluate their belief that orchid species growing in the wild were not able to cross-pollinate. With the realization that this not only could but apparently did occur, they began to see where certain orchids they had previously classified as species might in fact be natural hybrids.

On the other hand, while the botanists were busy reexamining the species, the hybridists were busy producing hybrids even more beautiful than their wild ancestors. Crosses were made in one genus after another and then, later, between genera. For example, a cross was made between a laelia and a cattleya to produce a laeliocattleya (abbreviated "Lc."); following this, a cross was made between a laelia, a cattleya, and a brassavola, which resulted in a brassolaeliocattleya ("Blc."). Then the addition of sophronitis to a cross between a laelia and a cattleya enabled hybridists to produce red cattleyas or sophrolaeliocattleyas ("Slc."). In these crosses the laelias added a brighter coloring to the cattleyas and the brassavolas gave a broad, heavily fringed lip.

As hybridists became more expert in their work they made crosses between many genera and eventually between the hybrids themselves. One great advantage in the fact that orchids are so slow-growing is that it provided sufficient time for the hybridists to keep accurate records, so that today it is possible to trace the ancestry of any hybrid right back to the original species.

Expanding on their work provided endless possibilities. By combining a summer-flowering plant with one that flowered in winter it was possible to acquire plants that would flower in spring or autumn. They soon found out, however, that hybrids are not as true to flowering schedules as are species. Instead of blooming at the same time each year or once in twelve months, they might bloom every ten months or even every eight months. And so on it went, one combination after another, with the results more and more fascinating.

By combining the dominant color of one parent with that of another, hybridists were able to increase the intensity of each and in some cases come up with a blend of the two or even a completely new color. It is in this way that we have seen the green and blue cattleyas come into being since the 1960s.

Of course, it was also true that undesirable characteristics could be inherited. But when crosses proved to have superior qualities and to breed true, any future crosses made by hybridists from them had not only superior flowers but also plants that were more vigorous.

All the plants that result from a cross are given a name. Some are named in honor of royalty or other rulers of countries, others after the hybridist or a member of his family. Some are named after ancient gods, while others get their names from the various color tones that appear in the flowers. To record each cross, it was registered with Sander's in England, which for years published *Sander's List of Orchid Hybrids,* a task that the Royal Horticultural Society of London has now taken over. To register a new orchid hybrid an application form is filled out by the originator of the hybrid or by someone else with his permission, giving the genus and the name being proposed for the hybrid. The parentage of the cross must be listed as well as the date the cross was made, the date of its first flowering, and a description of those flowers.

For example, a varietal name might be *Blc. Norman's Bay* var. '*Lucile,*' (with the varietal epithet always enclosed in single quotation marks). Then any time someone repeats the cross, the name that has already been registered for that cross is the name that must be used. It is only when a hybridist makes a distinctly new cross that he has the privilege of selecting a new name for it. Even so, today the number of hybrids is close to the 75,000 mark, with no end in sight.

THE WONDERS OF ORCHID REPRODUCTION

The manner in which orchids are reproduced, particularly in their native habitats, is one of the most fascinating examples of plant reproduction. It had long been thought by early botanists that the structures of the orchid flower made pollination an impossibility. However, in 1793 an obscure German botanist, Christopher Sprengel, wrote of having observed an orchid being pollinated by insects. Because Sprengel was not a recognized expert, little if any attention was paid to his report. It was not until long after he had died, an embittered man, that he received the recognition due him.

Dr. John Lindley, another botanist deeply involved in trying to unravel the mystery of pollination, finally reached the conclusion that fertilization took place when the pollen became attached to the stigma. But it was Charles Darwin who finally made the relationship between orchids and insects clear.

Darwin spent countless hours trapping the various bees and moths in his garden, where there were some terrestrial orchids growing. He examined the masses of pollen that had remained on the heads and bodies of these insects and recorded the fact that it took a certain type of insect equipped with a special proboscis to get into the deep column of some species. If you examine the column in an orchid flower closely, you will be fascinated by its structure. Every kind of orchid has its own distinct column. The cattleya column looks like a cylinder; the columns of other orchids can resemble birds or insects. Inside this column is the gland that secretes the nectar. Insects such as moths seem to prefer the white or light-colored flowers, which are known to give off a strong odor at night. Orchids are also pollinated by flies, by mosquitoes, and by hummingbirds as well as by certain bees.

Darwin was also intrigued by the way the genus *Catosetum* flings its pollen onto the body of an insect when the insect lands inside the depressed lip of the flower. The insect will fly away, but not before his head and body have become thoroughly covered with pollen.

When he was taunted with the fact that the nectary of the *Angraecum sesquipedale*, the "Star of Bethlehem orchid," has a nectar tube a foot long and the resulting impossibility of there being any insect that could possibly pollinate it, Darwin accurately predicted that someday an insect would be found that not only was capable of pollinating this orchid but that in fact did so. Sure enough, such as insect was found, years later, in Madagascar, where Darwin had predicted it would be found. The insect is a moth, known as Xanthopan Morhani Praedicta, that has a foot-long proboscis quite capable of reaching down into the long nectar tube of the *Angraecum sesquipedale.*

Once a hybridist has placed the pollinia or pollen-bearing structures of one orchid on the stigma of another—or an insect has done it—within a week or so the ovary will begin to swell and a seed pod will begin to form. When matured, this seed pod may contain millions of seeds that are so fine they look like dust. Nature may be lavish in the number of seeds she allows an orchid to produce, but the conditions she sets down for their germination make it highly improbable that orchids will ever overrun the earth. That more orchid seeds do not germinate is due primarily to the fact that, having no food stored within them, they must be provided with warmth and moisture along with a special fungus or special nutrients to enable them to grow.

Depending upon the type of orchid, the seed pod is left on the plant anywhere from a few months to over a year. Eventually the pod begins to turn yellow and starts to split. The seed should then be harvested and placed in a clean polyethylene bag or on soft tissues. The number of seeds in the pod can range from a few dozen to several million, some so minute that they can be seen only through a high-powered microscope.

It had long been felt that there was a connection between orchids and a minute fungus that grows on their roots. These fungi, which are known as mycorrhiza, feed on natural substances, digest them, and then pass these substances on to the developing seedlings, a kind of give-and-take relationship. This relationship between the fungi and the orchid seeds is called symbiosis.

For years many methods of germinating orchid seeds had been tried with but little success. The seed had been sown on sphagnum moss, on cork slabs, and on just about every other material enterprising growers could think of. Because many botanists felt that this close connection between the orchid and the mycorrhiza fungus was essential for the germination of the seeds, experiments were begun by sowing seeds in a nutrient agar solution. A double blind test was performed, with some seeds innoculated with the mycorrhiza fungus and others not so innoculated. Only the seeds where the fungus was present germinated.

An American, Dr. Lewis Knudson of Cornell University, suggested that the mycorrhiza released the carbohydrates and nitrogenous substances from the growing medium. In 1916, taking the idea a step further, Knudson developed an asymbiotic method of culture whereby the growing medium, now a nutrient agar, was provided only with the sugar (carbohydrate) that the seeds needed to begin the germination and no fungus was introduced. His seeds germinated in this completely sterile environment, and it is his method that is now used for the germination of the seeds of orchids. Unfortunately, since this—the only truly successful method of germinating orchid seeds—requires a laboratory with sterilizers and completely aseptic conditions, it is not something for the hobbyist, who would do better, therefore to buy his seedlings from professional growers. (See Chapter 5 for the growing of seedlings.)

Whether one is dealing with a species or a hybrid, the next problem is that of increasing its numbers. Until recently, the only means of doing this was the long, tedious culture from seeds or by division. This obviously is an extremely slow method of building up a supply of new hybrids. It also permits the passing of viruses from infected plants to succeeding generations.

The Meristemming Procedure

In order to furnish plants that are virus-free as well as to develop yet another method of propagation, the late French botanist Dr. Georges Morel in 1960 pioneered a new system known as *meristemming*—growing new plants from microscopic pieces of growth tissue—and thereby revolutionized the manner in which orchids could be propagated. Meristemming is also a method by which thousands of plants can be grown in a relatively short period of time and in which every new plant is exactly like the parent plant in every respect.

Actually, meristemming is an outgrowth of Morel's interest in finding some way to circumvent viruses in potatoes. It was just one small step from the eye of a potato to the "eye," or growing tip, of an orchid plant. Morel dissected the growing tips of orchids, layer by layer, almost cell by cell, until finally he reached the parallel rows of the rib meristem. He found that this portion, the apical

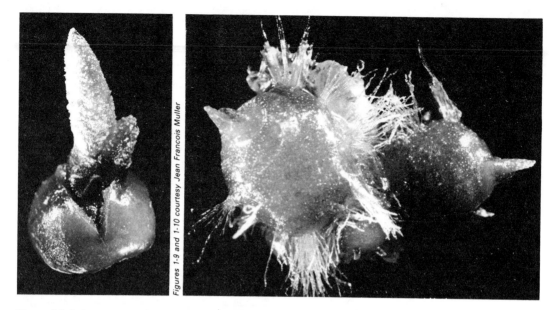

Figure 1-9 (left). A leafy shoot of a terete vanda growing out from the apex of a lateral bud after several months of cultivation.

Figure 1-10 (right). Many protocorms can be formed from a single meristem.

meristem, could develop into a new plant instead of just continuing to grow into a stem.

The entire meristemming procedure takes relatively little time. A $\frac{1}{16}$-inch cube or piece of tissue is removed from the growing tip of a plant. This is then placed in a special nutrient liquid and sealed in a flask. The flask is then placed in a squirrel-cage-like machine, where it revolves for some time. Instead of the many months it takes for seed to germinate, these tiny pieces produce knobby little growths within days, weeks at the most. When these new little structures, called *protocorms*, reach $\frac{1}{16}$ inch, they can be cut into four sections, and each section will then produce one growth. The four sections are then placed in the liquid in the squirrel cage and revolved, eventually to become sixteen little sections, and so on ad infinitum. So treated, the tissue continues to grow indefinitely, and an endless number of individual protocorms can be produced by continually dividing them.

Within just a few weeks these new little growths are ready to be placed in flasks. At the end of four to eight weeks, the original piece of tissue has developed from a protocorm into a number of plantlets that have their own leaves and roots and are well on their way to becoming vigorous, healthy, virus-free plants.

The process of meristemming not only makes possible virus-free orchids but also produces plants of outstanding quality at greatly reduced prices. Just think how many plants can be made from one particularly choice $3000 plant in a relatively short time. This is the miracle of meristemming. Although theoretically applicable to all orchids, to date it has probably been most successful with the cymbidiums.

The first commercial orchid firm to specialize in the

Figure 1-11. Some one-year-old cattleya meristem plantlets.

Figure 1-12. A worker in the laboratory at Vacherot & Lecoufle in front of a filtered and sterile air flow preparing flasks to be used in meristemming.

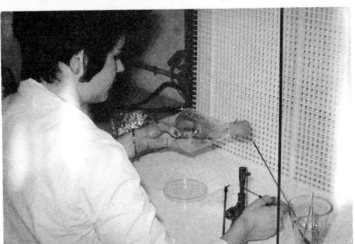

Figures 1-11 and 1-12 courtesy Vacherot & Lecoufle

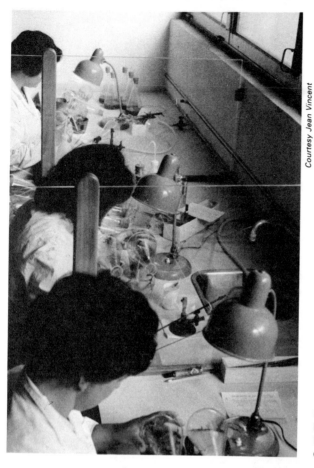

Figure 1-13. Workers in the laboratory at Vacherot & Lecoufle reflasking meristem cultures.

Figure 1-14. A revolving drum used in the laboratory at Vacherot & Lecoufle to revolve the flasks containing meristem cultures.

36

production of meristemmed plants was the old and distinguished house of Vacherot and Lecouffle, of Boissy-Saint-Leger, France. (In this country, Robert M. Scully, Jr., has been among the pioneers in meristemming.) To be certain that the plants used are absolutely virus-free, highly-trained virologists make microscopic examinations of every plant they consider for meristemming.

Leaf Tip Culture

Finally, before we leave the subject of propagation, there is one more method that should be mentioned. It is very much like meristemming and is called *leaf-tip culture*. This involves cutting out a somewhat larger piece of live growth than in meristemming and putting this into a flask containing the growing medium. This cut out piece will also form protocorms that develop leaves and roots and that can then be placed in a flask and grown through the various stages (as is done in meristemming) until they, too, become flowering plants.

SELECTING THE RIGHT ORCHIDS

Before concluding this opening chapter there is one more point we should touch upon: Where you intend to grow your orchids and the conditions prevalent there have a very great bearing upon the types of orchids you can grow. If you have a greenhouse, your choice of plants is almost unlimited, for in a greenhouse you have many microclimates, each providing different conditions of light, temperature, and ventilation. For windowsill culture, on the other hand, the height and width of the plants must be taken into consideration, making the miniature orchids and many of the species ideal choices. Miniatures such as the ascoscendas, *Laelia pumila*, *Cattleya walkerana*, and *Oncidium pulchellum* are particularly satisfactory.

In the house, if light can be provided from the south and west you can try growing warmth-loving plants such as the cattleyas, vandas, and dendrobiums. If the amount of light is limited, phalaenopsis and paphiopedilums might be better. On the other hand, if your available space is or can be kept cool, odontoglossums and cymbidiums will give a rich reward for little effort.

For growing under artificial lights, consideration should always be given to the size of the plants as well

37

as to the fact that the plants should be ones that do not need a high-intensity light. Paphiopedilums do exceptionally well under lights. Other kinds you might consider include the ascoscendas, some of the cattleya hybrids, lycastes, *Oncidium varicosum,* some of the phalaenopsis hybrids, zygopetalums, the smaller dendrobiums, and epidendrums.

If you are so fortunate as to live where you can grow orchids in the garden all year round, cymbidiums make excellent garden plants. They can be planted right in the ground. Their foliage is attractive, and the flowers are both showy and long-lasting. Many other orchids can be hung from the branches of trees or grown in a lath house or on patio blocks as described in Chapter 8.

Regardless of where they are grown, each type of orchid requires that you provide the conditions it needs in order to grow and to flower. These conditions are influenced by how and where the orchids grew in their native habitats. The more we learn about orchids, the more we realize how much more there is yet to be learned. With this in mind, let us continue through the book so that you, too, can join the large number of those who have found growing orchids a pleasant and soul-satisfying experience.

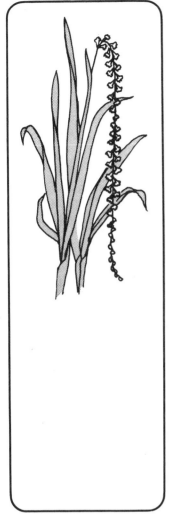

Temperature Conditions

No one aspect of orchid growing is more important than any other. All are interconnected. But since the orchids themselves are divided into three categories based upon their temperature needs, temperature should be considered first in a discussion of their culture.

Although most of the familiar types come from tropical areas, there are literally thousands of species that grow on mountainsides where the air is cool and brisk. Others come from plateau areas. In fact, with the possible exception of the Arctic and the Antarctic, orchids are found just about everywhere. Consequently, there will always be some kind of orchid you can grow without too much difficulty, regardless of your climatic conditions.

CHAPTER 2

While it is never possible to duplicate exactly all the conditions in which orchids grow in their native habitats, we can try to provide atmospheres as close as possible to those they have been used to. This is where temperature becomes important. It determines not only where orchids can be grown but whether certain kinds can be grown under the conditions you can provide.

Although they can grow in fairly strong light, orchids can tolerate neither excessive heat nor freezing temperatures. The requirements of most, if not all, the orchids you will ever grow indoors are as follows:

	Day	Night
warm orchids	70–80°F	65–70°F
	(24–29°C)	*(21–24°C)*
intermediate orchids	65–70°F	60–65°F
	(20–24°C)	*(18–21°C)*
cool orchids	60–65°F	55–60°F
	(18–21°C)	*(13–18°C)*

These are the temperatures at which both growth and respiration are best for each group. Temperatures can vary a few degrees either way and still give the same results. However, any time the temperature rises to around 95–100°F (35–38°C) they are in grave danger of becoming burned and of having their food supply depleted. For every 10 degrees Fahrenheit the temperature rises, the rate of photosynthesis (the process by which plants manufacture food for themselves) increases until the temperature reaches 90–100°F (31–38°C). Above this point it may actually decrease.

On the other hand, temperatures that are too low also cause many problems, such as blind growths and blotches on the leaves. New growth is particularly hard-hit by low temperatures, which not only turn it reddish and disfigure the plants but are not conducive to strong healthy plants. The flowers can also get brown spots on them. To be on the safe side, every effort should be made to keep the temperature at all times within the suggested limits for each kind of orchid either by increasing the heat or by decreasing it through letting in fresh air, misting the foliage with tepid water to cool the plants, and increasing the humidity.

Among the warm-growing orchids are the phalaenopsis, some of the cattleyas, the vandas, and the mottled-leaved slipper orchids or paphiopedilums (formerly known as cypripediums). The majority of cattleyas, epidendrums, dendrobiums, and oncidiums grow best in intermediate temperatures; miltonias, cymbidiums, plain-leaved paphiopedilums, and odontoglossums require cool temperatures both day and night to insure good growth and flowers.

EFFECTS OF THE SUN

Indoor temperatures always tend to rise when the sun is shining, reaching as high as 80-90°F (27-32°C) at midday under normal conditions. Then, as the sun sets, there is a natural return to lower temperatures. Therefore, indoor temperatures should always be kept at least 10 degrees cooler at night than during the daytime to insure the same temperature differential as under natural conditions.

Cloudy weather does not produce this differential. For short periods of time this is not harmful. However, during protracted periods the heat may have to be adjusted to bring about the needed difference. In such cases it is better to turn the heater down a bit at night than it is to turn it higher during the day, for without sufficient sunlight the plants cannot make as much food as they need, and the extra heat would simply tend to make them use up what food they already have.

During the day the combination of light and heat enables the plants to carry on two very essential activities, the making of food (sugar) and the use of that food for growth. During the night, when no food is being made, the food produced during the day is utilized by the plant for some growth but mostly for respiration. Thus it is a combination of temperature plus light that regulates these activities. Low temperatures slow down the process, while high temperatures speed it up. As you can see, if the temperature during the day is higher than recommended, the food may be used up as fast as it is manufactured, leaving no reserves for the night.

Conversely, if the temperature during the day is too low and the light insufficient, there will not be enough food made to nourish all parts of the plant. Since the leaves get most of what is available, the roots may be undernourished, and it is the roots that really determine how strong a plant is. In this respect, orchids are unlike most garden plants. When excessive heat causes water to evaporate from their leaves and the roots cannot absorb enough moisture to compensate for this, orchids do not wilt. Instead, the leaves and the pseudobulbs shrivel. (A pseudobulb is a thickened portion of the stem that resembles a bulb.)

High night temperatures are a major cause of bud drop and soft foliage, which, in turn, is much more susceptible to disease than the foliage of plants given a cooler temperature at night.

Although so-called "freak flowers," those with one or more parts missing, are thought to be caused by a genetic disturbance, it is also true that this abnormality can be caused by excessively high temperatures and extremely low humidity. With low temperatures (and extremely low humidity) the leaves become brittle and growth slows down. Even the plants' tissues can be damaged by low temperatures, resulting in watery black spots on the leaves. On the other hand, a combination of low temperatures and excessive dampness often results in disease and rotting. Uninhibited, this rot can work its way down into the pseudobulb, then into the sheath (the flat covering that protects the developing buds), destroying the buds and eventually killing the whole plant. Should this occur, slit open the sheath with a razor blade if you can do it carefully enough, and expose the buds to the air. This may save them. If the whole pseudobulb shows signs of rot, there is no alternative but to cut it off below the damaged part with a sterile knife.

On summer nights, even with plenty of ventilation, the temperature, particularly in greenhouses, will often remain 5 to 10 degrees higher than desired all night long. There is really no harm done in a situation like this, because during the day the temperatures have usually been the same 5 to 10 degrees higher, and the range between the day and night temperatures will be still sufficient for the needs of the plant. Thus, the plants are able to withstand somewhat higher daytime temperatures during the summer, if they can be assured of having the lower one at night. It is constant heat with no variation that depletes them.

So far, we have seen that temperature, humidity—which should range from a moderate 40–50% to a high of 70–80%, depending upon the needs of the particular orchid—and light go hand in hand to bring about good growing conditions. Along with the right temperature, there should also be a good circulation of air around the plants at all times. Seeing that they have this presents no problems. If the plants are grown in the house, the windows can be opened either in the room with the plants or in another room nearby. The goings and comings in the household stir the air up anyway.

In a small greenhouse we cannot always depend upon the air circulating by itself. Here the use of fans will help. Also, the ventilators should be opened every day, even in cold weather, just long enough to change the air without chilling the plants. This circulation helps to keep the temperature at a more stable level, and moving air keeps staleness from developing in the overall atmosphere. This is most important, because all orchids must have a fresh, buoyant environment to do their best.

At the beginning of each autumn the growths that have been made during the summer months must be hardened in preparation for flowering. For this there should be an increase in the amount of light available but not in the overall temperature. During the winter, when the sun shines brightly in spite of the cold outside, a greenhouse without ventilation could easily become an oven. So, when seeing that the plants are getting enough light, do not neglect to see that the temperature is kept under control by adequate ventilation.

Since greenhouses have much more glass than even the best of sunrooms and porches, the plants usually receive the greatest amount of sunlight during the winter. (In summer the greenhouse must be shaded for a longer period, so the rise in temperature of the plants themselves is usually due to the warmth outside and not to the sunlight. Even when summering out of doors they must be protected from the direct rays of the sun, so it is really in winter that the leaves get the most heat.

Small thermometers can be placed in and around the plants; a minimum–maximum thermometer will let you know not only what the temperature is but what extremes it has reached during the previous twenty-four hours without your needing to watch it constantly.

Since in full sun the temperature of the leaves is always hotter than the surrounding area, nothing can take the place of feeling the leaves to determine how warm they are. If they are too warm, put the plant in the shade and cool the leaves by misting them with tepid water.

Always remember, however, that orchids should never be subjected to sudden changes in temperature. This is why drafts raise such havoc with them. In fact, everything in orchid growing should be done in moderation, and temperature changes especially should be gradual.

43

TEMPERATURE AND FLOWERING

Temperature also has a bearing upon whether, as well as when, plants flower. Often plants will flower only when they have low night temperatures. In fact, cymbidiums will never flower unless the nights are cool.

Cattleya hybrids, on the other hand, particularly those that have the old species *C. labiata* not too far back in their parentage, must have night temperatures on the warm side, as recommended for warm-growing orchids, before they will initiate flower buds. Another favorite, *C. mossiae,* that is present in many a plant's parentage, also requires warmer temperatures at night to flower.

However, since most hybrids have a rather complicated ancestry, the only thing to do with an orchid is first to grow it at the temperature suggested for its type. Then, if it does not flower, raise or lower the night temperature until you hit upon the correct one.

It is also true that some orchids, being "short-day" or "long-day" plants, may need a change in the number of hours a day they receive light at a given temperature to get them to flower. This is just another indication of how closely light is tied to temperature. When the daylight hours are lengthened, either naturally or by the use of artificial lights, a commensurate increase in the amount of heat during these hours *and* at night is needed. The reverse holds true for the short-day plants.

Summing up, the atmosphere around orchids should always feel comfortable. The closer you can keep the temperature to that which has proven to be the best for them, the more vigorous will be their growth and the more profuse their flowers.

Light Requirements

Another cornerstone of orchid culture is proper light. Since orchids come from all parts of the world and grow under a wide variety of conditions, the correct amount of light available where we intend to grow any specific kind ranks high on the list of cultural necessities. However, we must not forget that *light* and *sunlight* are not necessarily the same thing. It is possible to have sufficient light even without the direct rays of the sun.

The place where you intend to grow orchids, whether in the home or in a greenhouse, must be one that has an abundance of light. It is relatively easy to decrease the amount of light by shading, but if the light is not there in the first place, short of using fluorescent lights you may find that orchids will never reach their full potential for you.

CHAPTER 3

Light is so important because the activity of the plant, the ripening of its growth, and the production of flowers are all dependent upon it. All orchid genera do not require the same amount of light. Some, like the thick-leaved cattleyas, can tolerate a high light intensity. Yet too much direct sun can destroy even these. Other orchids, such as paphiopedilums (cypripediums), odontoglossums, and phalaenopsis with their thinner leaves, seem to do better in dappled light, necessitating some shading in most cases. The only direct sunlight they really need is in the early morning. Early morning sunlight is a necessity for all orchids. It helps to open the stomata of the leaves and to promote the process of photosynthesis that increases the amount of food manufactured by the plant.

It is by photosynthesis that food is formed in the tissues of a plant. Although most of the photosynthesis is carried on by the leaves, any part of the plant that contains chlorophyll (and is green) and gets sufficient light also carries on the process. Also, the thicker the leaf, the more light the leaf can tolerate without burning.

We have already seen that as the temperature rises, the rate of photosynthesis also increases, until at temperatures of 90–100°F (31–38°C) there is no further increase; above this the rate decreases. This should be kept in mind when determining the amount of light a plant receives, because the higher the light intensity, the more heat generated. This is also why newly potted plants should be kept somewhat shaded until their roots have had a chance to begin to grow.

Unlike animals, which obtain their food from plants and other animals, plants must manufacture their food within their own tissues. Light, water, and temperature all work together in this process.

For the sake of convenience, the number of footcandles as measured by a photographic light meter, or even better a regular light meter that is calibrated in footcandles, may be used as a guide. Using a photographic light meter according to its accompanying instructions and with a setting of ASA 10 at $\frac{1}{100}$ of a second, the following f-stops can be converted directly to footcandles:

f/3.5	400 fc	f/7.0	1600 fc
f/4.0	500 fc	f/8.0	2000 fc
f/4.5	650 fc	f/9.0	2400 fc

$f/5.0$	800 fc	$f/11.0$	4000 fc
$f/5.6$	1000 fc	$f/12.7$	5200 fc
$f/6.3$	1300 fc	$f/16.0$	6400 fc

The light requirements of some of the more widely grown orchids are as follows:

Cattleyas. With their thick foliage and need for a high light intensity to grow and flower, these need between 2000 and 4000 fc. This represents about 30% of the full amount of sunlight, and hardened, mature plants can often tolerate up to 8000 fc without becoming burned if there is adequate ventilation.

Cymbidiums. While needing as much light as cattleyas, cymbidiums prefer a cooler and moister atmosphere. During the summer they can tolerate as much as 4000–5000 fc, providing this light intensity is built up over a period of some time. A reduction to 3000 fc is needed when they first show signs of developing buds.

Dendrobiums. Both the evergreen and deciduous types of dendrobium have light requirements between 1500 and 3000 fc. The evergreen type can stand greater intensity if adequate ventilation can be provided. The deciduous type, with its thinner leaves, always need protection from too much sun.

Phalaenopsis. These are low-light-intensity orchids. They do best in a soft, diffused light. Although they can stand more light during their active growing period, about 1000 fc is usually sufficient. Indoors they can do well with even less light, about 600 fc.

Paphiopedilums (Cypripediums). These are also low-light-intensity orchids and also like a soft, diffused light. During the winter, when the sun is bright, they can tolerate between 800 and 1000 fc if there is sufficient ventilation. At other times of the year, when they are not flowering, 600–700 fc is usually about right. The lady slipper orchids should never be exposed to direct sunlight except early in the morning.

Miltonias. These, too, are divided into two distinct groups. The Colombian can be grown right along with the paphiopedilums. They need between 1000 and 1500 fc in the summer, with a bit more light during the winter. The Brazilian group does better with more light, between 2000

47

and 3000 fc during the winter. Since they always need some shade from the heat of the sun, they will not need, nor should they have, as much light during the sumer.

Oncidiums. These grow in a wide range of light and can use 2000–4000 fc at all times. The heavier-leaved types can tolerate full sunlight, short of burning. As with any orchid that can tolerate a high light intensity and direct sunlight, they must always be shaded if the leaves become hot. Experience alone will tell you just how much sun and light an oncidium can tolerate.

Odontoglossums. While they like the cooler growing conditions of the cymbidiums and miltonias, odontoglossums nevertheless do need more light than the paphiopedilum group, but somewhat less light than do the light-loving cattleyas and cymbidiums. About 1200–1500 fc is right for the Andean group and between 1500 and 2000 fc for all others.

An eastern or northern exposure affords light without the hot rays of the sun. This is best for those orchids that need a low light intensity. Southern and western exposures, on the other hand, provide greater light along with additional heat from the sun. It is in these locations that some shading will always be needed.

Thus, you see, all orchids just cannot be grown side by side. Their individual needs must be met. Also, orchids should never be crowded together. Enough space should always be left between each plant so that the entire plant can benefit from an equal amount of light, with no shadows from the leaves of nearby plants cutting off any light.

THE NEED FOR SHADING

As the seasons come and go, the amount of sunlight a plant receives can be controlled by shading. All orchids need early morning sunlight. From mid-morning on they need partially filtered sunlight so that the leaves never become too hot. At noon more shading will be needed to reduce further the amount of heat on the plant. As the afternoon wears on, any shading on the plants can be removed so that they can once again have full sunlight.

In growing orchids everything should always be done on a gradual basis. During late autumn and early winter the need for shading is slight. In spring and summer, when the light intensity and heat are both greater, some kind of shading is always needed to temper the rays of the sun. Again, this shading should be increased gradually to the point where by mid-summer the plants will have the greater amount of shade.

The orchids themselves will show whether they are getting the correct amount of light. Pseudobulbs that are plump and hard and leaves that are firm and thick and of a good medium green indicate that the light has been just about as good as it could be. Leaves that are light yellow show that there is an urgent need for a reduction in light. Unless all traces of green have gone from a leaf (in which case it will eventually fall off anyway), it will return to a normal, healthy green when the amount of light is reduced by some kind of shading.

Well-developed, firm, long-lasting flowers, with strong stems, are also good indicators that the light has been adequate throughout the growing period. Too little light results in a spindly growth that is soft and dark green. It is one of the most frequent causes of failure to flower. Insufficient light also plays its part in creating an atmosphere that, when there is also too much humidity, is ripe for many diseases and fungi.

HOW AND WHEN TO SHADE

In growing orchids one cannot consider light without considering the need for shading. Some means of shading will be needed to reduce the amount of sunlight streaming in on the leaves. Yet since light is necessary for growth, the shading must only provide relief from the sun's heat, never eliminate all the light. Always remember, light is best when it is bright yet soft.

Where the shading is so heavy that it cuts down the supply not only of sunlight but also of skylight to a greater degree than advised, plants never develop a good root structure nor do they have many flowers. The leaves become soft and bent, the growth too lush. If, when in dense shade, the same watering and fertilizing schedule were followed as when the plants received more light, they would be unable to utilize the fertilizer and water as they should.

Slatted roller blinds on a greenhouse or thin curtains for the windowsill grower are excellent ways of providing shade. Even those orchids that receive the full rays of the

Light Requirements sun in their native habitat are unable to stand the scorching hot sun that becomes magnified through the glass in either house or greenhouse.

For shading, slatted roller blinds or laths are best. They let the plant receive dappled light where the sun filters through the slat openings. Then the movement of the air and the sun's movement allow the leaves to become shaded every few moments. This means there is no concentration of hot sun on any part of the plant.

If you plan to be away from home on days when you expect the sun to be hot enough to burn the leaves, the blinds or curtains should be put into place before you go. For a short period it is better to get along with less light than run the risk of coming home to scorched plants. Even on those days when the sun is maddeningly in and out, it is better to be on the safe side and to shade, for a plant scarred and yellowed from overexposure to the sun is never a pretty sight—and it need never happen.

Greenhouses can also be covered with a white or green wash to diffuse the light. However, the green wash in particular cuts down on the amount of light available at all times, so that especially on cloudy days the plants do not receive the light they should.

Figure 3-1. Slatted shading provides the filtered sunlight so necessary for orchids.

Courtesy Automatic Sunblind Installations

Courtesy Lord & Burnham, Irvington-on-Hudson, New York

Figure 3-2. These specially made shades for a greenhouse have sufficient space between the slats to let in filtered sunlight.

Many growers place sheets of clear 8-mil polyethylene on the inside of the glass to prevent heat loss. This also acts as an insulator between the cold glass and the plants, especially at night in winter. It does diffuse the light somewhat, however.

From about the middle of January through the middle of October the days are long enough and the sun's rays strong enough to make some shading a necessity. This is particularly true in the spring, when the combination of bright sun and a clear atmosphere can actually cause more damage than during the summer.

From the middle of October to the middle of January the amount of sunlight the plants receive can be gradually increased by providing shade for a shorter period each day. The gradual increase of light at this time of year produces well-ripened pseudobulbs and ultimately many flowers, and

Figure 3-3. The inside of the greenhouse can be lined with polyethylene to provide a barrier between the orchids and the cold glass.

it is this ripening or firming of the plant that helps it get through the winter months in good condition.

Finally, all plants in flower should be taken out of the sun to make the flowers last longer. Bringing the blooming plant into the living room out of the direct sun can add immeasurably to the life of the flowers as well as to your enjoyment of them.

DAY LENGTH

The term *day length* refers to the number of hours of light a plant receives each day. This has a great bearing on whether or not it flowers. For example, some cattleyas, because of inherited qualities, require a rather specific day length in order to produce flowers. *C. labiata* is such a plant—in this case a short-day plant. This quality exists also in the parentage of a great many of the cattleya hybrids. The flower buds are formed on these plants during the development

52

of the pseudobulbs in early summer and only start to grow in the sheath with the coming of the shorter days of autumn. Some orchids will not even start their flower buds as long as the days remain long.

A little experimenting is well worthwhile if you have a plant that consistently refuses to flower. Moving it to a darkened room several hours before sunset will give it the shorter day and longer night it might need to start the flowers. Ten to fourteen hours of darkness for a while might be all that is needed. Once the buds are up in the sheath, the plant can be returned to its usual growing place, since a longer day from then on will not stop the buds from developing. This effect of light on plants is known as *photoperiodicy*.

If the short-day, long-night treatment fails, try the reverse. One of these strategies is bound to work. Day length can, of course, always be stretched by fluorescent lighting. Also, no matter how lovely a conservatory, sunroom, or porch may look lighted at night, it may not be conducive to ideal growing conditions, particularly where some of the plants may require a short day length.

LEAF BURN

Leaf burn results from a combination of extremely high temperature and inadequate ventilation. It causes partial and sometimes complete damage to the tissues of the plant.

Severe burning shows up immediately. The leaf becomes soft and takes on a pinkish hue. In a day or two the entire leaf may become black. If the burn is relatively mild, all the plant tissues may not have been killed. Yet that leaf may still look scarred and wrinkled, and leaves that have been damaged are never able to contribute their full share to the growth of the plant and the production of flowers. This is why prevention is so important. If taken care of, orchids are long-lived plants.

The temperature of a leaf depends both on the temperature of the surrounding air and on the amount of heat from the sun. A continuous temperature of 105°F (40°C) on the leaves or a shorter exposure to a temperature of 110°F (45°C) usually causes burning. Burns usually occur near the top of a leaf, where the supply of moisture is less than on the rest of the plant. This is mostly because of its distance from the potting material and the roots, which receive their moisture directly when the plant is watered. Furthermore, the tip of the leaf often curls back toward the sun, which makes it even more vulnerable to burning and results in further dehydration.

Prevention of Leaf Burn

Prevention of leaf burn is accomplished in several ways: by eliminating excessive heat from the sun through shading, by providing adequate ventilation, and by cooling the leaves by misting with a fine spray of tepid water on bright, sunny days. On the other hand, a mature, well-rooted plant with adequate moisture at its roots can withstand short exposures to a hot sun with far less damage than plants just emerging from the seedling stage.

Whenever a plant feels hot, shade it at once. Then give it a misting. Shading itself always helps to cool off a plant, but misting in full sunlight is not recommended. Shade first, then mist.

Leaves whose tips have been burned can have the damaged part cut off with a sterile knife. This improves the appearance of the plant immensely, and even if the burned part comes well down on the leaf, it does not mean that the entire leaf need be cut off. Just the part that has been burned, for any living tissue can still aid in photosynthesis.

BLIND GROWTHS

Blind growths are those that have no sheath or buds. They plague all growers at some time. Most often they result from insufficient light and a temperature that is too high for the plant. Occasionally, buds die in the sheath as a result of the same conditions that caused blind growths—too little light and too high temperatures.

Air & Ventilation

Orchids need and enjoy the same comfortable environment that we do. Not one does well in a stuffy atmosphere, but all thrive where the air is fresh and buoyant.

Providing fresh air, therefore, is one of the basic requirements for good orchid growing. A free circulation of fresh air helps to prevent the development of those pockets of hot or cold dead air in which disease can get a start. It also helps to keep both temperature and humidity at the desired levels.

Some ventilation is always needed to help control a rising temperature and provide a healthy growing environment whether the plants are grown in the home or in a

CHAPTER 4

Air & Ventilation   greenhouse. With the exception of the frigid days of winter, a change of air is a necessity every day even if it can be for only a few moments.

WINTER

On warm, sunny winter days the ventilators on the greenhouse can sometimes be left entirely open from mid-morning to mid-afternoon. In order to keep some of the day's heat inside and save on fuel, they can be closed again before the greenhouse heating system turns on. On the other hand, there should never be any drafts or abrupt changes of air around orchids. This definitely checks their growth and may contribute to their dehydration.

Figure 4-1. An automatic ventilating unit allows the greenhouse ventilators to open and close as the temperature fluctuates.

At the same time, watch carefully any plants growing in baskets or from hangers near greenhouse ventilators on cold days so that they do not become chilled. This is one reason why ventilators should only be opened on one side, preferably the sunny south or west side and away from the wind.

Opening the ventilators a crack early in the morning before the sun's rays become strong enough to raise the temperature, and more as the greenhouse gets warmer, keeps a nice balance of fresh and warm air. It also insures a gradual rise in temperature, with none of those wide fluctuations so damaging to orchids.

Automatic ventilators in a greenhouse more than pay for themselves. Being controlled by a thermostat and gently opening and closing dozens of times a day, if need be, they keep the temperature and the atmosphere at prearranged settings. They are the only answer to having an adequate supply of air with no great sudden drops in temperature if you cannot be in or near the greenhouse at all times.

As indicated earlier, the deadly combination of stagnant air and high humidity is hazardous to orchids. In their natural habitat the air is always in motion, moving in and around the plants. This is nature's way of keeping them cool. Fresh air also helps to supply the carbon dioxide the plants must have to manufacture food.

Air that is kept constantly circulating goes a long way toward keeping under control both bacterial and fungal diseases, which thrive in a stale, damp atmosphere. Petal blight is just one of the many diseases that abound where the air is cold, damp, and inadequately circulated.

SUMMER

During the summer months, when the air tends to become heavy as well as hot, an electric fan may be needed, not only to increase the air movement but to keep the soaring temperatures down. However, the air circulated by the fan must be moist, or else by blowing dry air around the fan will just add to the overall dryness of the growing conditions. Damping down the floor of the greenhouse and misting the plants help offset such drying effects.

At the same time, the fan should never blow directly on the plants. Aim it at a place on the wall away from the plants or under the benches, where after a time the air will flow upward and circulate throughout the greenhouse. Also, the moving air should always be temperate, without hot blasts or frigid drafts.

Moisture soon begins evaporating into the air after watering and misting, and this increases the overall humidity. Up to a point this is desirable, but not to the extent of saturating the air. No orchid can possibly grow well in a damp, musty atmosphere. This is another reason why the plants must be provided with fresh air so far as is possible.

Increasing the moisture in an already stagnant atmosphere really courts disaster. Good air movement also keeps those plants in flower from spotting as a result of the moisture in the atmosphere collecting on the petals. This spotting condition is known as *botrytis.* When the air is fresh and well circulated, the plants tend to dry out at a faster rate, but frequent checking to see they have enough moisture is a small price to pay for the assurance of good growing conditions.

Both the windows in the home and the ventilators in a greenhouse should be left open at all times during the summer. An exception might be made for plants growing indoors. There, when the temperature outside is in the 90s, the windows might well be closed before the heat has had a chance to get in and then opened again at dusk. Night air during the summer, especially during a protracted heat wave, is a real tonic for all orchids, not just for those in a greenhouse but also for those on windowsills and those spending the summer outdoors.

About the only time the greenhouse ventilators might need to be closed in summer is during a hailstorm or hurricane. At such times the sun is not likely to be shining, and there is less buildup of heat. But never forget: a greenhouse tightly closed and with the sun's rays magnified by the glass quickly becomes an oven no matter what the time of year.

HUMIDITY

If the humidity goes down, if the atmosphere becomes dry and uncomfortable, the plants lose the water stored in their leaves and pseudobulbs. These then turn yellow and shrivel unless conditions are quickly changed.

As air grows warmer, the degree of humidity tends to increase, because warm air can hold more water than cool. This is one reason why damping down the greenhouse and misting the plants is best done when sunlight is warming the air. In a greenhouse the walls, benches, and floor can be wet down with a hose once or twice a day during the summer and once a day in winter. A pan of water in front of a heater also helps provide humidity, particularly when the greenhouse is heated by a forced-air gas heater such as a Dynavent.

The ideal amount of humidity ranges between 40 and 70% depending upon the requirements of the individual plants. More specifically, some of the most frequently grown orchids, such as the slipper orchids or paphiopedilums, which are terrestrial (ground-growing), need a moderate humidity of about 45%–55% during the day. Cattleyas, with their thick leaves, need a higher humidity, about 60–80% during the day. The thin-leaved oncidiums do well in the same moderate humidity as do the paphiopedilums. Cool orchids such as odontoglossums need a moist as well as a cool atmosphere, with the humidity between 45 and 60%.

A good rule of thumb to follow is that when the temperature is low, the humidity should also be low. When the temperature is high, the relative humidity can also be higher. Thus, during the night the humidity should always be less than during the day, just enough to counteract the drying effects of the heat.

In the house, trays full of pebbles and water placed under the plants and small dishes of water placed among them help increase the humidity around them. Daily misting of the plants in sunny weather also helps to increase the humidity, but do not become overenthusiastic and mist so heavily that you are, in effect, giving the plants an extra watering. Aim the mist at the leaves and pseudobulbs, not the potting material. However, during cloudy weather it is better to confine your efforts to keeping the surrounding area damp rather than to misting the plants themselves.

If it is inconvenient to mist the plants when they most need it, or if you live in an area that is arid, you might consider investing in a humidifier that can be set to release a fog once or twice a day. A small humidguide set among the plants will show at a glance the exact degree of humidity and prove a big help. Plump leaves that are solid-looking and free of wrinkles are always a good indication of adequate humidity.

59   Whenever there is insufficient humidity, not only will

Courtesy Lord & Burnham, Irvington-on-Hudson, New York

Figure 4-2. A humidity indicator is essential wherever orchids are grown.

the plants dry out much more quickly, but even the potting material will lose too much moisture. For newly potted plants this can be especially hazardous. In the case of mature plants, the sheaths sometimes stick together and do not open. Buds may fail to open, and even the tips of the flower sepals sometimes stick together. Although it is best never to allow such a dry atmosphere to develop, if it does happen and the situation is noted in time, it can be corrected by damping down and misting more frequently. Some growers, particularly those who grow orchids as house plants, place the plants on blocks of wood or plastic in trays of moist pebbles. The pebbles are kept constantly moist and raise the humidity around the plants, while the blocks keep the pots from standing in the water.

On the other hand, too high humidity—that is, humidity that is well beyond the needs of the plants—over an extended period creates an atmosphere where disease can flourish. This situation, if accompanied by temperatures that are also too high, generally results in weak plants that are unable to produce flowers.

Too much humidity in the atmosphere tends to condense on the foliage, and this is what paves the way for fungal diseases to become established. It also causes bud drop, spotting of flowers, and sheaths becoming black. Opening the ventilators in a greenhouse or the windows in the home will let in fresh air that will then circulate around the plants and dry out the atmosphere a bit.

Figure 4-3. The "Greenmist" humidifier, for increasing the amount of humidity, is a useful addition to a greenhouse.

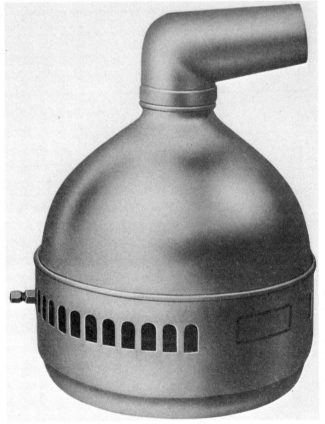

Courtesy Standard Engineering Co.

Experience has shown the following percentages of humidity to be best for the genera and species indicated:

high humidity 60–80%
Cattleya
Phalaenopsis
Vanda
Dendrobium (evergreen sorts)

moderate humidity 45–60%
Cymbidium
Paphiopedilum (Cypripedium)
Dendrobium (nonevergreen)
Oncidium
Miltonia
Some odontoglossums

low humidity 40–50%
Odontoglossum grande

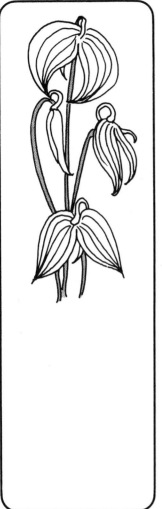

Potting Comes Next...

This is one of the most important and fundamental procedures in orchid culture. The growth and survival of the plant depend upon whether or not it has been potted in the correct manner, in a suitable potting material, and in a container that has provision for adequate drainage.

Because of their root structure, orchids unlike house plants, are rarely potted in soil. A visit to a commercial orchid firm to see how the experts pot their plants can be of great assistance.

Plants that have been improperly potted have little chance of growing well regardless of the otherwise good care they may receive. There are several ways in which

CHAPTER 5

Potting Comes Next . . . orchids can be potted, a variety of potting materials and containers from which to choose, and, above all, a correct time at which to do the potting.

CONTAINERS

First, we must realize that a pot is not a natural home for an orchid but rather a convenient receptacle to hold potting material and something that the orchids can cling to. The conditions under which orchids grow in their native habitat should always be kept in mind, however, for these influence both the type of container and the potting material used.

Clay and plastic pots are the most widely used containers, with the clay pots being used more with osmunda and both clay and plastic pots used with barks. If the clay pot seems to detract from the appearance of a plant in bloom, the plant can be temporarily set into a jardiniere or the pot itself covered with a pot cover that is available in attractive decorative colors. Under no circumstance should a clay pot be painted. This seals the pores and prevents the proper passage of moisture.

Orchids are extremely attractive when grown in baskets lined with sphagnum moss and then filled with osmunda or bark. Orchids can also be grown on tree fern logs, which have the advantage of closely resembling the setting in which the plants grow in the wild.

With either clay or plastic pots the hole at the bottom

Figure 5-1. Orchids grow well in baskets that provide good aeration for the roots.

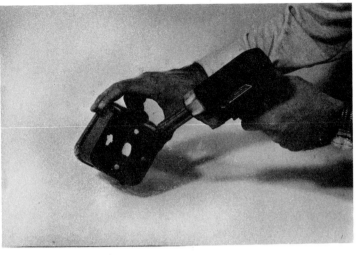

Figure 5-2. The holes in the bottom of a pot may have to be enlarged to provide adequate drainage.

Photo. Ralph Collins

must always be large enough to allow for adequate drainage. If the hole is too small, break the edge around it until it measures an inch or two in diameter.

Before using any pot, make certain it is scrupulously clean by soaking it in a solution of one part Clorox to four parts water and then rinsing it with clear water. New clay pots should be soaked in water for several hours or overnight before they are used to allow the pores of the pot to become thoroughly filled. In this way the pot will not absorb moisture from the potting material.

Obviously, the size of the plant determines the size of the pot used. Plants taken out of a community pot should go into 2 inch thumb pots. When they have outgrown these,

Figure 5-3. Notice the slits in the sides of these clay orchid pots, which provide easy drainage, and the chunks of osmunda in the appropriate sizes for each size of pot from seedling stage to mature plant.

Courtesy American Orchid Society

they can then be placed into 3 or 4 inch pots large enough to allow for two years of growth but no larger than this, because pots that are too large for a given plant easily lead to overwatering, which we shall discuss later in this chapter, under "Dividing."

No matter how carefully it is done, repotting is always something of a shock to a plant, and the flowers will not be at their best until the following year. Therefore, most orchids should not be potted every year.

POTTING MATERIALS

The purpose of the potting material is simply to hold the plant in place and not to provide nourishment, as is the case with the usual house plants. The material must also be porous to allow for good drainage, since orchids hate wet feet. The final criteria in the choice of a material are its availability, the ease with which you can handle it, and

Figure 5-4. An orchid should never be overpotted; there is a correct size of pot for every size of plant.

Photo. Ralph Collins

how well your particular plants grow in it. The reason garden loam is not used for most orchids, although it is added to bark and sphagnum moss for cymbidiums, is that the soft outer layer of the orchid root which takes up the moisture rots if confined in a pot containing soil. This is because soil is not porous enough to allow sufficient air to reach the roots and or to provide sufficient drainage.

Osmunda

Osmunda—the roots of the osmunda fern—is coarse and wiry. It allows a good circulation of air to reach the roots and provides excellent drainage. It was used almost exclusively by the old-time orchid growers because it was the nearest thing they could find to the medium in which the plants grew in their native habitat. Because of its nature, osmunda does supply some nutrients as it disintegrates. Therefore, plants potted in osmunda do not require additional feeding, and if they are fed, it should be with a smaller amount of food than plants in any of the other potting materials.

Before using osmunda, it should be soaked overnight and then squeezed out so that it is moist but not dripping wet. In this way it will not take moisture from the plant itself.

Osmunda can be purchased either in bales or in hobby-sized bags from most commercial orchid firms. It can be cut into the desired lengths with sharp shears or scissors. Since it does retain moisture for a longer time than most of the other potting materials, plants grown in it will require less frequent watering.

One way to tell when a plant in osmunda needs water is to look at and feel the fibers. If they are crisp, they have become too dry; if they are springy, watering can be delayed. It really does not take long for any grower to be able to judge when osmunda becomes dry, but it is important to learn how because if the osmunda is still wet when the plant is watered, the result is an overwatered plant, one whose roots may soon decay.

Bark

Bark is another widely used material for potting orchids. It is composed of small, uniformly sized pieces of redwood or fir bark. In recent years it has become the number-one choice of most growers because of its ease in handling. It comes in several sizes; a fine grade for seedlings; a medium grade for the majority of orchids; and a coarse grade for those with large, fleshy roots such as vandas.

Bark is also a good deal less expensive and easier to procure than osmunda. Unlike osmunda, however, it provides no nourishment. In fact, it tends to deplete the supply of nitrogen in the plant itself. Because of this, it is necessary when fertilizing to use a formula high in nitrogen. Bark needs nitrogen to aid its decomposition and takes about two years to decay. Osmunda takes a good deal longer.

Plants potted in bark also tend to dry out more quickly and require more frequent watering than those in osmunda. Root action appears to be the same in either material.

Figure 5-5. Mounting an orchid on a slab is the next best thing to growing it nature's way.

Tree-Fern Logs Tree-fern logs come from the fibrous trunks of tropical ferns of the Cyatheaceae family. They are available in many lengths and diameters and can easily be sawed into any size. They are ideal for many epidendrums and botanicals or species. The logs last for many years and need replacing only when their pores have become solidly filled with roots, leaving nothing more for the plant to hold onto.

Hapuu *Hapuu*, another material used in potting orchids, is the Hawaiian word for "tree fern." Depending upon the place from which it comes, it can be harder and more wiry than osmunda or softer, like some kinds of bark. It comes in slabs, which provide an excellent base on which to fasten orchids (plastic-covered wire will hold the plant to the slab). Fasten it securely so it will not wobble when it is watered. Eventually the roots grow in and around the slab itself, much as they would on a tree in the jungle. When cutting, make the slab large enough so there will be enough room for the plant to travel along it for at least two years.

Hapuu also comes in chunks and smaller pieces similar in size to bark pieces. Either form provides excellent drainage and aeration for the roots.

Orchid Mixes

Growers have come up with many variations of the basic potting materials of osmunda, bark, and tree fern. For want of a better name they refer to them as *orchid mixes*. These can be composed of bark and tree fern to which has been added some sphagnum moss to retain moisture. Perlite is sometimes added to give porosity. Even garden loam is added by some growers to make a mix specifically for cymbidiums and phaius orchids.

If your plants are growing well in a specific material, do not change it just for the sake of changing. Even if you visit other orchid growers and notice their plants flourishing in a different potting material, do not rush home and change your tried and true method. If you must experiment, try any new material on just a few plants at a time. Growing conditions and the care the orchids are given must be taken into consideration before any true comparison can be made. If, on the other hand, your plants lack vigor and have few flowers, changing the potting material might make all the difference in the world.

BASIC POTTING EQUIPMENT

Orchids will tolerate being confined to a pot much more readily if they have adequate drainage. Broken pieces of clay pot (known as crock), small pebbles, or coarse pieces of bark should be placed at the bottom of all pots to provide this drainage.

Pieces of crock are usually used with clay pots and osmunda, while pebbles are more commonly used with bark and other orchid mixes.

Florist's twine or twist ties cut to the desired length can be used for fastening pseudobulbs, leaves, and flowers to galvanized or wooden stakes.

Photo, Ralph Collins

Figure 5-6. All pots should be
crocked to provide adequate
drainage.

There are also special stakes that have the tops bent
into an open U-shape, which will hold the stems of the
paphiopedilums up straight. These stakes can also be easily
made from metal coat hangers.

Each plant should be labeled with its name, the names
of its forbears if known, the date potted, the date it flowered,
and the number of flowers it had. These labels can be made
of metal, wood, or plastic. They should be written on with
an indelible pen so that watering and misting will not
obliterate the information on them.

Another useful item is a potting stick, which is made
of either heavy metal or wood. It helps to push the bark
or osmunda firmly into the pots. Some shears or scissors
and either a bottle of alcohol or a spirit lamp to sterilize
70 the tools complete the basic equipment needed for potting.

Figure 5-7. Some of the many kinds of stake that can be used to hold the orchid growths upright.

POTTING AT DIFFERENT STAGES OF DEVELOPMENT

Potting Seedlings

Until recent years, when meristemming came into being, the most often used method of propagating orchids was growing them from seed. This was and is a time-consuming operation.

When a flower reaches its peak, hand-pollinating can begin. The pollinia from one orchid is placed on the stigma of another. After pollination, the flower wilts rapidly. To prevent decay from spreading down the column or stalk, it is best to cut the flower off at its base, leaving the stalk intact. In about a week's time the tip of this stalk becomes swollen. The pod that develops then continues to enlarge until it becomes ripe, which takes about three months to a year, depending upon the type of orchid. The pod then cracks open and the seeds are removed. These seeds are as fine as dust and are planted in sterile flasks filled with a solution of agar or a similar nutrient solution. In about a year the embryonic seed has become a seedling plant and is ready to be transplanted into a community pot.

Unless you are a serious and knowledgeable hybridizer cognizant of the genetic factors involved as well as the techniques of seed sowing, it is easier to buy flasks that have already been started by a commercial grower.

Community Pots

When the seedlings are $\frac{1}{2}$ inch tall, have developed two leaves, and are nice and plump, they can be transferred from the flask into a community pot. Open the flask, pour in $\frac{1}{2}$ cup of tepid water, and swish it around inside. Then pour out the water, and the seedlings that have come loose can be taken out with a piece of wire or a thin grapefruit knife. Removing some sections of the agar or other jelled substance may be necessary in order to get out the remaining seedlings.

Pluck the seedlings from the pieces of agar with sterile forceps and dip them, along with those that came out of the flask with the water, into a fungicide such as Wilson's Anti-Damp to prevent damping-off. The community pot can be any 4-, 5-, or 6-inch pot, or even a flat specially made for seeds, and should be well crocked at the bottom for drainage.

The potting material should have been soaked until damp all the way through. If you are using osmunda, cut the pieces up into strips and then place these strips into the pot vertically, using the potting stick to help force them

Figure 5-8. Cattleya seedlings ready for transfer to a community pot.

Figure 5-9. Paphiopedilums growing in an agar solution in a flask.

Figure 5-10. Cymbidium seedlings growing in a flask and ready to be transferred to a community pot.

in. When the pot is full of tightly packed osmunda, tip it to one side and cut off any straggly pieces with scissors so that there will be a flat surface across the top.

Then make a $\frac{3}{4}$-inch hole in the osmunda with an ice pick or small screwdriver. The hole should not be much larger in diameter than the seedling itself, so that when the seedling is put into the osmunda the osmunda will spring back around it and the remaining material in the pot will not be disturbed.

Continue to fill the pot with seedlings. One way to test whether each is snuggly in the pot is to take an ice pick and stroke it at right angles across a leaf. If the leaf bends but the base of the seedling remains rigid, that seedling is securely potted. If the seedlings are not put well down into the osmunda, they wash or gradually work their way out when watered.

The largest of the seedlings should be placed in the center of the pot, with the smaller ones around them at about 1 inch apart. All the leaves should be above the surface of the osmunda to keep them from damping off.

If you use bark or any of the orchid potting mixes, it is not possible to force the seedlings into the pot as tightly as it is with osmunda. Nevertheless, they must be put in as firmly as possible. Also, when you water those potted in bark, be sure the pieces of bark do not come floating out of the pot. When potting into bark or any of the mixes, the seedlings usually are placed in rows.

These tiny plants must now be kept moist. Placing a plastic bag over the community pot makes it into a miniature greenhouse, which will help to keep both the humidity and warmth constant—but always leave an opening in the bag so that there can be some circulation of air. The plastic bag itself will give a good indication of when watering is needed, since the droplets of moisture that collect inside evaporate as the moisture decreases. Never wait until all have disappeared before watering, however, because the seedlings at this stage need a moist atmosphere.

If algae accumulate on the inside of the bag, either replace the bag or wipe it clean. The seedlings should always have a clean, moist atmosphere with an adequate supply of fresh air. Seedlings also need warm temperatures, between 60 and 70°F (15–21°C), even at night. Temperatures can be slightly higher than this, but never any lower. Partial shade is also needed until they show signs of growth and

Potting Comes Next . . . new leaves appear. At this time the plastic may be removed and the seedlings given light, but not direct or hot sunlight.

Should any seedlings turn brown and watery-looking, spray them with a good anti-damping-off mixture according to the directions suggested for seedlings.

Many times you will see in advertisements the term *bare-root seedlings.* These are the ones that have just been taken out of a community pot and have not been put into their first individual pots. They are relatively inexpensive and are a good buy. In this way you do not have to purchase as many of one variety as you would if you bought either a flask containing dozens of plants or a community pot containing plants all of the same ancestry.

When bare-root seedlings arrive they often look rather dry. By placing them—leaves, roots, and all—at once in a bowl of tepid water they can be freshened up within a few hours. Then they can be potted, either in a community pot, if they are not very large, or in individual pots.

From Community Pots to Individual Pots

Growing your own community pot or buying plants in a community pot is one way to acquire orchids inexpensively. After all, it is you who will be growing them from infancy, so you will not have to pay for the time and care a commercial grower would have to expend on them. Although it is true that the seedlings in any one community pot will all be of the same cross, it is possible to exchange some of them with other growers, and thus you will be able to get plants you otherwise might not have.

After spending the best part of a year in a community pot, the seedlings should be ready for individual pots. Two-inch pots are the best size for this stage of growth,

Figure 5-11. Seedlings in community pots that are large enough for transfer to their first individual pots.

unless the seedlings are exceptionally large. A pot too large for the size of the seedling always results in overpotting. In such cases, not only is there danger of seedlings being overwatered, but their growth can be affected, since seedlings only grow well when their roots are near the sides and bottom of a pot.

Again, bark or osmunda will need to be soaked overnight so it will be thoroughly damp. Orchid mixes, on the other hand, need soaking for only a few hours. In either case, be sure that all excess water is squeezed out of the potting material, since it should never be soggy.

By slipping a knife around the edge of the community pot you should be able to lift out all the seedlings in one piece. Then gently separate the little plants. Broken roots should be trimmed off, and any seedlings still too small to go into individual pots should be put back into another community pot until large enough for their own pots.

Figure 5-12. All potting material should be thoroughly dampened before it is used.

Photo, Ralph Collins

Potting Comes Next . . .

Photo, Ralph Collins

Figure 5-13. Osmunda should
be cut into small chunks
before it is used.

If osmunda is used, cut it into pieces just long enough to wrap around the roots of each seedling. Then place the seedling, with its roots wrapped in osmunda, in a small pot that has been crocked for drainage. The base of the seedling should be $\frac{1}{4}$ inch below the top of the pot. If it is down too low, it might damp off. If too high in the pot, it could work its way out when it is watered. Continue pressing small pieces of osmunda into the pot until the seedling is firmly in. Finally, tamp in the osmunda with the potting stick. Label each pot and place it in a shady location. Grouping pots together helps to retain a moist atmosphere around them, and they will not dry out as quickly as when scattered about singly. They can all be set on one large tray that has been filled with pebbles kept constantly moist. As indicated before, damp pebbles help raise the humidity around the plants.

Plants in small pots always require more water than plants in large pots because the small pots dry out more quickly. At all times when you water, do it gently so the potting material does not come floating out. If that happens, put the plant back into the pot without disturbing the roots.

Mist the seedlings frequently with tepid water. This is an excellent way to provide moisture without soaking the roots through too many pot waterings, but mist before mid-afternoon so the foliage has time to dry before night. No plant should ever have wet leaves at night.

These little plants will then require shading for several weeks to recover from the shock of transplanting. Night temperatures at this time should still be no lower than 60–70°F (15–21°C).

Potting can always be done much more quickly if bark or one of the orchid mixes is used. The potting procedure is the same as with osmunda. The orchids should be potted as firmly as possible; however, since bark tends to move around more than osmunda, the plants should be loosely tied to small stakes to help anchor them into the pots.

If a fuzzy mold develops on the bark's surface, the atmosphere is too humid.

Seedlings never grow well in a stuffy atmosphere. They need just as good a circulation of fresh air as the older, more mature plants.

Some growers place their small pots in empty aquariums with a thick layer of pebbles in the bottom. As with older plants, the pots are then set on blocks of wood or plastic so they do not stand directly on the wet pebbles. If the aquarium cover is used, remove it at frequent intervals to allow for the circulation of air, it can even be left off entirely. The sides of the aquarium are high enough to retain the moisture.

After several weeks there should be a marked increase in root action. The plants can now be fed a weak solution of fish emulsion about once a month if potted in bark or in one of the orchid mixes. Seedlings potted in osmunda do not need any additional food at this time. In any case, a weak solution is advised, because too much fertilizer causes growths to become too soft and lush. All feeding, even foliar feeding (spraying a weak solution of fertilizer directly on the leaves) should be done only when the plants are out of the sun so there will be no chance of the tender young leaves being burned. Seedlings usually stay in their individual pots for about a year, after which time they are ready for their next move.

The Next Stage of Growth

Two or three years have now passed since the seedlings were first started in the flask. The roots should now be healthy and the leaves about 4 inches long. At all times when taking the seedlings out of their pots, try not to injure the roots, but any roots growing over the side of the pot should be cut off with sterile scissors. Attempting to force these roots into new potting material would only break them off.

At this stage in their growth the seedlings will probably need pots 3 or 4 inches in diameter. If they are potted in osmunda, some of this may still be attached to the roots; to avoid root damage, place such seedlings in the new pot with the osmunda attached. Since it has only been a year since they were placed in individual pots, the osmunda has not had a chance to decay, and it is not necessary to remove it all.

If the seedlings were potted in bark, it is, again, not wise to get every last piece from the roots. Little plants are not as vigorous as mature ones and need careful handling. If you plan to continue growing the plants in osmunda, again force the osmunda around the plant with the potting stick and keep forcing it into the pot until you positively can get no more in it. Potting firmly is important because it keeps the plants steady, and the roots will then not have a chance to pull out.

Place the plant in the center of the pot and add osmunda from the center of the pot toward the rim to help keep the osmunda from swelling up and coming out of the pot after the first watering. Place a stake against the leaves and tie them loosely to it. Again label the plant with name and the date of repotting.

Care at This Stage

The plants will need to be shaded for a week or so and the foliage misted frequently, especially on bright, sunny days. They will not dry out as quickly in these larger pots and will not need watering as frequently. The potting material should now be allowed to become almost dry between waterings, but never completely dry. The daily misting will help keep the atmosphere moist around them. Because they are now larger and more mature, there will be no need for the added protection of plastic bags around them or for them to be placed in aquariums. However, keeping them grouped together does maintain better humidity and makes it easier to care for them.

After several weeks, when they have recovered from the shock of repotting, they should begin to show signs of new growth. Then they can be moved from the shade to a brighter, sunnier location.

The Last Stage before Flowering

The time from the flask stage to flowering varies with the type of orchid and the growing conditions. On an average it takes from five to seven years.

Whenever the new growths begin to grow out over

the sides of the new 3- or 4- inch pots, or if the potting material appears worn out, it is time to repot the plants again. This time, repot into 5- or 6- inch pots.

Some of the plants may look quite large, having several good-sized leaves and growths, but this does not mean it is time to divide them. Repot the plant as before, taking all the same precautions. See that the roots are protected from injury, leaving small pieces of the old osmunda or bark attached if it has not decayed. Crock the pot with several inches of drainage material and a layer of osmunda or bark. This time, however, place the plant not in the center of the pot but to one side, against the rim of the pot and against the side of the pot from which new growth is not expected. This will enable the new growth, which consists of one or more eyes that show up as small swellings at the base of a pseudobulb or growth, to spread into the new potting material as it develops. At the end of two years the plant will probably need both dividing and repotting.

Plants grown in osmunda require little if any additional food. Those potted in bark should be fed about every three weeks, because the bark provides no nourishment.

Remember, you must keep a newly repotted plant shaded for a week and mist the foliage daily. New growth should begin to emerge in a short time. The plant should be watered just before it becomes dry. It is in this pot that the plant will flower for the first time. Since these first flowers are never as good as subsequent ones, be patient. The second flowering is much more indicative of the plant's potential.

REPOTTING THE MATURE PLANT

Every two or three years mature plants need to be repotted. By that time the potting material has usually become decayed, and the roots may be growing over the sides of the pot, for the new growths have no more room for further development. New live roots always grow along the rhizome as the plant grows. Thus, the feeding roots are ordinarily found beneath the lead growth, with very few live roots under the older growths and backbulbs. (Backbulbs are the old pseudobulbs found behind the actively growing pseudobulbs; although they often lack leaves, they are alive and may have one or more eyes.)

If the repotting of a plant were to be delayed and the

Figure 5-14. A mature cattleya badly in need of repotting.

new growth become jammed right up against the edge of the pot where it would have no place to grow and develop properly, the plant would not be able to depend on this new growth for sustenance and would be forced to rely on the backbulbs, which have little food or water left in them and may shrivel up.

Potting material that has become decayed may also damage the roots. All the plants enjoy fresh material in which to grow.

Even though repotting is always a shock to a plant, the shock can be minimized by doing it at the proper time, that is, when a new eye or growth is about 1 inch tall and the roots have started to grow once again after the plant has had a brief rest period in its growing cycle.

If you wait until the new growth has become several inches long, the shock of repotting the plant can be severe

Figure 5-15. Bandaging a tuft of osmunda under the new lead growth that has grown out over the side of the pot will allow the plant to flower without being disturbed by repotting.

enough to prevent the plant from flowering, as it may not have time to recover sufficiently before a bud would normally begin to develop. Between the repotting and the appearance of new buds, the drain on the plant's reserves could be enough to even hinder it from making any new roots—and roots are the most important part of any orchid. Never neglect to repot a plant when the time has come to do it.

When a plant is badly in need of being repotted and it cannot be done without interfering with the flowering cycle, a tuft of osmunda can be bandaged under the new long growth that has grown over the side of the pot. Another similar method is called "piggybacking." A pot the same size as the one the plant is already in is broken in half and one-half is snuggled up alongside the main pot. The two pots are then wired together. The "piggyback" pot is filled with the same potting material as the original pot until it reaches underneath the growth that has protruded. This growth will then have some potting material in which to grow and can eventually flower undisturbed.

In this way the risk of losing some of the flowers is

lessened. As a rule, orchids should never be repotted just before they flower. Neither should they be repotted when they are resting, before new growths begin developing. Then the backbulbs or older growths and the back part of the newer portions from which the new growth starts—and which contains the plant's reserves of food and water—are no longer adequate to carry the plant until the new roots and growth develop. Thus, disturbing a plant in its resting period upsets the whole cycle of growth.

Although it is technically true that orchids can be repotted at any time of year, they suffer less and recover more quickly when the potting is done during the warmer months, that is, spring, summer, or early autumn.

Figure 5-16. In "piggybacking," a second pot with the side cut off is attached to the main pot just below the protruding new growth and is filled with the same kind of potting material. This arrangement provides support and nourishment for the plant until it has finished flowering and can be repotted.

Unpotting

Before you can repot any plant you first have to unpot it. There is a correct way to do this. Healthy, well-grown plants have many roots that stick quite firmly to the inside of the pot. Consequently, if you were to take the plant in one hand, the pot in the other, and pull them apart, the roots so necessary for continued growth would be broken off. Roots that have been broken in this way stop growing at the breaks, and it takes a long time before they can develop new branch roots from these points.

On the other hand, there is no need to break the pot to get the plant out. The easiest way to do it is to water the plant well just before repotting, for roots that are moist loosen more easily from the insides of a pot than do dry ones.

Next, run a knife around the pot between the potting material and the pot itself. Then push a stick through the drainage hole against the pieces of crock in the bottom of the pot. The plant should then slip out easily with few or no broken roots. When it is finally out of the pot, examine it carefully. This is the time to correct anything that might have gone wrong since it was last potted.

Handling of Roots

While removing the old potting material carefully, check whether any of the roots have decayed. If they have, trim off all such portions. These trimmed roots will eventually

Figure 5-17. Carefully cut off any dead or diseased parts before repotting.

Photo. Ralph Collins

Figure 5-18. A plant that has developed long aerial roots will have to have them cut back to 1-inch stubs before repotting.

branch out and give renewed vigor to the whole root system. If left on, the decay would always be present and might eventually spread to other parts of the plant. Don't forget, too, that at the same time the new roots make their appearance the older ones also experience a wave of activity.

Many plants develop aerial roots, some of which may grow rather long. They look so healthy it is always a temptation to preserve them, but it is almost impossible to get them into the new pot without severely injuring them. And even if you did manage to get them in, they probably would not survive because they are what their name implies—air roots—and detest being buried in potting material. Even when the tips of these aerial roots do get into the potting material on their own, the portion of the root behind the growing point always remains in the air.

It might be heartrending to a new orchid grower who

85

Potting Comes Next . . . is so proud of the fine cultural technique that has resulted in all this root growth to cut them back to a 2-inch stub, but this is exactly what is needed. These stubs will send out new little aerial rootlets which, together with the roots in the pot, will assure the plant's optimum growth. These new roots are even more important than the old ones in maintaining the health of an orchid.

Orchid roots really look quite attractive. They have a light green tip behind which they are covered with a snow-white substance known as *velamen*. This covering protects the roots, helping them absorb both food and water.

Repotting Gently pull away all the old potting material that you possibly can. Some can be left around the newest growth so that it will have something familiar to hold onto. Leaving it also prevents any injury to the roots if it should prove to

Figure 5-19. Remove as much of the old potting material as possible from in and around the roots.

be difficult to remove. Be certain that any material that is left on is in good condition. If there are any signs of decay, it should be removed.

This is the time to cut off any dead or yellowed leaves and to check the plant thoroughly for signs of disease. If the paper-thin tissue covering a pseudobulb is loose, it can easily be taken off if it is moistened first. This thin tissue is called *cataphyll,* and it often provides a hiding place for scale, which is one reason it should be removed if it can be done easily. However, you should never *tear* it off the plant, particularly when it is still brown, because the new eye or growth emerges through this cataphyll, and tearing it off could easily break off the new growth.

Cut away any areas that are diseased or show signs of rot with a sterile knife or shears. By using only sterilized tools you insure that viruses and fungi are not transmitted from one plant to another.

When a plant has seven or eight pseudobulbs or growths, repotting four or five of the newest ones is better than just moving the whole plant into a larger container. An exception is when the plant is a choice one that blossoms profusely and makes a good specimen plant. The care and handling of specimen plants is discussed in more detail in Chapter 8.

One reason for not placing all plants into larger pots is the matter of convenience. It is easier to lift and water 5- or 6-inch pots than huge containers. If space is limited, it is also possible to have a greater variety of plants when all of them are in moderate-sized pots.

Aftercare of the Mature Plant

After potting, plants should always be kept in a shaded place out of the direct rays of the sun and not pot-watered for a week to 10 days. Instead, rely upon misting the leaves and the top of the potting material to supply the needed moisture. If some of the pseudobulbs or growths begin to shrivel after potting, this does not necessarily mean the plant is in need of water. Just continue misting until the new roots develop, and then the pseudobulbs and growths will become plump once again as the new roots take over the functions of supplying the plant with food and water.

Root action is the energy-maker for all plants. If the roots die from having had too much water, there is no means of supplying food and moisture, and the plant soon dies.

Normally roots should begin to show signs of developing from the newer growths, and the older leaves, pseudobulbs, and growths will begin to plump up again within several weeks.

As the plant begins its new growing cycle, its need for water increases. In fact, in its entire growth cycle it needs the most water when the new growths are forming. Always remember, plants that have many roots in good condition always need more water than those in less-than-perfect health.

If any of the leaves fall off after repotting, no harm is done. Those leafless pseudobulbs and growths that still have roots on them are the storage places for water, and they can still contribute their share to the growth of the plant. The next time the plant is repotted, these leafless growths and pseudobulbs can be cut off at their base.

The yellowing of leaves is also a natural process on older growths and does not indicate that the plant is dying. For mature orchids, follow the suggestions given earlier for light, temperature, humidity, and watering for each type.

Finally, the plants need as much fresh air as they can get safely, for good air circulation eliminates the stagnant atmosphere in which rot and disease thrive. As long as a plant is medium green and the growths and pseudobulbs are plump, the humidity and light have apparently been in the right proportion.

DIVIDING When a plant has many growths, dividing often becomes a necessity. This entails breaking the plant into two or more sections. To do this, cut through the rhizome or between the growths with a sharp, sterile knife or shears. One section should contain four or five of the newer growths and the other two or three of the older ones. Make the cut a clean one with no jagged edges. There should be live eyes or growths—that is, swellings about 1 inch tall—at the base of at least one pseudobulb or growth on each division.

Many plants, however, develop only one new lead (new, young vegetative growth) a year, so that every time a plant is repotted it is not necessary or even desirable to divide it. A plant should be divided only when it has become too large to handle comfortably or has too many dead growths in its center.

The front or lead division with its roots trimmed off is now ready for potting. If the other division has a live eye or the start of a new growth, it, too, can be potted as a separate plant. However, if there are no live eyes or new growths, this section is known as a *backbulb.* Its handling will be discussed in Chapter 9.

Choose a pot large enough to leave room for two or more new leads to develop. Orchids should never be put into pots that are larger than needed to accommodate the growth of the next two years, because the potting material would then have a tendency to stay wet, particularly in the center of the pot, which is the last place to dry out, while around the edges it may be dry. When this happens the plant never has time to dry out between waterings, a common cause of diseased and rotted roots. Since we should always try to duplicate the natural growing conditions of orchids as closely as possible, the roots must have a chance to dry out between waterings just as they do in the wild.

To repeat, every pot should be thoroughly scrubbed with a solution of 1 part Clorox to 3 parts water. Then it should be soaked in plain water overnight. This fills the pores of the pots so that they do not take moisture from the plant itself. This is especially important with clay pots.

Old clay pots often have a grayish white appearance that is the result of fertilizer salts that have accumulated on their surfaces. If this is not scrubbed off, any roots that come into contact with them may become burned.

USING THE POTTING MATERIALS

Osmunda

After enough pieces of crock have been placed in the bottom of the pot to ensure adequate drainage, put a small piece of damp osmunda on top of the crock. Hold the plant in one hand and lower it into the pot, making certain that the rhizome is level with the top of the pot or just a bit below the back of the oldest growth. The back part of the plant should be firmly against the inside edge of the pot. As mentioned before, a mature plant is always potted away from the center of a pot and off to one side so that there is room for new growths to develop over the next two years.

Gently spread the roots apart with your other hand. Then pack the previously cut-up chunks of osmunda vertically around the roots. By placing the osmunda vertically in the pot instead of horizontally there is less chance of

Figure 5-20. The back part of
the plant should be set firmly
against the edge of the pot,
allowing room at the front for
several years' new growth.

its working its way out when the plant is watered. Force
the osmunda into the pot with the potting stick until there
is absolutely no room for more.

Finally, put your finger between the pot and the
osmunda. If there is any space there, take a chunk of osmunda
and this time lay it horizontally across the pot and then
force it down into the pot vertically with the potting stick.
This will fill any space between the rim of the pot and
the osmunda. If necessary, continue doing this all round
the pot.

Old-time growers used to lift the plants up by their
leaves to test the firmness of the potting. Any plant that
wiggles has not been properly potted. Such loose potting
is one cause of a plant's leaves and pseudobulbs shriveling,
because it leads to a poor distribution of water.

If the plant is one that has a rhizome, this should

always be flat with the surface of a pot, and new eyes should always be visible just above or close to the top of the osmunda. Burying the eyes can cause them to rot, and any new eyes that might develop would come out way above the osmunda. The back portions of the plant should never be placed too deep in the pot. As far as possible they, too, should be level with the surface of the osmunda to prevent rotting. If this back part were put in too deeply, the front growths might emerge right up into the air, above the potting material, and any roots that developed from this elevated portion would have no potting material beneath to hold onto and thus would be unable to get sufficient water and nutrients for a time; they would also make the plant lopsided.

No plant can reach its full potential when it is incorrectly potted, so take the time to do the job right. If you do not, then all future pottings of that plant will be difficult, because you will be forced to try to correct the lopsided growth and in many cases will not be too successful in doing so.

If, when you are potting, the rhizome starts to hump up, remove a few pieces of osmunda and settle the plant down again. If that does not help, the only thing left to do is to start the potting all over again, for a humped-up plant will only hump up more when you water it, and before you know it the new growths and roots will all be up in the air. Before finishing, tie the leads to a stake and label the plant.

Bark or Orchid Mixes

When using bark and similar products, pots should be crocked with gravel, pebbles, or crock. Again, hold the plant against the side of the pot with one hand, then pack in the bark or orchid mix around the roots with the other hand. Neither bark nor an orchid mix need be tamped in as forcefully as osmunda. When the pot is filled with the new material, tap it gently on a smooth surface. This will help settle the material and allow more to be added if necessary. Repeat this until the pot is tightly packed and full of potting material.

Before you finish, check to see that all rhizomes or growths are on or just a bit below the surface of the potting material. A clip-on stake is more useful for plants that have been potted in these softer, more porous materials. If the plant is still wobbly—and this is often the case when there

Figure 5-21. Put a layer of
bark in the bottom of the pot,
over a layer of crock or stones,
before setting in the plant.

are not enough roots to anchor it—place a piece of U-shaped
wire across the rhizome and anchor both ends of this wire
into the potting material.

How Long Potting Materials Last

Osmunda, bark, and the orchid mixes last for varying lengths
of time, but they all break down more rapidly when the
atmosphere is humid or when there is an overabundance
of water. As a rule, these potting materials should remain
in good condition for two or three years.

When the osmunda has become soft and spongy instead
of crisp, or the bark or the mixes show signs of decay and
become compacted, the material is no longer in good condition. In such cases the only good roots will probably be
those in the upper part of the material. Those in the bottom
of the pot, where there has been little or no air, will probably
have died. Then, if the potting material decays at a faster
rate than has been suggested, it might be wise to reevaluate
both the level of humidity and the frequency of watering.

Figures 5-22 and 5-23 courtesy American Orchid Society. Photos. The Staggs

Figure 5-22 (below). Pack the potting material in and around the roots.

Figure 5-23 (above). Tie the plant to a stake to keep it from wobbling until the new roots have developed. Notice the two new eyes about 1-in long developing from two of the pseudobulbs.

Moving Plants from one Medium to Another

Because of the scarcity of osmunda and its high cost, many growers have turned to bark or to one of the many orchid mixes that are available. When changing from one material to another, if it is possible, leave a bit of the previous material attached to the plant, provided it is still in good condition. Other than this, all traces of the old material should be removed from in and around the roots. If every last piece cannot be removed without breaking some of the roots, it will be necessary to leave these pieces on the plant.

If while transferring a plant from osmunda to bark you must leave a piece of the osmunda around the plant, be sure that it is a small piece. Osmunda holds water longer than bark, and leaving on too large a piece tends to retain water in that area while the bark around it dries out. In such a spot decay can easily start.

...& Watering

Because so many orchids come from areas that experience extensive amounts of rain, an erroneous impression has been created that orchids must live in an environment that is constantly wet to the point of saturation. However, in their native habitat orchids are not confined to pots, and their roots are not encased in potting material as they are with us.

The epiphytic orchids, such as the cattleyas, grow right on the trunks of trees, and their roots are completely exposed to the air. These orchids receive moisture from the copious rainfall, which then runs right off the plants. This rainfall also keeps the humidity at a high level. The plants always dry off rapidly when the sun shines again. This whole process of sun and rain is continuously repeated; frequent rain-showers interspersed with equally frequent periods of sunshine enable the plants to have a sufficient amount of moisture but never to become soggy.

This is the condition that we try to duplicate when we allow the plants to become almost dry between waterings. Whenever watering, be certain that the potting material becomes thoroughly wet. The roots of the plant can then take up the moisture and pass it on to the pseudobulbs, growths, and leaves, which act as the storage places for the water for times when the plant may not have enough moisture.

Orchid roots need air as well as water. This is why it is stressed over and over again that potting material must be almost dry before a plant is rewatered. It is only when the potting material starts to become dry that air can circulate through it, for obviously air and water cannot occupy the same space at the same time.

HOW TO TELL WHEN WATERING IS NEEDED

You should always lift a plant up before you water it. If it feels light this is a sign that water is needed. On the other hand, if it feels heavy, watering can be postponed for awhile—until it has had a chance to dry out a bit more. Lifting the pots provides a better indication of whether a plant needs water than just depending upon how dry the top of the potting material looks. If the pot is heavy and the potting material already wet when the plant is watered, the sodden mass that would result could cause extensive rotting of the roots.

It is through capillary action that the top of the potting material becomes damp during the night. The morning, before the plants have had a chance to dry out again from the heat of the sun, is the best time to check on whether or not they need to be watered. In this way there is less chance of overwatering. Furthermore, damp potting material always absorbs water faster than dry.

Every plant will not need watering at the same time. It is never advisable to decide that since you are going to do some watering you might as well water every one of them. There is no other activity in orchid culture that is performed as often as watering. While you are checking

each plant to see whether or not it needs water, also take

time to check for signs of pests or diseases. If this is done faithfully, there will never be any large infestations on the plants. This is also a good time to see whether any of the pseudobulbs need to be straightened. If they do, they can be tied to rigid stakes with twist ties. If there are sheaths that show signs of rotting or buds that have become cramped inside a sheath, now is the time to take corrective measures. By making watering a leisurely activity, you will get to know your plants well, and corrective measures taken in time prevent serious problems from developing. The result will be healthy, well-grown orchids.

Plants that are resting, that show no signs of new growth, need very little water, but they do need their pseudobulbs and leaves misted frequently. Remember that growth must always precede watering—never attempt to force the new growth through watering.

When the new growth does start, the eyes begin to form and pseudobulbs or growths to develop. The plants will then require more water than at any other period in their growth cycle. Any plants in bud should never be allowed to dry out, because the buds would then not be able to develop into proper-sized flowers. Instead, they would be thin, stringy, and of poor substance. Cramped buds inside a flower sheath are often the result of a lack of moisture at the roots at a critical stage in the plant's development. Moisture, either from watering or from misting, should not remain in the axils (the main stems) of the leaves, for this sets the stage for rot. Fortunately, such excess water can easily be removed with a tissue or a swab stick.

To continue watering as often when a plant has matured and ripened as when it was just developing can actually postpone the flowering cycle. In some cases, the flowering stage is skipped entirely and the plant just sends up another growth. In fact, with such care it may keep on sending out one new growth after another, none of which flower.

Until such time as the buds become visible in the sheath, give the plant less water. Failing to do this could cause a dramatic decrease in the number of flowers it will have. After flowering is completed, most plants go into a resting period, at which time the need again is for less water. At the end of the resting period, the cycle of growth starts all over again, with the developing of new growths and new roots.

97

Plants that have many roots both in the potting material and growing out all over the sides of the pot will always absorb more water than those with only a few roots. Watch the former closely for any signs of dehydration.

TERRESTRIAL VS. EPIPHYTIC ORCHIDS

The terrestrial or ground orchids, such as the paphiopedilums, whose roots have no protective covering, should always be kept moist and never be allowed to become completely dry.

Still, since all orchid roots must have air, even the terrestrials must not be subjected to a potting material that remains wet. They, too, need to dry out somewhat between watering, but not as much. One way to do this is to give them a somewhat more earthlike medium to grow in.

The epiphytic orchids, on the other hand, those that grow attached to the trunks of trees, need a potting material that is porous and capable of becoming almost dry between waterings. As indicated before, these orchids have roots that have a thick protective covering of velamen. This covering makes these roots much tougher than the roots of the terrestrial orchids. When the roots of the epiphytes are dry, they become snow-white and their tips are usually a light green. Whenever these roots become too wet over too long a period, they become a dull green color. Continued overwatering may eventually turn them brown and could cause them to rot off.

Pseudobulbs or growths that have become wrinkled during a plant's resting period do not necessarily need more water in order to become plump once again. The problem can also be caused by roots that have rotted from too much water. Thus, additional water on them will just kill more of the roots and finally kill the plant itself. What is needed is more frequent misting, less pot-watering, and time to allow the new roots to develop.

Orchids are different from the usual house plants in that they have roots that can live indefinitely on atmospheric moisture without becoming dry. In addition, the pseudobulbs and the leathery leaves, when present, hold reserves of water that the plants can draw upon when needed. Therefore, surprising as it may seem, orchids die less often from dryness than from too much water.

All plants, both terrestrial and epiphytic, that have just been potted are better off if set off by themselves to recover from the shock of potting. They should not be watered until such time as an eye or new roots emerge, and it is better to rely upon misting to keep them from drying out. By grouping them together you can watch them more closely, and they will also create their own atmospheric moisture. Carrying this a bit farther, all plants in clay pots should be placed together and all those in plastic pots together. Obviously, plants in plastic pots need to be watered less frequently than those in clay, and if not kept separate, it would be very easy to underwater those in the clay pots and overwater those in the plastic pots.

Those plants that are growing on tree-fern slabs or logs and those hanging from branches of trees during the summer do not retain water for very long. The water seems to run right through them. The weight of the tree-fern slab or log when lifted is a better indication of the need for water than the look of it. If the slab feels light, it should be watered. The underside of the slab or log should be watered and misted as well as the topside. However, unless all watering is thorough, any fertilizer salts that might build up on the slab will not leach out and could eventually kill the roots.

KINDS OF WATER

We all take water so much for granted that few of us give any thought to whether it is hard or soft or contains any unwanted chemicals. Old-time growers collected rainwater in barrels and used that exclusively to water their orchids. They felt it gave the plants the same kind of water they received in their native habitat. Unfortunately, today, with air pollution so widespread, even rainwater may not be the panacea it once was. Fortunately for most of us, however, the water supply in most communities or from our wells is safe for orchids and also contains some nutrients.

A proper pH balance—a balance between acidity and alkalinity—is important. A medium pH of 6.2–7 is ideal, but a slight variation either way does no harm to most orchids. It is not the pH balance of the water that causes the problems, but the salt content. A high chlorine level in the water supply may make it mandatory to find another source or even to revert to using rainwater. Chlorine retards root action and can kill plants if enough is present. Fluorides in municipal water systems, however, do not appear to be harmful to orchids.

So-called "hard water" is water high in calcium and magnesium salts. If this is the only water available, be sure always to water liberally, flushing the pots out thoroughly to prevent any buildup of these salts. The water softeners often used in regions that have hard water may be excellent for laundry purposes, but they are strictly taboo for orchids. For the most part, these water softeners just exchange sodium salts for the calcium and magnesium salts and are just as toxic to orchids. Aerial roots, for example, will turn brown and wither, then become black and die from these highly soluble sodium salts; a demineralizer should be used to treat softened water. As a result, hard water that has not been treated by water softeners is always preferable to water that has been so treated.

If the available water supply is good enough for you, the chances are it will be good enough for your orchids.

HOW OFTEN TO WATER

Any potting material used for orchids should be sufficiently porous to allow water to flow freely through it and then out through the bottom of the pot, which has been crocked to facilitate this drainage. Fresh potting material will require more water more often than potting material that is several years old. Osmunda, for example, retains water much longer than does bark, which has a tendency to dry out rather quickly. Orchid mixes, which are composed of bark, tree fern, sphagnum moss, and the like, fall somewhere between osmunda and straight bark in their water-retention properties.

When bark becomes bone-dry the water will run right through it, and the pot will still feel light when you lift it, because bark that is too dry cannot absorb the water readily enough. This is one reason that bark should always be soaked overnight before it is used.

Whenever a plant that has been potted in bark does become too dry, water the plant thoroughly and let it drain for a short time. Then rewater it—even water it a third time if necessary. The spacing of these waterings will dampen the material slowly, and eventually the moistened bark will be able to retain sufficient moisture.

On the other hand, any of the orchid mixes that retain water too long should have more bark, osmunda, or tree fern added to increase their porosity. This may necessitate potting the plant all over again in the altered mix. Allowing the plants to dry out between waterings is the only way that roots encased in the pot are able to get sufficient oxygen.

Atmospheric conditions also have a bearing on the frequency with which plants are watered. If the air is humid, the plant will receive additional moisture from the air and will not dry out quite so rapidly. Watering under these conditions might be needed only every week or 10 days.

During protracted spells of cloudy weather there is less need for watering, for then there is no hot sun to dry out both plants and air. In fact, it is never a good idea to water during cloudy, rainy, dark weather. Try to do it on bright, sunny days only, and finish before midafternoon so that the foliage will be able to dry off before night.

During the long periods of dry weather in summer or whenever conditions seem to be drier than usual— including winter, when the heating system is going full blast—it is necessary to water more frequently. In summer, in particular, this could be as many as three or four times a week.

In any case, each and every watering should be thorough. The top of the potting material should never be just sprinkled. It is essential to water deeply so that all the fertilizer salts or even any salts that may be in the water supply itself will be leached out.

Figure 6-1. Soak the potting material thoroughly when watering the plants.

Courtesy American Orchid Society

The size of the pot will also determine how frequently a plant needs to be watered. Large plants in 7- or 8-inch pots, depending upon atmospheric conditions and the type of potting material, can go as long as two weeks between waterings. Under the same conditions, smaller pots dry out faster, and the plants in them sometimes need to be watered as often as twice a week. Under average conditions, however, the time between waterings is about a week.

HOW TO WATER

Plants in a greenhouse are frequently watered with a hose. The potting material is flooded with water, which then drains out through the bottom of the pot. Orchids growing indoors as house plants are best watered by submerging the pot in a container of water.

When using a hose, be sure to water only the potting material and to continue watering it until the pot becomes flooded. If you do not splash it over the plants, there is less chance of its remaining in the leaves or sheaths, for a few drops of water left there give disease and rot a chance to start. Similarly, the leaves and pseudobulbs should merely be misted rather than watered.

A $\frac{1}{2}$-inch piece of sponge cemented to a spatula makes an ideal tool for taking up any water that has become lodged among the leaves.

Whenever you put a plant into a bucket of water, the rim of the pot should be level with the top of the water, particularly if the potting material is bark or one of the orchid mixes. If the pot is not level with the water, you may end up with the potting material getting loose and floating around in the bucket. If this happens, it must then be put back in around the plant and firmly packed in. Also, when you pot-water, hold the pot in the water until all signs of bubbling have stopped. This takes only a minute or two. Then set the plant on a raised piece of wire that has been placed on a tray and let it drain.

WATER TEMPERATURES

The water used on the plants should always be tepid. It should feel comfortable on your hands. If you use rainwater, particularly during cold weather, let it stand a day or so until it reaches room temperature.

Tap water should also be warm. A mixing faucet for hot and cold water is a real necessity in a greenhouse, for water that is too warm may cause the roots to become soft, while water that is too cold may shock the plant and retard its growth. Still, there are growers who are of the opinion that water as low as 45°F (7°C) is not harmful to orchids. However, it does seem kinder to the plants to see that they are not shocked with a cold bath.

Cold water that drops down on the plants from the top of the greenhouse, particularly in cold weather, can also cause serious problems, such as damping-off of the new growths, black rot, and spots on the leaves. These calamities can all be treated with an antidamping compound, but it is much better if the plants are moved away from areas where the water can drip on them.

RESULTS OF OVERWATERING

Overwatering, which in orchid culture means watering while a plant is still wet from a previous watering, quickly breaks down the potting material into a sodden mass and makes repotting necessary more often. Potting material that has become waterlogged also kills off the roots, because water-soaked material leaves little or no room around the roots for the air that orchid plants must have to survive. Also, it contributes to black rot.

Soggy material takes a long time to dry out, and if more water is continually applied to it before it has a chance to dry out, the results can be fatal to the plant.

As indicated earlier, plants that have been potted into too-large containers are easily overwatered. Therefore, always match the size of the pot to the size of the plant. It should be just large enough to allow for two years of growth. Oversized pots dry out slowly, leaving the material in the center of the plant wet most of the time, even when the potting material has become dry around the edges.

When any of a plant's roots have died from too much water, the leaves dependent upon these roots for their moisture turn yellow, become watery-looking, die, and drop off. The deadly disease known as basal decay, which particularly affects paphiopedilums, is caused both by overwatering and water standing in the axils of the leaves. Furthermore, the old rotting flower stem at the base of these leaves also makes an ideal place for this kind of decay to develop.

Once roots decay they cannot renew themselves, and any nutrients given plants that have been overwatered are wasted, because the decaying roots are not able to utilize the food.

Remember, too, that while it is easy to get potting material too wet, it is a lot harder to dry it out. The only cure is to let it dry out completely until it becomes crisp once again. If this seems to take too long and the plant is getting worse, take the plant out of the sodden material and repot it in fresh material. Then keep it partially shaded and rely on misting to try to get new roots and growth started rather than relying on watering. The length of time an orchid takes to start growing again after having suffered this damage varies depending upon the kind of plant and how much damage has been done. Orchids are very tenacious of life. So give any plant at least six months to show signs of recovery before giving up hope.

RESULTS OF UNDERWATERING

Potting material that has not been firmly packed into a pot lets the water run right through with no chance of retaining any of the moisture. Consequently, the growths are then forced to rely upon their stored supply of water, and when that is gone they begin to dehydrate. There are other conditions that also cause pseudobulbs and growths to wrinkle, but an attempt should be made to restore their plumpness by frequent misting with a fine spray of tepid water before resorting to other measures.

Whatever the cause, not having enough moisture adversely affects new growths in particular. They tend to become stunted and withered. Insufficient water also causes the roots to become weak and thin instead of plump and strong, and plants with no active roots are forced to live on moisture wherever it can be found—usually from the pseudobulbs and leaves, which depletes the moisture in them and again results in the shriveling described above.

MISTING

Misting means spraying a fine cloud of water on the leaves, pseudobulbs, and growths. When the underside of a leaf is misted, the water becomes even more available to the plant, because the underside is more absorptive and does

not have the waxy substance found on top.

The commercial misters have nozzles that can vary the spray from fine to coarse and can be attached to a hose for use in a greenhouse. Indoors, smaller brass misters or air-freshener bottles that have been thoroughly cleaned make excellent devices for spraying the foliage. Under ordinary conditions, plants should be misted at least once each day, although during bright, warm weather it may be necessary to do it several times a day.

The additional moisture that misting provides also helps to keep the plants from shriveling by raising the humidity around them. Thus, as we mentioned earlier, all newly potted plants, even when grouped together, tend to dry out quickly and therefore need misting several times a day. But, only the leaves, pseudobulbs, and growths should be misted. If the potting material is also moistened, it results in overwatering.

The aerial roots, the long roots that grow out into the air, often do not get watered when the plant does. They, too, will remain in much better condition and be better able to contribute their share to the plant's growth if they are also misted every day.

Flowers and buds, however, should not be misted. The flowers may become spotted and in some cases turn brown. Furthermore, the plants may accumulate moisture in and around the buds which, if left there, may cause them to rot.

DAMPING-DOWN

Spraying water on the floor, walls, and benches of a greenhouse to wet them thoroughly is called *damping-down* and is not the same as watering or misting the plants. Watering wets the growing medium; misting moistens the plants. Damping-down adds to the total humidity of the air in the greenhouse, which again helps the plants and particularly the aerial roots to absorb additional moisture from the air.

The frequency and amount of damping-down that is necessary is, of course determined by both the temperature and the season of the year. It can vary from just once a day during the winter, when both the sun and the heater have some drying effects, to as much as three or four times a day in hot summer weather—to no damping-down at all on damp, dark, cloudy days. However, greenhouses should never be wet all of the time. They need to dry out once in awhile, if only to keep the algae under control.

It is important, too, that damping-down always be done

before mid-afternoon. This allows the greenhouse to dry out a bit before night. It is also important to remember that a greenhouse is never as warm during the night, even with the temperature at 65–70°F (18–21°C) as it is during the day, when the heat of the sun is on it. Leaves that are wet the first thing in the morning indicate that the moisture during the night has been overdone and could lead to fungi developing on the leaves. The reason for this is that during the night, when the temperature has dropped markedly from its midday high and the house is tightly shut up, the humidity tends to rise.

RESTING

Resting is that period after flowering when an orchid is inactive—when no new roots or growths have yet appeared. It will be discussed in greater detail in Chapter 8. However, we should mention here that the resting cycle calls for a drier atmosphere, with lower humidity and less need for watering and misting than at other times.

Feeding Your Orchids

In their native habitat orchids receive nourishment from the vegetative matter that accumulates around their roots and that is constantly being replenished by falling leaves and other decaying matter. The nutrients in this material are then dissolved by the rains and carried onto the roots of the plants.

Since we grow our plants in pots or baskets or on slabs of tree fern, and since in most climates orchids cannot remain outdoors all year round, the only way we can be certain they will have sufficient nutrients is for us to supply them in the form of fertilizer. Both the amount and the kind of fertilizer used are largely determined by the potting medium and the type of orchid grown.

Osmunda, being a natural substance that slowly decays, is able to provide orchids with some nutrients through its decomposition. Thus for many years growers did not feed plants that were potted in osmunda. Even today, plants potted in osmunda can grow fairly well without any additional fertilizer. However, a weak solution of a water-soluble fertilizer (about one-quarter the usually recommended strength) sprayed on the leaves of the plants as a foliar feeding appears to improve both the size of the growths and the quality of the flowers. In spite of this, there are still many growers who feel that to add any fertilizer at all to plants growing in osmunda will result in overfeeding.

In recent times bark has become the most widely used material for potting orchids; since, however, it provides no nutrients, plants growing in it must always be fertilized. Not only is the bark itself low in nitrogen, but as it decays the bacteria tend to use up what little is available, even taking it from the plant if need be. But since bark is such a wonderful material for potting, being so porous and providing such good drainage, having to feed plants occasionally with a fertilizer relatively high in nitrogen is a small price to pay for the good culture bark encourages.

Orchids potted in tree fern or on tree-fern slabs or logs or in *hapuu* (Hawaiian tree fern) will benefit from occasional light foliar feedings with a balanced fertilizer. Plants potted in any of the various orchid mixes composed of bark, fiber, sphagnum moss, and the like need some supplemental feeding. In fact, plants growing in any material other than osmunda need a fertilizer fairly high in nitrogen.

FERTILIZERS

Now for the fertilizers themselves: All contain the three basic elements—nitrogen, phosphorous, and potash—plus any trace elements the manufacturer may add. However, these trace elements are not always essential in an orchid fertilizer, because frequently there is enough in the water or as impurities in the fertilizer to supply the needs of orchids.

Nitrogen is the first number shown in any fertilizer formula, and it is the substance that gives orchids their healthy green color. It is also essential for vegetative growth. Yet too much nitrogen can cause excessive growth, which becomes a dark green color, and growth that is too lush and that is readily susceptible to rot. Too much nitrogen can also delay or even prevent flowers from developing. On the other hand, when there is not enough, growth becomes stunted and the whole growing process is retarded. This lack of nitrogen often first becomes apparent when the older leaves on a plant turn yellow. Some may even turn bronze or red, and if uncorrected this condition may progress through to the newer leaves. At the same time, new growths are slow to develop, and what growths do emerge are small. The leaves also lose their sheen and become dull-looking and feel hard when touched. If the deficiency is not remedied, these leaves may eventually lose all of their green coloring (chlorophyll).

To distinguish between those plants that exhibit symptoms of nitrogen starvation and those whose symptoms, although more or less similar, are due to overwatering, to injury by a buildup of fertilizer salts around the roots, or to being burned by too much hot sun, one should remember that the pseudobulbs and growths of nitrogen-starved plants do not show excessive shriveling, because their roots are still in good condition. In fact, sometimes the condition of the roots is the only clue to the difference.

Plants that are pot-bound, with roots growing out all over the sides of the pots, may also show some of the same symptoms, even when well fertilized, because in such cases there may not be enough viable potting material left to retain the nutrients and the plants become starved. Even foliar feeding of these aerial roots may not be sufficient to supply food to the whole plant.

Naturally, an adequate feeding with a high-nitrogen fertilizer eliminates some of the symptoms of nitrogen deficiency in plants potted in bark, but it is only in the new growth that the leaves and growths will be completely green and show no signs of either stunting or discoloration. The older leaves will always show some evidence that at one time they did not receive sufficient nitrogen.

In attempting to correct a nitrogen deficiency it is not enough just to have the first number of the fertilizer formula showing a high percentage; this first number should also be higher than the other two. For example, a 20-10-10 formula will supply more nitrogen to a plant than a 20-20-20 formula, in which the three elements are equal.

Phosphorous is always the second number in any fertilizer formula and is needed to initiate buds and stimulate flowering. Phosphorous also aids in the ripening and maturing of the plants. At the first sign that a bud is being formed or when you want to induce buds, you should use a fertilizer higher in phosphorous than in the other two elements—for example, 10–30–20. The directions that come with many orchid fertilizers stress the fact that phosphosous alone or in a higher percentage than the nitrogen and potash should never be used on a continuing basis. In fact, it should not be used more than two or three times in succession. A real deficiency in phosphorous is seldom found in orchids. It seems to develop only when straight nitrogen is the only food given over a long period.

The sign of a phosphorous deficiency is the development of a reddish pigmentation in the leaves of plants with colored flowers. (White orchids develop a yellowed look to their leaves.) Without enough phosphorous, new growths do not attain their normal size, and the plants may never flower. Unfortunately, a deficiency in phosphorous can take as long as a year or a full growing cycle to be remedied, since it takes that long for a plant to get back to its normal growing and flowering schedule.

Potash (or potassium) is the third number in the fertilizer formula. Its chief function is to build strong roots. Osmunda, bark, and most orchid mixes seem to contain enough potassium—and trace elements—which, together with what is in the water itself, provide sufficient potassium so that a deficiency of this element is seldom encountered in orchid culture. However, if the color of the flowers becomes paler with each succeeding year and the number of flower buds keeps decreasing, a deficiency in potassium might be worth looking into.

KINDS OF FERTILIZER

Orchid food comes in both dry and liquid forms as well as in pellets. The liquids are obviously water-soluble and can be either organic or inorganic and are the safest to use with orchids. They come in several formulas—for example, 30–10–10, which, being high in nitrogen, is ideal for plants potted in bark. A fertilizer high in nitrogen is indicated not only by a high first number in the formula but also by the amount of phosphorous and potassium available. A 30–20–20 fertilizer does not have the differential that a 30–10–10 fertilizer does.

Liquid Fertilizers

A fertilizer formula that is evenly balanced, such as a 10–10–10 or the stronger 18–18–18 or 20–20–20, is good for the general feeding of plants in orchid mixes. Sometimes a 10–10–10 formula may not seem to be supplying enough nourishment to a particular plant. When this is the case, change to a more potent formula, but always increase the strength of any fertilizer gradually. This can be done by using less than the amount the manufacturer recommends until you have had a chance to see whether or not this formula might result in overfeeding—or underfeeding—the plant.

Fish emulsion, which is water-soluble, is a 100% organic fertilizer containing, in addition to the three basic nutrients, salts and hormones that are most beneficial to orchids and are not generally available in standard inorganic chemical fertilizers. Its nutrients are rapidly available and the plants do maintain a healthy green color. It also increases root action, thereby helping the entire plant to become stronger and more vigorous. In general, fish emulsion seems to provide just the right amount of nourishment without forcing the plants into soft, lush, unproductive growth. As a result, many growers feel it is the best of all the fertilizers for orchids.

Dry Fertilizers

As a rule, dry-applied fertilizers, whether organic or inorganic, are not considered safe for orchids. The exception to this might be with cymbidiums that have been potted in a mixture of loam, sphagnum moss, shredded bark, and sand. But even here its use is debatable. If it is used, no more than a teaspoonful of dry fertilizer should be spread on a 6- or 8-inch pot. Then the plant should not be fertilized for at least three months. Dry fertilizers should only be used when the plants are growing vigorously and the potting material contains some loam.

Another type of dry fertilizer, dehydrated manure, contains large amounts of salts, and these make it inadvisable for use on orchids. In fact, any dry inorganic fertilizer whose ingredients are quick-acting tends to begin working much too quickly and is used up rapidly. Dry fertilizers that lack any slow-release organic components are generally too highly concentrated, and the roots may very easily be burned by them.

Food Pellets

In a search for quicker, easier, and less frequent methods of fertilizing, industry has come up with food pellets. These provide a form of food that is released slowly and has proved

111

successful in feeding orchids. Osmocote, QUE, and MagAmp are such products. Since these pellets supply nutrients over a long period (anywhere from 3 months to a year), they do eliminate some of the time-consuming part of fertilizing and can be a help to the busy person who would rather spend what time he has with his orchids in other ways.

Two points to remember: a little fertilizer goes a long way, and too much is always harmful, especially to orchids. The nutrient content of an orchid is only 1% of the green weight of the whole plant. Therefore, orchids, except those growing in osmunda or tree fern, must have some fertilizer, but the amount needed is minimal compared to what is needed by other types of plants.

WHEN AND HOW TO FERTILIZE

Never fertilize an orchid that is dry. The best time to fertilize is right after watering, when the potting medium is wet and can better absorb the nutrients. At that time there is also less chance of the roots becoming burned. Fertilize with a water-soluble material in solution that will become immediately available to the plant from the moist potting material. (If you use a dry fertilizer or fertilizer pellets, wet the potting medium, apply, and then water the materials in thoroughly.)

Water-soluble fertilizer can be mixed in a gallon jug and then poured from the container right on the potting medium. Or a special proportioner, which threads onto a hose and delivers a predetermined amount of the fertilizer that has been put into it, can be used; in this way the fertilizer will be diluted to the exact strength needed, and gallon jugs do not constantly have to be refilled.

In order to be certain the hose-end appliance is dispensing the fertilizer in the proportion desired, one of the Peters Orchid Fertilizers, which are colored blue, can be used. Collect the blue solution as it comes through the hose from the proportioner into a glass jar. Then mix another glass of the water-soluble fertilizer in the exact proportions recommended and compare the color. This will tell you if you are getting the right amount through the proportioner.

It is always better to use a small amount of fertilizer at every second or third watering than to use a large amount just once a month, since orchids need a constant supply of food to assure good root growth and strong stems capable of sustaining the flowers. Small and frequent amounts of fertilizer help a plant to grow steadily with no feast or famine periods.

Whenever watering, always flush the pots out thoroughly so that any salts that may have accumulated from the fertilizer will be leached out. Thorough watering does not mean frequent watering. It means letting the water pour freely through the pot. If you did not do this, there might be a concentration of water-soluble salts that could kill the roots or inhibit the plant's growth.

Bear in mind, however, that the plants should be fertilized only when they are actively growing. This is the time when the plant builds up its strength, and with most plants this occurs during the spring and summer, although there are some plants that literally never stop growing. Fertilizer can be a poison to a sick plant, because such a plant lacks the strength to sustain the increased growth the fertilizer might encourage.

Feeding is regulated by the amount of light that is available to the plants. The more light there is, the more food the plants can use. Light also regulates the process of photosynthesis whereby carbon dioxide is united with water to form sugar. When the amount of available light is cut down, as it is during cloudy, overcast weather, photosynthesis may be reduced by as much as two-thirds. As a result, plants cannot utilize the same amount of food during cloudy weather that they can on bright, sunny days.

Any plants that have growths that are soft or blind do not need fertilizer. Very likely, they could not utilize any more than they already have. It is best, therefore, to discontinue all feeding for a season and let the plants grow on their own. When the growths become normal, once again, feeding can be resumed, but at one-quarter to one-half the previous amount, and only half as often.

Compared to other plants, orchids are slow-growing. They also have so-called rest periods—sometimes long, sometimes short, depending upon genetic factors—when no active growing takes place. Yet even during these periods they can still absorb nutrients in small amounts and store them in their tissues and pseudobulbs for future use.

FOLIAR FEEDING

Foliar feeding means using a water-soluble fertilizer diluted to the proportion suggested by the manufacturer for this purpose and spraying it on the leaves with a mister or sprayer with a fine nozzle. The fine-spray nozzle of a hose-end proportioner can also be used for this purpose.

Foliar feeding is an excellent way to be sure newly potted plants and seedlings will have some nutrients available until they have a chance to grow new roots and before these new roots have become long enough to be able to use a pot feeding.

In foliar feeding it is the leaves that absorb the food. In fact, a plant can absorb food more rapidly through its leaves than it can if it has to wait until the roots absorb it and then send it along to the leaves. Scientists have tracked the trail of fertilizer from the leaves to the stems, to the roots, and back again with the aid of radioactive isotopes. About 90% of the fertilizer applied directly to the potting mix is washed out, leaving only about 10% to be absorbed. With foliar feeding, 90% is absorbed and only 10% is wasted.

The thin underside of an orchid leaf always absorbs more food than the thicker upperside, making it most important that the undersides be sprayed when foliar-feeding. Do not foliar-feed plants in the hot sun or when the leaves themselves are hot. Be sure to wait for some sign of new growth to develop before feeding any orchid that has finished flowering or has just been repotted.

RESULTS OF OVERFEEDING

The fact that water may run out of an orchid pot quickly and freely does not mean that the nutrients also run out at the same speed. A portion remains attached to the potting material and on the roots for some time. It is easy to overfertilize orchids, and the damage this does may take a long time to overcome. Too much fertilizer causes damage to the tips of the new leaves first, because the fertilizer is taken up from the roots to the leaves by moisture, and as the moisture evaporates from the leaves, if there is more fertilizer there than the plant can use, the excess remains and tends to clog up the plant's circulating system. This results in the leaf tips becoming brown and burned.

New growths on plants can also be burned by too much fertilizer, either by too great an amount at one time or by too frequent applications. Yet if the potting material is leached out at every watering and the roots are not too badly damaged, eventually new growths appear at the base of the injured ones. Roots that are completely dead cannot rejuvenate themselves.

Pseudobulbs and sheaths have been known to burst from an excess of fertilizer. When you notice that there are dead roots on a plant, this is an indication that it might be wise to change your brand or formula of fertilizer and reduce the amount.

FERTILIZING PLANTS GROWN IN DIFFERENT SETTINGS

House Plants

Orchids that are grown as house plants require fertilizing less often and in more dilute amounts than those grown in greenhouses, mostly because they do not receive anywhere near as much light. Again, the less light available to a plant, the less food that plant needs. Use about a quarter to a half as much as the recommendations call for on the fertilizer package.

During periods of cloudy weather these indoor plants will need even less food. It is not easy to leach out fertilizer salts that have accumulated in a pot as a result of overfeeding. Using less fertilizer helps to keep down the accumulation.

Plants in Greenhouses

Almost any book—and this one is no exception—tailors its suggestions on feeding to those plants growing under optimum conditions, namely in a greenhouse. Since a great variety of orchids can be grown in the many microclimates of a greenhouse, suggestions about feeding will be found under each genus in Chapters 12 and 13.

Plants in Gardens

It is only in the warmer, frost-free areas of the world that orchid growers can keep orchids in their gardens year round, in lath houses, specially prepared beds, or tubs. Depending upon location and temperature, the amount of light that is available to the plants will always regulate the amount of food that will be needed by them.

Such garden-grown orchids, because they are exposed to all the elements, either have abundant rainfall that quickly leaches out any fertilizers and thus makes more frequent feeding necessary, or they experience periods of drought where dehydration becomes a problem and consequently need less food. During dry periods, it is up to the grower to make sure that his plants have the necessary amount of water. The frequency and amount of feeding then must be tailored to the conditions. Nevertheless, foliar feeding outdoors about every two weeks usually helps produce excellent growth, but in the last analysis it is the conditions under which each plant is grown that determines its need for food.

Dry fertilizers, either organic or inorganic, however, do have a place in outdoor orchid gardening, particularly where specially prepared beds have been set up for the orchids. Dry fertilizers should always be thoroughly and completely watered into the potting material and not just scattered across the top of it.

Plants Summering Outdoors

Plants that have been taken from a greenhouse, windowsill, or conservatory and placed outside for the summer seem to do best when hung from the branches of large trees where they have some shade. This is similar to the conditions that they were accustomed to in their native habitats. They can also be placed in tubs where there is dappled sunlight.

In any case, it is important to remember that on hot summer nights high temperatures tend to deplete the plants rather quickly because they produce a drain upon the plants' food supplies manufactured during the day. This, plus the leaching-out of the fertilizer by showers, necessitates feeding the plants more often than when growing them indoors sheltered from the elements. But the concentration of the fertilizer should not be increased—rather, the frequency with which it is applied should be increased.

Because of their greater need for food, foliar feeding with a balanced fertilizer once every 10 days is usually an enormous help to the plants.

Plants Growing under Artifical Lights

Orchids under high-intensity fluorescent tubes will grow faster and need more food than those grown under average fluorescent lights. Nevertheless, in such cases the overall condition of the plants themselves must serve as a guide to how often they need food and how much they should be given. Fish emulsion, water-soluble 18-18-18 (30-10-10, if the plants have been potted in bark), even a 10-30-20 when the buds begin to form—all must be used in more dilute proportions than is recommended for greenhouse or windowsill culture. Again, constant but small amounts of food seem to give the best results under fluorescent lights.

Care at Different Stages & Times

By now it has become apparent that orchids, by their very nature, have cultural requirements not common to the growing of other kinds of plant. There are also aspects of their growing cycle that are unique: the care that will be necessary to assure that the buds formed in the plant's sheath will emerge unscathed to produce handsome, well-formed flowers; the ways in which these flowers can be made to last as long as possible on the plant; the need for a resting period before the plant commences another growing cycle; the advantages of orchid plants being able to spend the warm summer months of the year outdoors where the growing conditions will more nearly approximate those of their native habitats. An understanding of each of the phases in an orchid's development will go a long way toward making their growing an easy, enjoyable, and rewarding experience.

CARE AT DIFFERENT STAGES OF DEVELOPMENT

Plants in Sheath and Bud

To any orchid grower the sight of a plant with a bud in its sheath is a joyous occasion. It is the culmination of all his efforts. The sheath, of course, is the thin green envelope that contains the buds and protects them in the early stages of their development. As the buds grow, the top of the sheath splits and the buds emerge. The sheath then continues to act as a support for the buds until they have grown heavy enough to require staking. (It is also possible—and often happens—that the buds of some orchids develop and grow without the sheath.)

Occasionally a bud becomes cramped inside a sheath. This may be because the bud is too big for the sheath, or the sheath itself may be too tough to split open. Then, unless the bud is able to burst out, it may die inside the sheath. If this danger exists, slit the sheath with a knife or tear it down the sides. A lack of moisture at the roots when the buds were forming is often the reason for this difficulty.

Sheaths may also turn yellow and look dry. The buds inside are not usually affected by this and should continue to develop. The exception to this is when soft rot develops and turns the sheath brown, then black. In this case the buds may also die in the sheath. This seems to occur more often in some species and hybrids than others, leading to the assumption that it may be genetically caused. Nevertheless, insufficient light, air pollution, and perhaps the fact that the plant itself may not really be healthy are all contributing causes. Prompt cutting open of the sheaths all the way down to the tops of the pseudobulbs is the only way such buds might possibly be saved.

There are certain plants that always produce a double sheath. The cause is either genetic (the plant may have *Cattleya labiata* in its ancestry) or one that has not yet been identified. In any case, the outer of the two sheaths can be cut away, leaving just one to enclose the flower buds. The top of the lone sheath can then be cut off just above the bud. This allows air to get into it.

118   When buds die in a sheath it is often an indication

that the plant's strength has been depleted, perhaps as a result of the night temperatures being too high, because of too much watering too frequently, or because of too much shade.

Ethylene gas, which is harmful to orchids, can cause buds to turn pink, then brown and drop off. Buds that have become chilled or too hot from being too close to the window may also drop off the plant. Water standing in the sheaths is the prime cause of bud rot.

Flowering Plants

Orchid flowers open slowly. First the sepals and the petals stretch out from tightly enclosed buds. Then the lip emerges, followed by the wider opening of each flower part. Finally, the flower opens fully, and the color intensifies during the next few days while the petals become firmer.

Flowering plants kept cool and out of direct sun usually keep their flowers in good condition a long time. Some flowers, such as those of cattleyas, may last for three weeks or more, while the flowers of paphiopedilums and cymbidiums may remain in good condition for three or four months.

Careless watering and misting may spot the flowers, leaving them with brown spots and speckles. Plants in flower should not be where there is any danger of sudden changes in temperature, which could cause the flowers to wilt. This is particularly important when you move a plant to another location so that the flowers may be enjoyed. Always remember, the flowers are the most delicate part of the orchid and do require careful handling.

There are things that can shorten the lives of orchid blooms. If the overall condition of a plant is poor, the flowers may be thin and lack the sturdiness they should have. This is one reason why attention must be given throughout the growing cycle to see that the plants always have the proper temperature, sufficient light, and enough humidity and water. Good-quality flowers can only come from well-grown plants.

Temperatures that are too hot, particularly at night, also cause flowers to be short-lived, while temperatures that are too low may prevent the flowers from developing the way they should. In addition, an atmosphere too damp and cool may cause water spots on the sepals, with the spots eventually turning pink or brown. This condition is known as *botrytis* and is a disease. Flowers so affected should be cut off, not only because their looks have been spoiled, but more important, if they are left on the plant the disease could spread to other flowers.

During the warm months insect pollination can also be suspected whenever flowers fade rapidly.

Resting Plants

Resting is that period, usually after flowering, when a plant is not actively growing. An orchid does not have to shed its leaves like a tree and look dormant to rest, although a few orchids, like the deciduous dendrobiums, do that. Most orchids look no different when they are resting, except there is no visible activity such as new roots or growths developing.

The majority of plants take some time to regain their strength after flowering. It is at this time, when there is no active growth, that they rest. Not all orchids rest, however. Some start new eyes or new growths at the same time that their buds open.

The resting of orchids after flowering was a standard practice in the early days of orchid culture, when most orchids grown were species with definite built-in rest periods. Today, however, when so many orchids are hybrids, many have no well-defined dormant periods—each of the crosses used to make the hybrid had its resting period at a different time of the year and the plant is "confused."

Yet unless a plant does have some rest, the tendency to constantly produce new growths could eventually exhaust it. The resting period, however, can as well be a very short one of days or weeks, as a long one of, perhaps, many months. A plant is resting until it shows signs of new roots and new growth.

Usually a resting cycle calls for temperatures a bit lower than those for a plant in active growth, a less humid atmosphere, and watering less often. But less water does not mean no water. Resting plants are not completely without activity, and misting the plants helps keep the leaves and the pseudobulbs from becoming shriveled.

Newly Acquired Plants

It takes vigilance to keep a collection of orchids healthy and disease-free. For this reason, no matter where you get a new plant, you should assume it may be harboring some viruses, bacteria, insect pests, or the like and isolate it. If the plants are grown in a greenhouse, keep the new one in the house. If yours are grown as house plants, place the new one in another room or otherwise away from the other plants.

Otherwise, give the new plant the same light, temperature, and humidity needed for that particular orchid. Mist the foliage frequently. Check the plant over minutely for any signs of pests lodged beneath the leaves or deep inside the sheath. Also, look it over carefully for signs of rot or decay and take the necessary corrective measures at once for any potential sources of trouble (see Chapter 11).

Then, when you are sure the new plant is completely free of any problems, it may be placed with the other plants. For a period of at least two or three weeks, you should go over the plant with the proverbial fine-tooth comb each day.

GROWING SPECIMEN PLANTS

There is nothing quite so impressive as a specimen plant, a large, well-grown orchid completely covered with flowers. Any plant that is to be grown to specimen size not only should develop many new leads that consistently flower, but these leads should break from the center of the plant as well as the outside, for no specimen can be attractive unless its center is as full of flowers as the outside. Not every orchid lends itself to becoming a specimen plant.

One way to increase the number of center growths is to cut a V-section—not more than a third through—out of a rhizome behind a leading pseudobulb. This will force it to send out a new growth toward the center of the pot. Then, instead of dividing a plant that is a vigorous grower and a prolific bloomer into several small plants at the time of repotting, the entire plant can be put into a container a size larger than the one it has been in. This shifting can continue at each repotting time until the plant has reached really mammoth proportions.

Cattleya mossiae, an old but beautiful lavender cattleya that blooms in the spring, is an example of an orchid that easily adapts itself to growing into a specimen-sized plant; another is *C. skinneri*. Well-grown specimen plants literally covered with blooms are a truly spectacular sight.

Some of the paphiopedilums, such as *Paph. maudiae*,

and the cymbidiums can also be allowed to grow into large plants. *Epidendrum fragrans* and *Dendrobium aggregatum* are outstanding examples of small orchids that can be grown into very large plants of outstanding beauty.

Such large plants always require more care than the average plant growing in a 6-inch pot. Specimen plants also tend to retain moisture much longer, particularly in the center of the pot, because the potting medium does not dry out as quickly or as completely at its center. This makes the amount and frequency of watering more difficult to gauge and makes overwatering a greater hazard. Always check the potting medium thoroughly before you water. Since such plants are often too heavy to lift to test for dryness, poke your finger into the potting medium. To water such a plant before it has had a chance to dry out causes the roots to become both diseased and rotted. The length of time that large, healthy plants can go without water is truly amazing. Several weeks to several months is not at all unusual.

Specimen plants always look especially attractive planted in baskets filled with osmunda or in large-sized pots that have been fitted with heavy galvanized hangers and then hung from the sash bars of a greenhouse. Round, lightweight plastic baskets are ideal, for they have plenty of open spaces where air can get to the roots of the plants. (Some come with a plastic lining, which should be removed before filling them with osmunda.) Usually there is no need to crock a basket, because excess water is able to pour right through the osmunda and out through the openings of the basket. This type of container also allows the roots to grow more freely and permits good circulation of air, and there is less chance of the roots rotting.

The potting procedure for placing a specimen plant in a basket is the same as that for any orchid in a basket. Pot firmly. However, if the plants are to be potted not in baskets but in large pots, then provision must be made to ensure adequate drainage. Since large pots are heavy, a lighter crocking material such as polystyrene broken into small pieces will make the pot easier to lift. Frequent misting will help keep the leaves and roots in a healthy condition and prolong the intervals between pot waterings.

The amount, strength, and frequency of feeding for specimen plants depends upon the type of orchid grown. There is no basic difference in the food requirements of a specimen plant and those of an average-sized plant of the same kind, because whenever you feed a specimen plant the entire container is exposed to the fertilizer and all the potting medium benefits from it.

With proper care, specimen plants can be enjoyed for many years, and the abundance of flowers will always, even to a long-time grower, present a breathtaking spectacle. When the center of the plant finally becomes bare and there are many leafless pseudobulbs or old, dead growths, the plant can be removed from the container and divided, and the largest section started on its way to becoming another impressive specimen, while the smaller parts will enlarge your collection by that many more plants.

SUMMER CARE

Even though your orchids have been growing beautifully all during the colder months on a windowsill, on a porch, or in a greenhouse, the heat and extra sunlight during the summer mean that they may need increased watering and misting, more ventilation, and, of course, extra shade, whether kept under cover or put out under the trees.

As explained before, food is made only during the daylight hours, but growth and respiration during the night can use up this food unless the temperature is lower at night. If the night temperatures remain too high, particularly over a long period, the growth becomes soft, lush, and not conducive to the production of good-quality flowers. The increased air that plants get in the warm weather, along with the extra amounts of sun and light, mean an increased need for watering. Again, do not forget to lift the plants before watering, and remember that if they feel heavy, they do not need to be watered. Ordinarily, misting at frequent intervals will help to provide the additional moisture needed. At the same time, too much water even at this time of year could cause roots to rot at the very time they should be growing vigorously to help to strengthen the plant.

Care of Indoor Plants

House Plants

Summer heat and additional sunshine call for extra misting, more watering, more ventilation, and, of course, increased shading. Since most plants are growing actively at this time, it is necessary to do everything possible to promote good growth. Although sunshine is a key factor in orchid growing, bear in mind that the plants must have some protection from the hot rays of summer. Thin curtains are often sufficient. So tread the fine line between enough sun and enough shade.

The plants should not start to harden until late summer or early autumn. Increased amounts of sun at that time will allow the hardening process to begin, whereas giving the plants too much sun earlier in the growing season may result in premature hardening of the pseudobulbs, growths, and leaves.

Plants grown in a northern exposure do not receive much sun anyway, and shading there is probably not needed. It is the south and west exposures that allow the temperatures to build up. Here the plants will always need some shade from mid-morning to mid-afternoon, but since they will not receive direct sun during these hours, it becomes important that they receive every bit of the early morning sunlight.

Sometimes it is difficult during the summer for the night temperatures to drop 10 to 20 degrees lower than they were during the day inside a house, but this is essential. However, during the day you should never go to the other extreme of shading the plants too much in order to keep them cool. An overabundance of shade and copious watering combine to produce troubles, not the least of which is the rotting of roots.

If the plants are on a porch, bamboo drops lowered at mid-day can be used for shade. In general, the plants do best with early morning sunshine, then some shade for several hours at mid-day, and no shade for the rest of the day. Cloudy days, of course, give you respite from pulling down and pulling up the shading.

With indoor plants it is also a good idea to shut the house up before the heat of the day has a chance to raise the temperature, but let the plants have plenty of air all night, since there is nothing like cool night air to rejuvenate them after a hot summer's day. The cool air also lowers the temperature the 10 or 20 degrees the plants must experience to produce flowers.

Plants in the Greenhouse

It is often quite an undertaking to put all the greenhouse plants outdoors for the summer, and it is nigh on impossible if the greenhouse is a large one. Many growers are thus understandably hesitant to move them. Nevertheless, if the greenhouse is somewhat shaded by trees and roller blinds, the ventilators are left wide open day and night, screens are used in the doors to allow for further circulation of air, and perhaps some fans are added, the plants may be happy enough inside. But it is important to see that the fans blow air on the walls or beneath the benches, never on the plants themselves. Frequent misting and damping-down also help cool the atmosphere.

In areas that experience oppressive heat, a greenhouse owner who wants his plants to grow well has no choice but to install an evaporative cooler. If it is installed at one end of the greenhouse, the outside air pulled through it will come into the greenhouse quite a bit cooler. One or two fans can then be used to circulate this cooler air and expel the warm air through the ventilators.

Thus, in warm climates the need for evaporative coolers or greenhouse air conditioners is simply the other side of the coin to a heating system.

Air Conditioning

Air conditioning and orchids are not incompatible, although a few adjustments may have to be made. Most units reduce the humidity as well as cool the air, so the humidity will have to be carefully checked. The plants should never be placed directly in front of any air conditioner, because it dehydrates them with the breeze as well as chilling them unnecessarily.

Several small containers of water placed among the plants, or growing the plants on trays filled with damp pebbles, helps increase the humidity. Frequent misting of the foliage also increases the overall humidity around the plants and helps prevent the shriveling of the leaves and pseudobulbs that occurs when the humidity is low. A humidguide or a hygrometer will help you tell at a glance when the humidity is too low to support good growth.

Another problem with air conditioning, although not insurmountable, is the difficulty in getting the night temperature lower than the day. The air conditioner must be turned down lower at night to allow for a temperature differential. Either that or it can be set at a higher temperature during the day.

125   Where provision has been made to assure that there

is always an adequate amount of humidity, air conditioners can be a help in growing the cool-type orchids such as odontoglossums, plain-leaved paphiopedilums, and some of the miltonias. In fact, without air conditioning it may be difficult, if not impossible, to bring an odontoglossum through the summer in hot climates.

The warmth-loving cattleyas, which require both heat and humidity, might be better off outside during the months when the air conditioner is in use.

Care of Outdoor Plants

If none of the above suggestions for taking care of the plants in their usual growing places in summer is feasible, the only other alternative is to put them outside, giving them a real summer vacation. Fortunately, most plants do enjoy a summer outdoors. Nevertheless, always remember that all plants are affected by changes of location. So proceed carefully.

During medieval times there was a saying that "city air makes men free." Now, unfortunately, it makes them cough. Air pollution presents problems with smog, smoke, gasoline fumes and so forth for the plants growing outside. It can be a real nemesis in some locations, making it necessary to keep plants indoors at all times.

Orchids can add tremendously to the decor of a garden if they are strategically placed to take advantage of both the plant's needs and the setting. Pots can be hung from the lower branches of tall trees where there is enough shade from the leaves to prevent the foliage from becoming burned by the sun. Do not hang the plants so high that it is inconvenient or impossible to check on them at least once a week.

On the patio, plants can be attractively arranged so that the sunlight reaching them is filtered and they are assured of protection from the hot sun. People enjoy breezes, but it may be necessary to erect some kind of a windbreak to protect the plants from drying out too quickly. In any case, the plants should always be put into planters or on patio blocks rather than directly on the ground. In this way there is less chance of slugs getting into the pots.

Unfortunately, insects multiply rapidly during the warm weather and may become a problem. Here prevention is better than a cure. A weekly spraying with Malathion will control most pests. A biweekly soaking of the potting

Figure 8-1. A patio can serve as an extension of the house where orchids can be grown to perfection and where the grower can relax and enjoy them.

medium with metaldehyde will take care of any slugs. It is important always to check the insecticide label to be certain that the product is one that can safely be used on orchids. Spraying with an insecticide in summer is best done in the late afternoon, when the temperature is somewhat cooler, yet is still early enough in the day for the plants to dry off before night.

There are always spells of dry weather every summer, and during these periods the humidity can be increased by frequent misting of the plants and the surrounding area.

A regular schedule of fertilizing, according to the needs of the individual plants, should also be part of outdoor culture.

127

The fact that plants should have a chance to dry off after watering and spraying before night is continually stressed, but what if it rains during the night? The plants are then thoroughly soaked. The difference between plants being wet in an enclosed area and plants wet outside is that outside there is air circulation, and sometimes brisk winds, and when the air does not become stagnant, diseases that result from night wetness in a greenhouse are often not present outside.

In Lath Houses

Another way to grow orchids outside in summer is in a lath house. This can be either a temporary or a permanent part of the garden, is easily built, and can be most attractive. It can be painted to match the house, even covered with a grapevine to provide additional shade for the orchids.

A lath house is easy to make, but one must make sure that the slats are spaced several inches apart. Otherwise, the slats would block out too much light. Benches can then be fitted inside to hold the plants, and perhaps another

Figure 8-2. A lath house provides plenty of fresh air and filtered sunlight.

might be added for sitting and enjoying the plants. Some of the plants can be fastened to the slats themselves in an attractive and decorative manner. Others can be hung from the top. (This also leaves more space on the benches for additional plants.) If the lath house is large enough, it can also provide space to do some potting.

Watering in a lath house could not be simpler. All one needs is a hose. Be certain that all the plants can drain properly and do not sit in any accumulation of water. A misting nozzle attached to the hose makes misting so easy and fast that it is no chore to do at frequent intervals.

In Screen Houses

Screen houses are enjoying a return to popularity both for outdoor relaxation and as a place in which plants can grow free from insects during the summer. The screening does cut down somewhat the amount of sunlight available to the plants, and it is therefore necessary to experiment a bit, for with a solid roof there is no dappled sunlight as there is in a lath house. This is especially important with those orchids that need an abundance of sunlight.

Probably the greatest advantage of a screen house is that it eliminates the insect problem. This alone makes it desirable. Otherwise, plants growing in screen houses will need the same watering, misting, and fertilizing routine needed in a lath house.

In the Open

We must not forget that plants that are growing in all kinds of weather need a different culture from those in the security of a house or greenhouse. For example, a prolonged spell of drought, which is a frequent occurrence in the summer, means the plants will have to be assured of enough water so that they will receive no setback. Summer winds that cause dryness must also be compensated for. Several times each day the plants will need to be misted. As for watering, there is no hard-and-fast rule as to when and how often to water plants outside. Everything depends upon the weather, but always check the potting medium first to be safe.

Rainfall is marvelous for all plants. But like all good things, there can be too much to it. Constant rain with no sunny breaks in between can lead to soggy conditions. The roots can rot and the potting medium deteriorate faster than is desirable. Adequate drainage is the only way to thwart this.

In their native habitats, many orchids cling to the trunks of trees, not as parasites in search of food, but merely for support. Their roots, not bound in pots, enjoy ideal drainage.

The combination of rainfall and watering leaches out fertilizer. Thus, whenever there is a long period of rain the plants must be fertilized more often.

A spraying program is also needed to take care of any insects. But before you spray be sure you need to spray and know what you are spraying for. Slug damage, for instance, is noticeable even when you do not see the culprits. They leave holes in the flowers, buds, or leaves. If you have any doubt that slugs are the culprits, put a saucer of beer near several plants just before it gets dark and in the morning you will see the little demons dead or nursing bad hangovers.

Thunderstorms, even hailstones, are other hazards associated with summering orchids outside. Although there is not much you can do to protect the plants against either one, the amount of damage is usually minimal, with heavy showers doing little more than giving the plants a thorough soaking.

As for hurricanes or tropical storms, there is usually ample time before they strike to bring the plants back into the greenhouse or the house itself. Since this is just a temporary move, no cleanup of plants and pots is in order as is the case when they are brought in for the winter.

Bringing Plants Back Indoors

Finally, several weeks before frost is due to arrive and the night temperatures get down to around 65°F (18.3°C), plans should be made for moving the plants back into the house or greenhouse. In the meantime, of course, the greenhouse should have been thoroughly cleaned, painted, and repaired where necessary, for it is far easier to clean an empty or half-empty greenhouse than one that is filled to capacity.

Each plant should also be thoroughly examined before it is brought inside. Check it for scale insects and, if any are present, spray with Malathion or remove as many of the scales as you can with a swab or a toothbrush soaked in Malathion. The leaves should also be sponged with water and a soft tissue used to remove any dust or film that might clog the pores. (Hard scrubbing may cause abrasions and damage to the epidermal cells.)

The pots should also be thoroughly cleaned and scrubbed and, even if there are no signs of slugs, be on the safe side; water the plant thoroughly and then douse the potting medium with metaldehyde according to the manufacturer's instructions.

Weeds that might have grown up in the potting medium should be removed. Then if any of the plants need repotting, this is a good time to do it, before they are brought inside. (It is easier, much more pleasant, and a lot less messy to do this outside on a nice sunny day than indoors). Each plant should be in as good condition as possible so that it will be able to start its new life indoors in good health and free of all diseases and pests.

How to Vacation and Still Grow Orchids

Summer vacations need not be given up when you grow orchids. A little planning can make summer an enjoyable time for you and a period of undisturbed growth for your

Figure 8-3. Orchids can be hung from the branches of trees to get the benefit of a summer outdoors.

plants. Orchids can be put outside during the summer, or perhaps a reliable neighbor will look after them for you. But don't trust to memory. Meticulous written instructions, covering not only their routine care but every possible eventuality, should be left, including how and when to water, fertilize, and spray for pests; under what conditions added shade is needed, and when and for how long the ventilators should be open if in a greenhouse or under lights; and finally, the name and phone number of your plumber and electrician.

SUMMER CARE BY TYPE OF ORCHID

Intermediate Types

Cattleyas

Summer is the time when cattleyas make their most rapid strides in the production of new growths. Whenever a plant shows signs of new buds forming, it needs extra moisture at its roots. However, the potting medium in which cattleyas grow should always become almost dry between waterings. This is why when they are outside for the summer they should not be hung so high that it is impossible to check the condition of the potting medium. Increasing the moisture at this time helps cattleyas develop long flower stems.

Cattleyas, in particular, enjoy the warm, buoyant atmosphere of summer. This is one reason a summer spent outdoors does them so much good. Also, cattleyas need more light than most orchids, but not necessarily bright sun. Rather, they should be shaded before there is any danger of the leaves becoming scorched. The dappled sunshine that comes through a tree or lath house is ideal.

On the other hand, having too much shade indoors results in soft, lush, sappy growths that are dark green. Instead, the plants should be firm and healthy and a medium green.

Thunderstorms can usually be counted upon to break up protracted spells of intense heat. The freshness of the air after a rainstorm and the cooler temperatures that follow are a real treat for cattleyas. The cooler night temperatures are also a tonic for them. You will notice in a short time how much healthier the plants look. Summer also brings with it a higher humidity, which is just what cattleyas need.

Whether grown indoors or out, keep an eye on the pseudobulbs of cattleyas, particularly on warm, windy days. Wind tends to dry out the plants, and the pseudobulbs can start to shrivel and the leaves wrinkle. This is a sure sign that the humidity is too low. Increased misting of the foliage is the way to counteract this. More watering is not necessarily the answer. In fact, the problem may be too much water that results in the roots rotting.

At this season, particularly, cattleyas potted in bark need to be fed a high-nitrogen fertilizer every two or three weeks until the buds begin to form. Then switch to a fertilizer low in nitrogen and high in phosphorous, such as 10–30–20. Cattleyas potted in one of the orchid mixes should be fertilized with a more balanced formula at the same intervals as those in other potting materials.

Then, between pot feedings the plants can be given a foliar feeding, but only when they are not in direct sunlight. This acts as an additional stimulus, especially if you are careful to spray the undersides of the leaves.

The only exception to this feeding schedule might be after a protracted rainy period or when several inches of rain have fallen in a relatively short time. Because the extra water is likely to have leached out the fertilizer, an additional feeding at this time may be necessary.

Epidendrums and Oncidiums

The same summer care given the cattleyas is also right for epidendrums and oncidiums. The growing medium, especially, might need a bit more water.

Paphiopedilums

Somehow or other most growers hesitate to put paphiopedilums outside for the summer, preferring instead to keep them inside where they are protected from the wide swings in weather outdoors.

Whether they are growing inside or outside during the summer, paphiopedilums like a cooler atmosphere than cattleyas. They should be kept moist at all times since they have no pseudobulbs in which to store water. Neither the cool-growing, plain-leaved sorts nor the warmer-growing, mottled-leaved paphiopedilums should be grown in strong sunlight or even in strong light. The hot summer sun can cause extensive damage to the leaves and weaken the plant itself. Paphiopedilums prefer to be where there is partial shade and soft, filtered sunlight.

133

Because of the shadier conditions under which they are grown, paphiopedilums require less food than most other orchids. A dilute solution of a balanced fertilizer such as 18–18–18 every three or four weeks will usually be sufficient.

Any foliar feeding you do needs to be done cautiously so that the water does not become lodged in the axils of the leaves and cause basal rot. This is the only real problem that paphiopedilums seem to have. This is also one of the reasons many growers hesitate to put them outdoors in summer, especially during rainy weather.

The warmer outdoor temperatures plus the drying winds tend to cause the potting medium to dry out rather quickly, and since the roots of these plants must always be moist, the plants need to be watered more frequently than when growing indoors.

Dendrobiums

As you soon learn when you grow dendrobiums, somehow or other they do not seem to respond to any generalized cultural suggestions. Each plant requires its own special treatment with regard to location, amount of water it receives, day and night temperatures, amount of food it can use, and percentage of humidity right for it. But once you have hit upon the right combination for a dendrobium, stick with it. Because it has a different ancestry, another dendrobium growing right beside it may need entirely different treatment. Overall, however, dendrobiums seem to like the same basic environment as do cattleyas.

If you decide to put dendrobiums outdoors for the summer, keep an especially observant eye on them during the first few weeks. If they do not seem to do as well as they did indoors, do not hesitate to put them back inside at once.

Dendrobiums should never be allowed to dry out completely, and during a dry spell they need to be watered more frequently and the leaves misted several times a day. Bear in mind, however, that there are two basic types. The deciduous dendrobium sheds its leaves at the end of each growing season, while the evergreen type keeps its leaves intact. The culture of both during the summer is about the same. Both can remain outdoors until night temperatures drop down to 60°F (15.6°C), at which time they should be
brought indoors.

Most dendrobiums make only vegetative growth during the summer and develop their flowers in the autumn or winter. Thus, buds and flowers will not, as a rule, be in evidence during the summer. But should a terminal leaf (a leaf at the end of the growing stalk) appear, heralding the arrival of buds, the plant will then need less water but not to the point of allowing the canes to shrivel. When the flower spike does appear, the amount of water can be increased for a time. Then, just before the buds appear on the spikes, decrease the amount of water once again.

Dendrobiums are rapid growers. They grow almost like weeds and need a proportionately large amount of fertilizer. A balanced fertilizer twice a month assures good, healthy growth, and as light-loving plants they need only enough shade to prevent their foliage from burning.

Warm Types

Vandas

"Aloha" and leis are always brought to mind by the incredibly lovely vandas and their miniature relatives the ascoscendas. Vandas like light, and plenty of it—even more than cattleyas, if that is possible. They should be shaded just enough to prevent their leaves from burning. They also require large amounts of water. They have some of the thickest, fleshiest roots of any orchid. Their roots hang out all over the sides of the pot and are true aerial roots. For best results, the roots as well as the leaves should be misted several times a day during the summer, for it is through these thick aerial roots that vandas get much of their moisture and food. This is one of the reasons they respond so well to foliar feeding.

Vandas are truly heavy feeders, needing a balanced fertilizer at weekly intervals. Even when they are potted in bark, a balanced fertilizer such as 18-18-18 appears to give much better results than a fertilizer high in nitrogen. In fact, the latter seems to cut down on the number of flowers produced. Vandas also need rather high humidity and good air circulation.

Phalaenopsis

Since phalaenopsis plants come from the really hot areas of the Pacific and Asia, summer presents no serious problems for them. They like warm weather. As long as they are protected from excessive heat and an oppressive atmosphere, they will do quite well.

Indoors or out, they need to be shaded from the hot sun yet allowed an adequate amount of light. They should be misted frequently and watered sufficiently often to prevent the potting medium from drying out. Phalaenopsis like to be kept moist but never wet.

On the other hand, excessive humidity on cool, cloudy days is conducive to crown rot and bud drop. On days such as this, the foliage should not be misted; it is on warm, sunny, windy days that the plants need more moisture. It is always helpful to have the temperature at night lower than during the day. This helps rejuvenate phalaenopsis and is also necessary to assure that they will flower.

Their temperature requirements range between 65 and 90°F (18–32°C); therefore, if they are put outdoors for the summer, they should be brought back indoors before the temperature goes below 65°F (18.°C) at night. While phalaenopsis enjoy air that's warm and humid, the air should also circulate, so they do especially well in a lath house during the summer.

Phalaenopsis are not particularly heavy feeders; for those potted in bark a high-nitrogen fertilizer, such as 30-10-10, usually gives the best results. They need to be fed about once a month except when growing vigorously, when twice a month may be necessary.

Cool Types   *Odontoglossums*

Probably no other orchids so well characterize the cool-growing type as do the breathtakingly beautiful odontoglossums. It is doubtful that they will survive outdoors in the summer except, possibly, in a cool pine grove. Their temperature range is between 45 and 70°F (7–21°C) at the absolute maximum, and most sunny days have temperatures in excess of this.

If you want to grow these orchids and do not have air conditioning in the house or an evaporative cooler in the greenhouse, it is difficult to keep them as cool as they should be. During the summer odontoglossums barely hold their own, and since cool night air gives them such a lift, whenever possible leave the windows open at night. They even look fresher in the morning for having had the benefit of this cool night air. It is also wise to keep the windows closed during the day to keep out as much heat as possible.

In any case, the use of fans and blowers, plus frequent misting of the plants, will help in keeping them cool. When the cool, crisp days of autumn arrive, odontoglossums take a new lease on life. They then begin to grow new roots and turn a fresh green.

Odontoglossums also need to be kept moist, but the potting medium must not become waterlogged or the plant will have leafless bulbs in a remarkably short time. For this reason, sufficient crocking should always be placed in the pots to provide for drainage. Since they are light feeders and grow in dappled light that is somewhat on the shady side, odontoglossums require only a small amount of fertilizer once a month.

Cymbidiums

Not only do cymbidiums do best when put outside for the summer, but it is almost a necessity, for they must have low night temperatures to enable them to initiate flower buds. The better air circulation outdoors also helps keep them healthy, for they are a cool-growing orchid, even though the miniatures do like a temperature a bit warmer than the standard. As with most other cool orchids, cymbidiums prefer sunlight that is partially filtered. The more light they receive, the more the plants tend to dry out and need water. Cymbidiums require copious amounts of water, yet the potting medium must have an opportunity to dry out somewhat between waterings.

From the middle of August until cymbidiums are brought indoors for the winter, the potting medium should be kept somewhat drier to force the plants to develop flower spikes by halting their vegetative growth. Frequent misting of the foliage also helps control red spider mites, which seem to thrive best in dry weather and dry surroundings.

Because of their large size, it is impractical to hang cymbidiums from the branches of trees. They do, however, add immeasurably to the decor when they are grown in pots on a patio or on a bench in a lath house. Always place the pots on blocks of stone or similar material to discourage slugs from getting into the pots.

Since cymbidiums do require copious amounts of water throughout the year, fertilizer leaches out rapidly. They will need to be fed every ten days to two weeks. The amount of rainfall also has a bearing on how often they need to be fed. In periods of frequent rain this may be as often as once a week. Plants kept indoors do not have to cope with excessive rainfall, and their feeding schedule can be kept on a definite biweekly basis.

Cymbidiums potted in bark or mixes containing a large amount of bark need a fertilizer high in nitrogen during early summer. Towards the middle of the summer, a change should be made to 10–30–20 or 6–30–30, high in phosphorous. This helps the plants start their flower buds.

While other orchids are brought back indoors before the night temperatures reach 60°F (15°C), cymbidiums should be allowed to remain outside until temperatures drop to 50°F (10°C).

Miltonias

Miltonias are the lovely pansy orchids, some of which are the cool-growing Colombian type and others, the warmer Brazilian kind. Both types need to be kept shaded and moist throughout the summer. Their need for water is much the same as that of the paphiopedilums; that is, they should be moist but never soaking-wet.

Early morning sunlight is best for miltonias, because at that time the sun is never too warm, making lath houses ideal places to put miltonias outdoors, provided they can be placed in a shady spot in the lath house.

Misting the plants at frequent intervals helps keep them cool and also helps raise the humidity around them. As with the paphiopedilums, care must be taken that water does not remain at the base of the flower stems to cause rot. This is one reason many growers prefer to keep their miltonias indoors during the summer, or, if they are put out, to take them indoors during periods of heavy rain or showers. Finally, miltonias are not heavy feeders, and a small amount of fertilizer once or twice a month will take care of their needs.

As with all orchids, experience will show you how often to mist, how often to water, and whether the plants should have more or less shade. This constant challenge is what makes orchid growing the fascinating hobby it is.

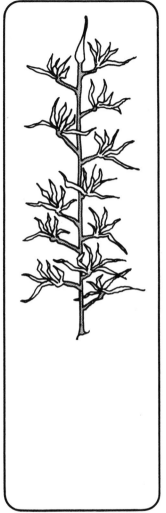

Increasing Your Collection

No orchid lover ever has all the orchids he would like. The constant desire to acquire more and more plants and to have an ever increasing number of different kinds is all just part of the mania that develops with growing orchids. But that is part of the fun. And with over 30,000 species and an even greater number of hybrids from which to choose, it is doubtful if in any one lifetime anyone could acquire more than a small selection of the many orchids that are available.

In any case, there are many ways of increasing the size of a collection. Probably the simplest and the least expensive way is by dividing your plants when they need repotting and thereby getting several extra plants. Saving

CHAPTER 9

backbulbs and letting these develop their own root systems is another way. Succumbing to the lure of the advertisements in orchid catalogs and sending away for either mature plants or less expensive seedlings, swapping plants with friends, buying plants from dealers who are going out of business, sending to faraway places for hard-to-find and exotic species, or, the most enjoyable way of all, taking a trip to where orchids grow and acquiring and shipping home your very own choices—these are just a few of the ways in which a collection can be enlarged.

Some growers choose to specialize in one particular kind of orchid and try to get as many of that kind as possible. Others seek to broaden the scope of their collection by including as many different genera as will grow under the conditions they can provide for them. From ascoscenda to zygopetalum, the choice is limitless.

DIVIDING PLANTS

Dividing a mature plant that has many pseudobulbs or growths is one of the most common ways of increasing the number of orchids a grower has. In fact, unless the plant is one that can be developed as a specimen, it is better not to repot more than three or four of the newer bulbs or growths of any plant in any one pot. The remainder of the bulbs are known as backbulbs.

However, every time a plant is repotted, it does not necessarily need to be divided. Dividing is only done when a plant has become too large or too cumbersome for the container, or if you want another plant of the same kind, or when the rhizomes or growths have crisscrossed each other, which allows rot and decay to get a start.

After taking the plant out of its pot, gently remove as much of the old potting medium as possible and carefully examine the entire plant. Decayed roots should be trimmed to 2-inch stubs. With a sharp knife that has been sterilized, cut away any area that shows signs of decay. By always using sterile tools, you will prevent the transmission of viruses from one plant to another. Then cut off the dead and yellowed leaves. Moisten the pseudobulbs and remove the paper-thin tissue that covers them, if this can be done easily. This tissue, called cataphyll, is a favorite hiding place for scale insects.

Next, determine whether it is possible to separate the

Figure 9-1. To separate a plant, cut through the rhizome with a sharp, sterile knife (except for paphiopedilums, which should be gently pulled apart).

newer growths from the older ones so that there will be one section that will have three or four of the newer growths. Make a clean cut through the rhizome or the connective tissues with a sharp, sterile knife or shears and then separate the plant into two or more sections. By dusting powdered sulfur on the cuts, virus infection can be prevented.

If there are any live eyes or any signs of new growth on each of the separated sections, you will now have two plants instead of one. Each plant then develops its own new leads and new growths, making it possible to have many more flowers from the original plant. When dividing, try to make each division into as strong a plant as possible.

Along with increasing the number of plants, these new divisions are easier to lift and water than was the case with one huge one. When plants have grown too large, the buds tend to remain dormant on the older growths. Separating the lead growth from the back growth often lets one or more of these buds on the older section spring into life.

Figure 9-2. A plant that has been separated into two sections: a smaller one, with a new live eye just developing; and a larger one, with no signs of new growth, that becomes known as the backbulb section.

Photo, Ralph Collins

Having split the plant into sections, you should now try to separate the roots, being careful to avoid breaking them. Finally, pot the section or sections with new eyes or growths as you would pot any mature plant. Then give each newly potted section, which is now a plant on its own, the same care you would a newly potted mature plant.

GROWING PLANTS FROM BACKBULBS

When a plant is divided, the back portion of the plant often has no visible live eyes and not too many roots. The eye is that small triangular swelling at the base of a pseudobulb or growth that develops into the new growth. If the eye is alive, it should be light green. If dead, it looks withered and brown or black. The back portion of a plant is called the *backbulb* or *backbulbs.*

Without live roots, the backbulbs do not contribute anything to the plant. In fact, they may even take food from the front section. If there is not enough food to sustain the entire plant, leaving these backbulbs untouched can result in the whole plant suffering nutritionally. In a short time, if the backbulbs are not severed from the front section, first one and then another of the leaves on the oldest backbulbs may turn yellow and fall off anyway. At the same time, the backbulbs would continue to drain the plant until they ceased to function and died. For years some growers felt that these backbulbs stored water that could be used in an emergency, but without live roots of their own, rather than helping the plant, they become a drain on it.

Backbulbs that are not in good condition, have rot, or are diseased should always be discarded. There is nothing that can be done with them. If, however, they are in fairly good shape, they can be encouraged to start growing some roots of their own. At times it is even a good idea when cutting away this back portion of a plant to see if it is possible to include a part of the front division that has a live eye or new growth in this section. This gives the back section a head start in growing on its own and enables it to flower possibly within two years.

The mere fact of giving the backbulbs a shock when they are severed from the main plant is sometimes enough to start them growing. Before they were severed they were, for the most part, parasites, living on the front portion. Now they must either develop new growths and become

143

sturdy plants or fall by the way and die. As long as they remain green, there is a chance they will grow. It is only when they have become brown and lifeless that hope is gone.

The backbulbs, however, should not be potted in the same way you pot active, mature plants. For the time being they need only to be propped up in a pot that contains some well-moistened, loose osmunda or bark. Then place the pot in a polyethylene bag, close the bag tightly, and tie it with a string or elastic band. The pot should then be placed where it is cool and shaded and checked once in a while to see that the potting material remains moist. In time, a new growth and some new roots may show signs of developing. It is a slow process, one that can take many months, but giving the backbulbs both shade and moisture will encourage dormant eyes to swell and grow.

Finally, when new growth and new roots have become visible, it is time to take each backbulb out of its polyethylene bag and put it into another pot. For this, choose a pot large enough to allow for the traditional two years of growth. Then proceed to pot them as you would mature orchids. The plants will undoubtedly be wobbly because the roots are still not very vigorous, and so staking may be needed. In any case, backbulbs should always be potted firmly so that they will not move around in the pot when they are watered. Nothing discourages root growth more than having a plant wobble all over the pot.

At this time the roots are probably not long enough to go very deeply into the potting medium, and this means they will not need a great deal of water. Lightly mist both the foliage and the top of the potting medium instead of giving the plant a pot watering. This should be done only until the new growths have grown several inches long and the roots have become stronger. Then the plant should be given a regular schedule of watering along with the older plants.

A backbulb division that has a well-developed root system may sometimes flower on its first growth. More often, however, it does not flower until its second growing cycle. Any way you look at it, you now have another plant that has cost you nothing but time, care, and patience.

Some commercial growers sell some of their surplus backbulbs each year. If these have not shriveled, still have some leaves, and, most important, come from superior plants, buying these can be a very economical way to obtain a division that might otherwise be too expensive to purchase as a mature plant.

When these backbulbs arrive they should be dunked at once—pseudobulbs, leaves, and all—into tepid water. Then, after putting the plants into pots containing loose bark, peat moss, and perlite, put the pots into a bucket so that the bottom third of each pot is standing in the water. When the potting material has become thoroughly soaked, the pots can be taken out and allowed to drain for several hours. Then the pots can be placed into their own polyethylene bags and treated as described above for backbulbs until they begin to show signs of developing new roots.

BUYING BARE-ROOT SEEDLINGS

The purchase of an orchid is always an exciting experience. Catalogs have been pored over or, happiest of all, a commercial grower has been visited and the plant personally selected. So far, so good. If you have seen the plant in flower, you know exactly what you are getting. However, if you buy unnamed seedlings, you have only their ancestry to guide you and the integrity of the grower to assure you that you are getting plants of good quality. *Bare-root seedlings* are seedlings that have not flowered. An educated guess can be made as to what they will look like, but there is no guarantee. Yet the chances of getting some excellent plants are sufficiently high to make their purchase worthwhile.

These bare-root seedlings are always less expensive than are mature plants for many reasons, not the least of which is that they are shipped without pots. This saves tremendously on transportation costs. Thus, having a few bare-root seedlings of any one variety is much more practical than a community pot containing several dozen, all of which are of the same variety, since there are not many who want a whole collection of only one kind of plant.

Especially when such seedlings arrive from a distance, they will undoubtedly look—and are—rather dry. Even though the grower has done everything possible to ensure a perfect shipment, the radical temperature changes, careless handling, and delays in delivery, even with air transportation, can take their toll.

145   As soon as the seedlings arrive they should be dunked

into tepid water. Within a few minutes each seedling will begin to look fresh and bright green. They are now ready to be potted. The size of the pot will depend upon the size of each seedling. Never use a pot that is too big. Crock the pot well before filling it with potting medium that has been thoroughly soaked and had any excess water squeezed out of it, for the potting medium should be uniformly damp but never soaking-wet.

If the seedling is small, it should be placed in the center of the pot and will need one or two more pottings before it reaches the flowering stage. If it is of good size, it can be placed to one side of the pot so that there will be room for new growths to develop for a year or two. Always pot seedlings firmly, staking them if necessary. Then label them with the plants' numbers, parentage, and the date you acquired them. Many of these bare-root seedlings do not have names, only the numbers assigned by the grower, but with these numbers the grower can look back in his records and locate the names of the plants that made the crosses and the dates it was done.

Such small plants tend to dry out quickly. Therefore, they should be grouped together so they can be misted and watered without disturbing the more mature plants, for misting the foliage helps to keep the seedlings fresh and the humidity high.

BUYING MATURE PLANTS

Visiting a commercial orchid range and selecting the plant you want is the ideal way to buy an orchid. There are so many different kinds and varieties of plants and so many in bloom that it is like visiting a flower show. If visiting a commercial grower is not possible, catalogs will give you an ample selection from which to choose. They also contain many helpful hints and bits of advice on growing orchids that are well worth heeding.

When it arrives, the plant should be a vigorous grower with plump bulbs and growths and leaves of a good green, since the color of the leaf is a good indication of the health of the plant. A light green leaf may merely mean that the plant has been grown in strong light, but yellowing is suspect. A plant like that needs to be given extra shading for a time and requires extra care to bring it back to a healthy green. There should be no shriveling or any signs of diseases or pests. The shriveling of the front growth, for instance, may indicate that the plant has had poor culture that resulted in a loss of roots.

A plant should also show signs that it will continue to produce new growths. Look for swellings at the bases of the pseudobulbs or growths that give promise of developing into new leads. If there are backbulbs still on the plant, they should be firm and sturdy.

When the plant blooms, how often it blooms, and how long the flowers last are all facts worth considering, for it is always desirable to have orchids in bloom each month of the year. Something should also be known about its parentage, for it costs just as much in time and energy to bring along an inferior plant as a potential award winner. The plants should also show signs of having blossomed recently as indicated by having some part of the old flower spikes or stems still attached to the last growth. In any case, beware of so-called "bargain plants." Their quality usually matches their price.

Another point to remember is that all plants from one cross are rarely all alike, unless they are meristem-produced. Some can turn out to be award winners, others duds. In any batch of plants from seeds it is usual for one or two to show outstanding qualities. These are distinguished by being given a cultivar name along with their registered one. An example of this is Blc. Norman's Bay 'Lucile,' a truly outstanding brassolaeliocattleya.

In addition, local orchid societies often have plant sales. Also, the members are usually most willing to exchange plants, thus affording everyone a chance to increase the variety of his collection and obtain plants he might otherwise not be able to.

IMPORTING PLANTS

The growing of orchids readily leads to dreaming of faraway places where they are found growing in abundance. Whether you are fortunate enough to visit these places and do your own collecting or can only visit them through the pages of catalogs offering orchids for export, an import permit is required before any orchids can be brought into the United States. Therefore, if you contemplate getting orchids from a foreign country, the first thing you must do is apply for a permit to:

Permit Unit
Plant Protection and Health Inspection Service
U.S. Department of Agriculture
Federal Building
Hyattsville, Maryland   20782

There is no fee for this permit, and when your application has been approved, a permit number is issued to you. This number identifies you by name and address. It remains on file at Hyattsville and at each of the inspection stations located at the various ports of entry to the United States. You will also receive a set of instructions pertaining to the importation of plants. Upon request, the Permit Unit will also supply mailing and shipping labels.

If plants are being shipped by mail—and it is strongly recommended that they be shipped by air mail if possible—a mailing label sent you by the Permit Unit should be used. This has your permit number, and it will save considerable time by directing your shipment to the inspection station named on the label as well as providing all the information necessary for the Plant Inspection Service.

The manner in which the plants are to be shipped should also be agreed upon by both you and the exporter in writing. The place from which the plants are shipped and the place where they will arrive will determine the mode of transportation, but the fastest possible routing should be selected.

Although you are free to import only one or as many plants as you wish at any one time, it is often faster and much less expensive, if a large shipment is contemplated, to have it broken up into small parcels and sent by air mail or air parcel post, rather than all at once by air freight or air cargo. In this way, everything is taken care of by the Postal Service, from going through customs, delivering, and picking up the plants at the inspection station to sending the plants on their way to you. Any duty due is paid when the shipment arrives at your door.

Air freight or air cargo, on the other hand, can present problems, not the least of which is the amount of time consumed. There is also a minimum charge for both from foreign countries, which makes it prohibitive for one or two plants. It is necessary to engage the services of a broker, at an additional fee, to take the shipment from the port of entry through customs, bring it to the plant inspection station, pick it up after it has been inspected and cleared, pay the duty, then bring it to an airline to be shipped to you.

Imported plant material is not allowed to go overland to an inspection station nearer your home. The plants must be inspected at the station nearest the port of entry. The purpose of this regulation is to prevent foreign plant pests from escaping from a shipment, entering this country, and possibly causing untold damage to agriculture.

Figure 9-3. A highly trained inspector at a U.S.D.A. plant inspection station looking for signs of pests and diseases with a magnifying lens.

Courtesy U.S.D.A., APHIS Division

149

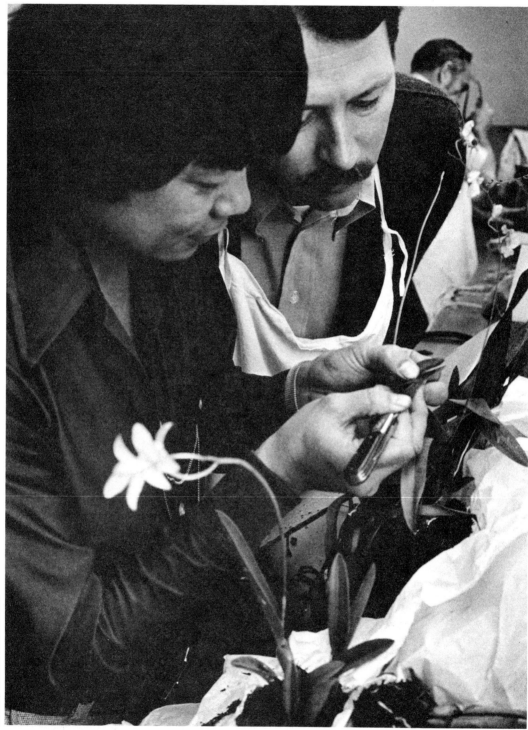

Figure 9-4. Workers at a plant inspection station inspecting orchid plants for leaf borer before clearing them for entry.

After the plants are unpacked at the station, they are thoroughly inspected, under magnification if necessary, but it is usually only the plants that have been collected in the wild that are in the high-risk category. All plants are then processed one at a time to prevent any mixup, and all parts of each plant are examined. Any parts that show signs of infection or infestation are removed by the inspectors.

Any plants found to be infected or infested are then subject to treatment by the method that will cause the least harm to the plant. The treatment may be fumigation, a hot-water dip, an insecticidal dip, or defoliation.

Unfortunately, there are times when a shipment, particularly one that has been collected in the wild, is so badly infested that there is no choice but to refuse it entry. At each step records are kept of the date and the condition of the plants upon their arrival at the inspection station, any treatment given, and the date of their release from the station. These records are available upon request to the importer.

For importation to be successful you should buy only those types of orchid you feel you are capable of growing. Make certain that the exporter is reputable and has had

Figure 9-5. A worker at a plant inspection station making out a report on his findings on a group of orchids imported from South America.

Courtesy U.S.D.A., APHIS Division

Figure 9-6. Live plants being placed in the fumigation chambers at one of the plant inspection stations.

experience in packing and shipping orchids long distances. Keep tabs on the whereabouts of your imports from the time they leave the exporter until they are delivered to your door. Finally, do not be too hasty in placing the blame for shipments that arrive in poor condition upon the plant inspection station. More often than not the cause is with the exporter.

When the shipment does arrive it should be examined at once. If there are any plants that have been damaged, remove the injured parts with a sharp, sterile knife. Then dip the cut areas into a fungicide to prevent infection.

If the plants are dry and wilted—and they probably are—lay them in a basin of tepid water for several hours. Then let them drain on soft tissues. If they should arrive in really poor condition, it might be necessary—after they have had time to soak up some moisture—to place them into polyethylene bags that contain some well-moistened osmunda or bark. When the roots begin to grow they may then be taken out of the bag and potted. They still need some shade for the first few weeks and will also need to be misted frequently to keep them fresh.

Growing under Special Conditions

We have seen how in the beginning orchids were grown exclusively in greenhouses where the temperature and humidity could be kept at the extremely high levels it was felt were necessary. As time went on, growers began to realize that when they let in some fresh air and lowered the temperature the plants actually grew better. It was then that orchids began to be grown in conservatories and even on windowsills.

Modern advances in technology, particularly through the use of fluorescent lights, have now made it possible not only to grow orchids in places never before thought possible but also to advance the flowering dates of many genera. This has enabled orchid growers to have plants in flower not only for all of the holidays throughout the year but also for those special times when an orchid makes any occasion really festive.

GROWING UNDER FLUORESCENT LIGHTS

Perhaps the idea of growing orchids under lights came from a grower who was successful in maturing seedlings at a faster rate with the use of fluorescent lights than would otherwise have been possible. Being adventurous, he then expanded the idea to his more mature plants.

Whatever its beginnings, growing under artificial lights has made the growing of orchids possible for many who otherwise would never be able to do so. Since the 1950s it has become an increasingly important and widely used manner of culture.

This method has the advantage of providing an almost completely controlled climate, with no need to be concerned

Figure 10-1. Orchids growing under lights where growing conditions are all electrically controlled.

Courtesy American Orchid Society

about cloudy days or hot sunlight. Even vacationing is made easier, for the plants can be left without care for longer periods than those grown as house plants or in a conventional greenhouse.

The automation of so many cultural procedures when gardening under lights means that the time spent in routine chores is so shortened that even extremely busy people find that they, too, can indulge in growing orchids.

Unused rooms, hallways, basements, living and dining rooms, dens, kitchens, just about any place can be made a suitable and often attractive place for fluorescent-light gardening. Whatever place is chosen, it should be free from drafts and someplace where doors will not constantly be opening and closing. And, perhaps most important, the floor should be able to withstand the splashing or dripping of water without being damaged.

Generally, basements seem to be the most popular choice, probably because there is sufficient space available, the water supply is usually nearby, and the surrounding area is not readily damaged by the moist atmosphere needed to grow orchids. Walls that have been painted a flat white give the entire area a brighter, more inviting look, as well as increasing the amount of light available to the plants. On the other hand, plants are frequently grown under lights in one place and displayed in bloom in another and more luxurious setting.

It is important to remember, however, that whenever the plants are moved from one place to another or even from the end position on a tray to the center, they should be given the same orientation to the lights that they have been accustomed to. In other words, plants always grow toward a source of light, and if they are moved and the orientation or facing is altered while the buds are forming, the whole blooming process may be interrupted. Another point to remember is that since there are usually fewer plants in a display area, each one can be taken away and watered, misted, and fertilized elsewhere to protect the surroundings from possible damage.

Equipment

Most of the equipment needed to start indoor-light growing can either be made by the grower or purchased from companies that specialize in these items. It can be as simple

Figure 10-2. Hardware cloth on benches allows free drainage of water
and also both bottom hear and air.

or as elaborate as your taste and pocketbook dictate. Even
portable plant carts already equipped with fluorescent lights
can be purchased to harmonize with one's decor, and tables
also come so equipped.

Stands, benches, cabinets, and wardian cases can also
be utilized as the nucleus of the growing center. Not only

Figure 10-3. Flat benches with cypress laths are an improvement over
stone-filled benches.

carts but also large cabinets can be equipped with casters to make moving them about much easier in case you want to change the growing location at any time. The only stipulation is that the dimensions of the growing areas themselves be the same length and width as the fluorescent light units so that light will always be shed on every plant.

Within the growing area, trays filled with pebbles that are kept constantly moist can be put on top of the shelves, tables, or benches. This helps maintain the needed humidity, while a wire rack or piece of hardware cloth placed over them will keep the pots from standing in water. Upturned saucers or plastic blocks can also be used for this latter purpose.

Most of the cattleyas, the small species orchids, some oncidiums, the majority of paphiopedilums, some phalaenopsis, the ascoscendas, and the dendrobiums all grow well under artificial light.

Light Fixtures

The fluorescent lightbulbs themselves are, of course, the heart of the light-gardening unit, but reflectors are also needed, for then the plants receive their light both from the tubes themselves and from the reflectors. The fixtures that hold them must be able to be readily raised or lowered over the tops of the plants by pulleys or by chains to adjust to the size and needs of the plants.

Here two precautions are important. Since the fixtures are exposed to a rather high humidity, they should be sprayed with a moisture-repellent material, and for safety's sake no fluorescent tube should ever be handled while it is lit.

The tubes themselves should be ones that have been designed especially for growing plants. These are the tubes that also produce the red and blue areas of the spectrum necessary for photosynthesis. They include the far-red area of the spectrum needed to initiate bud formation. GRO-LUX, the wide-spectrum tube made by Sylvania, and PLANT-GRO, made by Westinghouse, are probably the best known, although there are others such as the Duro-Lite line that have many ardent supporters. These tubes emit enough red radiation so that there is no need for any additional incandescent lightbulbs to provide these red rays. While some feel that the combination of ordinary fluorescent light plus incandescent bulbs properly handled are as effective, many

157

are convinced that incandescent lightbulbs always give off too much heat, and in a small area this extra heat can raise the temperature to unhealthy levels.

Four 40-watt tubes mounted over an area 40 inches long by 38 inches wide provide sufficient light for orchids like cattleyas, which require a bright light. Two 40-watt tubes can be used instead for those that need less light, such as the paphiopedilums, which need to be grown under a lower light intensity. In any case, the total amount of light provided by the fluorescent tubes must never be less than 5 watts for every square inch of space. A plant that would receive 1500 footcandles of light in a greenhouse for 7 hours will need fluorescent lighting for 16 hours to receive the equivalent amount of light.

The fluorescent tubes are usually placed 3 or 4 inches apart. The reflectors, which should have a coat of flat white paint on the inside for added reflection, are placed side by side above the light tubes. The whole unit can then be hung from the ceiling by a chain or pulley. This enables it to be moved up or down easily to accommodate the light requirements of the various plants.

The plants should never be crowded. They should be spaced in such a way that there will always be an overlapping of light on each plant, and no plant should ever be where any part of it will receive too little light or, worse still, no light. Remember, too, that plants at the end of the growing area will always receive less light than those at the center, and plants beginning to show buds should be put in the center.

There are two ways that light intensity can be increased: by adding light tubes or by lowering the tubes closer to the plants. To decrease the light intensity, do the opposite.

Checking Light Intensity

It is easy to become so accustomed to the lights that you are not aware of the fact that they are losing their original brightness. Checking with a light meter is the only accurate way to measure light intensity. Without it you must watch the tubes closely, for as fluorescent tubes age they tend to darken along their entire length. When its ends become black, the life of a tube is just about over for the plant culture. Ordinarily these tubes last 1000 hours, but never wait until the light from the tube has become dim before replacing it. All tubes should be replaced routinely every year.

Amount of Light Needed

The whole purpose of growing orchids under lights is to ensure that they will receive the same amount of light for the proper number of hours each day. To make certain the amount of this light does remain constant, clean the tubes and fixtures once a month.

As for timing, the lights are usually left on between 14 and 16 hours a day on the average. (The length of time compensates somewhat for the lack of intensity in the artificial light.) The exact number of hours is determined by how the plants react. For some, long hours of light are essential if they are to flower. For others, the "short-day" plants, fewer hours of light are necessary to produce blooms, and this must be taken into consideration in determining the number of hours the lights will be left on.

It quickly becomes apparent, therefore, that all types of orchids cannot be grown side by side without regard to their differing heights or light requirements, and also that all cannot be grown at the same distance from the lights.

Fluorescent tubes should never be closer than 2 inches from the top of the leaves. It is always possible to find a place among the taller orchids that need a high light intensity for those that need a low light intensity, providing these are smaller and therefore lower, which means that they will be getting the lower light intensity they need.

In terms of their light requirements, orchids are generally divided into three groups. First are those needing a low light intensity, such as paphiopedilums and some phalaenopsis. With these the tubes can be raised from a few inches to a foot or more from the top of the leaves to get the desired light reading, and instead of using four 40-watt fluorescent tubes two 40-watt tubes are more likely to provide the correct amount of light. Check the number of footcandles needed for each type of orchid with the list in Chapter 3 and try by adjusting the lights to come as close as possible to the amount that has been suggested.

Two 40-watt GRO-LUX tubes on an hour-a-day schedule

will provide the following light intensities (reflectors, however, substantially increase this amount):

Distance of Plants from Tube, in inches	Footcandles
1	1100
2	860
3	680
4	570
5	500
6	420
8	330
10	280
12	240

This means that orchids that need a high light intensity of 1500 to 3000 fc can be grown under four 40-watt fluorescent tubes with the tubes about 2 inches from the tops of the leaves. Any orchids that need more light than this must be put in a growing area that can be equipped with more light tubes.

Experience has shown that orchids in the low-light-intensity group do the best under artificial light. Experience also shows that where the growing area is relatively small and growing the largest number of orchids of as many types as possible is desired, those orchids that have long, drooping leaves, such as cymbidiums, or those that grow extremely tall, like vandas, are too large for the limited space available.

One major difference in growing orchids under artificial light is that there are no seasonal changes to cope with, no cloudy days, no hot sun—just regular, controlled lighting. Yet the plants still seem to have natural seasonal reactions with respect to flowering, at least for the first few years they are grown under lights. Thus, by controlling the amount of light they receive you can, in effect, control their blooming period. Increased light always stimulates the growing cycle, just as spring and summer do for windowsill and greenhouse plants.

Some growers even try to imitate nature and vary the length of time the lights are on to correspond to the various seasons:

15 hours	January–February
16 hours	March–August

15 hours   September–October
14 hours   November–December

New fluorescent light tubes are constantly being developed. Some high-output tubes provide greater light intensity with less wattage. In others, the reflector is an integral part of the tube. Still, regardless of the type of light used, the basic light requirements for orchids as measured in footcandles are still the means of determining the amount of light needed.

Light is not the only consideration in growing orchids. Temperature, ventilation, humidity, watering, feeding, and even pest control all are equally important.

Temperature

In most instances the heat from the house's heating system is more than ample to keep the area warm. This, along with the heat from the tubes and ballasts, can usually assure enough warmth for even the warmest-growing orchids. However, if it does not, as might be true in a basement, an electric heater can always be used to supplement the heat.

Since the environment is so completely controlled under artificial conditions, several good, accurate thermometers placed among the plants should be all that is needed to tell you whether the temperature under the lights is what the plants require.

As we indicated before, each type of orchid has its own temperature needs, ranging from very cool to very warm (see Chapter 2.) The same differential (10 to 20° cooler when the lights are off) is needed to preserve the balance for photosynthesis. So while there is a natural decrease in temperature when the lights are off, if this decrease is not enough, then either the heater, if used, will have to be turned down or some cool air introduced in a way that does not cause a draft.

Ventilation

The ballasts on fluorescent light fixtures always give off some heat—and so to some degree do the tubes themselves.

In fact, enough heat may be generated to burn plants that

are too near the tubes. Therefore, there must always be enough circulation around the plants to dispel this heat. Allowing enough space around each plant is one way to help.

Since the plants are probably growing where there is no opportunity to give them fresh air directly from a window, a fan may be needed to keep the air circulating. This fan can be hooked up to a timer that will turn it off and on at the same time as the lights. The fan can also be used to pull in fresh air, since orchids must have some fresh air each day, even if it means opening a window in another room and letting the fresh air filter in from there.

The fresh, buoyant atmosphere helps prevent both fungus and rot, while stale air is generally deadly to orchids. Hanging a piece of ribbon from the light fixture will provide a visual means of checking the air circulation.

Humidity

The amount of humidity should never be guessed at but checked carefully with a hygrometer or a humidguide placed in among the plants. For best results this humidity should run between 50 and 60% when the lights are on and about 30 to 40% when they are off. Naturally, when the plants have been watered or misted there is a rise in humidity. Then, as this moisture evaporates, the humidity gradually decreases. So there should be no problem in obtaining lower humidity at night, for all the watering or misting is taken care of while the plants are lighted, thus giving the plants time to dry off a bit.

The water around the pebbles under the plants is a big help in maintaining the humidity. However, if there ever does develop any difficulty in maintaining sufficient moisture, one solution might be to enclose the growing area in polyethylene. In fact, some of the commercially made floral carts come with such plastic tents as part of the unit. An opening must always be left in any such covering to allow for some fresh air and circulation. In a large growing area a frame can be built that will enclose the whole area and to which the polyethylene can be stapled, but always leave the top and a part of one side open for ventilation.

When the atmosphere is too dry, a humidifier is useful. Leaving the fan on after watering also helps keep the atmosphere moist. If there is room, a table fountain with its own circulation pump is both an attractive addition to the growing area and a good way to increase the humidity when the plants are being grown in one of the living rooms.

As a precaution, however, any fluorescent tubes, timers, electric heaters, and thermostats should all be checked out to be certain that when all of them are plugged in at the same time they will not blow a fuse. Each electrical aid should be equipped with a mercury switch to withstand the water and humidity. They can be plugged into several outlets by using waterproof extension cords. If there is any doubt, it might be a good idea to have an electrician go over your requirements and suggest ways of distributing the load evenly throughout the system. This is particularly important if you are away from home a great deal.

Watering

The same general watering guidelines apply when growing under lights that do elsewhere; the potting material should be almost dry before it is watered. However, paphiopedilums, which need to be kept slightly moist at all times, should be kept moist under lights as well.

When growing under lights, plants have a greater rate of transpiration (exhaling moisture), perhaps because the long hours of light stimulate the growth processes. Yet this does not mean that they dry out so quickly that you can water indiscriminately. Never water an orchid unless it needs to be watered. Every plant does not need water at the same time. Keep water out of the axils of the leaves, where it becomes the main cause of basal decay in paphiopedilums. To prevent overwatering, check each plant carefully. Put your finger deep into the potting material and feel just how dry it really is. Then, if it needs water, go ahead.

Since these plants are used to a sheltered, pampered existence, they should never be shocked with cold water. Always have it at room temperature.

As elsewhere, small pots will dry out faster than large ones, and plants in the center of the growing area (where the light is strongest) will also dry out faster. Therefore, water these more often.

How you water your plants under lights also depends upon where the plants are being grown. In a basement a hose is probably the easiest way. In this case, there must be some means of draining off the excess water left on the trays or shelves, especially after flushing the plants. One way is by draining the water into a sink by means of a tube; another is by siphoning it off into a bucket. A drain in the floor under a growing area alone is not the complete answer, because the upper shelves also need some means of getting rid of their water.

In smaller growing areas in the living rooms, where the use of water might cause some damage, the plants can be either pot-watered separately by placing them in a bucket of water and then on a draining tray or watered with a small-sized watering pot.

As you can see, it is impossible to give any hard-and-fast rules for the amount and frequency of watering. Nevertheless, no orchid should ever become waterlogged; neither should it become bone-dry. A happy medium to fit your particular conditions can only be arrived at by trial and error.

Finally, never for one moment forget when you are watering these plants that there are electrical sockets and cords all around you. Exercise caution.

Feeding

Feeding, too, is different. The amount of food needed by a plant growing under artificial lights is not only much less than that needed by one in a greenhouse, but it is less than half of that needed by those growing on window-sills. The usual high-nitrogen formula can be used for artificial-light-grown orchids potted in bark, with an occasional feeding with a balanced fertilizer, but whether to use one higher in phosphorous is something you will have to determine on your own. In fact, the whole fertilizing program depends entirely upon the amount of light the plants receive. The more light, the more food they need, but heavy feeding is always a danger to orchids, and especially to orchids grown under lights. The amount of light they receive from fluorescent tubes can never equal in intensity that provided by the sun.

Foliar feeding also comes into its own in under-light growing. It gets the food onto the leaves and pseudobulbs, where it is quickly absorbed and put to use. Every other watering can double as a very light fertilizing, which, together with foliar feeding once a month, should supply enough nutrients. But remember, what you want are strong, sturdy plants—so do not overfeed.

Once a month all pots should be flushed out thoroughly with plain water to get rid of any fertilizer salts that may have accumulated.

Potting

The manner in which a plant is potted takes on even greater significance when growing under lights. Overwatering can be just as hazardous to the fluorescent-light grower as it is to the greenhouse or windowsill grower. Often the potting material will look and feel dry halfway down in the pot, while the lower part is still soaking-wet. To get around this condition, a lighter, more porous material should be used than when potting for conventional culture. Large-size bark that is not tamped in is good, but until the roots develop sufficiently to hold the plant up you will have to rely upon tying the growths to one or two stakes. As expected, the more porous potting material gives the roots room to breathe, and then there is less chance of their rotting.

When it comes time to repot, such plants are also easier to remove from the looser potting material. Tip the pot up, carefully ease the plant out, and shake off or gently pull off the old material. Then crock the pot well and pot as you ordinarily would, except that you do not tamp down the material.

Small orchids on tree-fern slabs do not take up too much room and also make a nice change from too many pots.

Pests and Diseases

The fact that orchids are growing in a controlled environment does not mean that they cannot fall prey to diseases and pests. Unfortunately, they can and do, and mealybugs, red spiders, and fungi seem to present the greatest problems under artificial lights. Still, they are easily controlled by applying the proper sprays when needed. (See also Chapter 11.)

Generally, all spraying should be done as early in the day as possible and finished at least six hours before the lights go off. Also, there must always be adequate ventilation so that any toxic fumes will have a chance to dissipate. This is particularly important in cold weather, when there is a limit to the amount of fresh air that can be let into a house. If the smell of an insecticide, such as Malathion, is unpleasant in one's rooms, spray and keep the plants elsewhere—the basement, for example or attic—until it is dissipated.

After orchids have been growing for a number of years under lights they seem to ignore the usual seasonal changes. Often not only does the blooming period occur at a different time each year, but they seem to have a very short resting period, if any at all.

Growth seems to be constant under the lights. The periods between flowering, particularly with paphiopedilums, seems to be shortened. Although it is not necessary to move any plant to a special resting area after it has flowered, it can be placed for a time over near the edge of the growing area where the light is not as strong until the new growths and roots have had a chance to develop.

Summer Care

There are two schools of thought concerning whether or not it is advisable to put plants that have been growing under artificial light outdoors for the summer. Some growers feel a summer outside is extremely beneficial, while others just as vehemently claim that once grown under controlled conditions they should not have any change from it. This is something each grower must decide for himself. If put outside, the plants obviously get more light and fresh air than if they remained inside, but they are also subject to the vagaries of the elements.

If they are summered outdoors, put them in a relatively shaded place where they are protected from the direct sunlight until they become accustomed to being outdoors. Sunlight, with its accompanying high temperatures, can readily cause burning, for no matter how strong the fluorescent lighting is, it does not match the sun in intensity.

When you first start to grow orchids under artificial lights, have patience. It will take the plants at least a year to become accustomed to the environment. During this first year they may only make vegetative growth, and it will not be until the next year that they will reach their flowering potential. Experiment, try out different ways of doing things. Growing under lights is a comparatively new field, with plenty left to learn. You can contribute to this learning process by your own experience.

What could be more beautiful or more exotic than an orchid in your window? However, the term *windowsill growing* should not be taken too literally. As used here, it includes the care of all those orchids grown as house plants, whether directly on a windowsill or not, for most sunrooms and porches also have enough light. The latter also frequently have the advantage of having windows on three sides that give three different exposures. But wherever they are grown, orchids add beauty to their surroundings.

Before embarking upon indoor culture, realistically assess the location and choose only those orchids most likely to do well in the temperature and light that is available. If you do this properly, you will find orchids are no more difficult to grow than many other house plants.

The suggestions in the preceding chapters on general culture will need some modification for windowsill culture, mainly because the amount of light under these conditions is seldom as great as in a greenhouse, which also has the added advantage of overhead light.

Temperature

Not only does the temperature in most houses compare favorably with that in a greenhouse, but in some instances the warm-growing orchids do better in the house. But they should never be grown too near a radiator or an outside door where there might be blasts of heat or cold drafts.

Unless your house is cooler than the average or you have a room that can be kept cool and that also has an abundance of light, cool-temperature orchids such as odontoglossums will just not do well.

Because to most people the cattleya with its showy flowers seems to fit their idea of what an orchid should look like, it has become the favorite for beginners. There are literally hundreds of hybrid cattleyas available and worth trying. *Paphiopedilum maudiae,* a green-and-white lady slipper orchid, is another favorite fairly easily grown indoors. Many of the botanicals (orchids not grown commercially for their flowers), phalaenopsis, and some of the oncidiums may do well. So you see, you have a large selection from which to make your choice.

To make them easier to care for, the orchids should be small or medium in size. Large plants like cymbidiums or huge vandas are just too large for the average indoor

167

grower. A 6-inch pot is about the largest size that can easily be handled for watering or moving from one spot to another.

Getting that necessary 10–20° differential between day and night temperatures is usually no problem. Both the plants and the room where they are growing cool off rapidly once the sun has set. On cloudy days when there is no buildup of heat during the day, turning the heater down at night will bring about the decrease needed for the night temperature. Whatever the temperature in your home, if it is comfortable to you it will be comfortable for some type of orchid.

Ventilation

Orchids must have fresh air. Most of the year this presents no problem indoors, since windows can be left open. But during extremely cold weather, the change in air might have to come in a roundabout way, perhaps from a window in another room. During warm weather, windows should be left open all night, for cool night air is the best tonic an orchid can have. This is one reason why those who grow orchids inside all winter like to put them outdoors in the summer.

For the same reason, never crowd your plants together. Each should have enough space around it for good circulation of air. If space is a problem, grow the small orchids like ascoscendas (which are really small vandas), miniatures like *Oncidium pulchellum,* or any of the small botanicals. Besides having compact growth, these little plants have flowers that are both beautiful and unusual and that last a long time.

Light

After determining that the temperature available will be adequate for the orchids you select, the next thing to be considered is the amount of light they need and whether the light that is available is sufficient. In looking for a place with the maximum amount of light, a windowsill is probably the best, providing the plants will be neither chilled nor roasted near the glass. It is always much hotter or cooler right next to windowglass than it is a foot or so back.

This is where Thermopane glass is a great help. Without storm windows, it is a necessity in winter in the cold northern states.

Figure 10-4 (opposite). A phalaenopsis growing on a windowsill adds its own charm to any room.

Orchids that need a high light intensity, warmth, and long hours of sunlight can be grown in a south or west window. Those that need more shade and low light intensity can be grown in an east window. A northerly exposure is rarely suitable, for the light is never quite strong enough there and the plants do not have the benefit of the early morning sunlight they need.

Sunlight plays an important role in growing orchids. The growth of the plant itself, the ripening of growths, and flowering all are dependent upon it. Watch the color of the leaves for an indication of whether the light is strong enough or perhaps too strong. Dark green leaves always indicate that there has been far too little light available, while yellow leaves have had all the chlorophyll bleached out of them by too much light. The leaves should be a medium green.

Shading

Some shading from the hot rays of the mid-day sun is usually needed from the middle of January to about the middle of October to keep the leaves from burning. Thin curtains, slatted blinds, and bamboo drops are all good ways to shade. They can also be used to keep the plants from becoming chilled on frosty nights. But try to get these shades up as early in the morning as possible so that the plants will get the benefit of the early morning sunlight. Needless to say on excessively cold nights orchids should be moved away from a window to a nearby table. Shading should always be removed by mid-afternoon so that the plants will be able to get the full benefit of the waning sunlight.

The plants can be moved from one window to another during the various seasons of the years to take advantage of the difference in light. In the summer they can be taken out of a window that faces south and grown in a more easterly exposure. By thus moving them around you can take advantage of both sunlight and shade throughout the year.

During the summer months, screens on the windows not only help the plants to get plenty of fresh air but also act as a form of shading, particularly if the screens have been painted green or black.

Insufficient light is always one of the prime causes of a failure of orchids to flower. On the other hand, even though growing conditions are pretty well controlled in a house, there is another area where you might inadvertently slip. Having a light on in the same room with the orchids may, if close enough, extend the number of hours a plant receives light. This amount, small as it may seem, might be all that is needed to prevent flowering, particularly if they happen to be short-day plants. (This also holds true for the light given off by street lights.) No matter how inviting it may look, rooms where orchids are growing should not be lit at night.

Unlike plants growing with fluorescent lights, where 16 hours of light is the average amount they receive, house plants get the full intensity of the sun's rays, which means they need light for a shorter time.

Humidity

The humidity in most homes is far too low—not only for orchids but for people. Consequently, a humidifier will be most helpful if it raises the humidity to 50 or 60%, or small dishes of water can be placed among the plants. Today most windowsills are not deep enough to accommodate trays of moist pebbles on which the plants can be grown, but if the light is still strong enough back a little ways from the window, growing the plants on such trays placed on a table does help keep the humidity up. As mentioned before, the bottoms of the pots should be raised on blocks above the moist pebbles so that no plant stands in the water. For accurate measurement, a small humidguide nestled among the orchids will help keep you aware of the true situation.

Remember, however, that a plant's leaves can look dry even though the potting material is moist. This is one indication that the humidity is too low. For your own health as well as that of the orchids, the humidity should never be less than 40%.

Watering

Probably the best and most convenient way to water an orchid indoors is by placing some polyethylene over the rugs and under both a plastic bucket filled with tepid water and a draining tray. A wire rack can be fitted over the tray so the plants can drain easily. Taking the plants to the sink for watering is also a popular method—and safer for the furnishings.

No matter where orchids are grown, the potting material

must always have a chance to dry out before it is watered. The exceptions are orchids such as paphiopedilums and phalaenopsis, which should be slightly moist at all times.

When you water, water thoroughly. It takes just a few minutes for a plant submerged in a bucket of water to become wet. When the bubbles stop, it can be taken out, for this is the sign that the potting matterial has absorbed all the water it can.

Feeding

The amount of food needed by plants growing in a house is just about half of what is recommended for a greenhouse. This is because the light that is available in the house is not as strong as in a greenhouse, and the amount of light controls the amount of food that is needed. As in general culture, too much fertilizer always causes lush, green, unproductive growths. Thus, feeding once a month, either directly in the pot or by foliar feeding, is sufficient. When you do feed, make up in a jug a solution of water-soluble fertilizer at half the strength recommended for greenhouse growing and apply as needed.

Again, the type of fertilizer you use depends upon the material the plants are growing in. Plants in bark always need fertilizer higher in nitrogen to offset that which the bark takes up in breaking down. In other situations, a balanced 18–18–18 can be used.

Potting

The procedures suggested in Chapter 5 are also applicable to the potting of orchids growing as house plants. Even though these orchids are being grown in what amounts to a decorative environment, they should not be grown in glazed or ceramic pots. The clay or plastic pots are better, with the plastic pots retaining moisture longer than the clay ones do.

Tree-fern slabs have a tendency to dry out rather quickly in a house, and therefore need more watering and more frequent misting. Yet *Epidendrum fragrans,* so small and exquisite, does extremely well on a slab of tree fern. Use a piece of fine wire or twist ties to fasten the plant to the slab until the roots have finally embedded themselves in the tree fern and these fastenings are no longer needed.

Orchids in hanging baskets can be most attractive in a window. However, they do need frequent misting and may have to be taken to the sink when the time comes to water them. Here, too, the water should run through the potting material until the latter has become completely wet. Then let the basket drain before hanging it up again.

Because these baskets are near the ceiling and heat tends to rise, they have a warmer environment than those grown on windowsills or tables. During the winter, when the house heating is going full blast, take these baskets down at night and place them on the floor. This will help give them the needed differential between the night and day temperatures that is so important in getting orchids to flower.

Pests and Diseases

Each day, as you mist the plants, look them over carefully for any signs of disease or pests. Always be sure to do this before you plunge a pot into a bucket of water for watering. If a plant were to be put in the same water that an infected plant had just been in, it would suffer the same ailment in short order. If a plant that has a disease or is insect-infected is inadvertently put in a bucket of water, that water must be discarded and the bucket thoroughly cleaned before it is used again.

Isolate infected plants in another room until you are certain they are completely disease- and insect-free. A daily check of your plants goes a long way toward keeping troubles under control. (See Chapter 11.) Also, to be on the safe side, isolate all newly acquired plants until you are certain they are disease- and insect-free.

The pests most likely to attack orchids in the home are scale, mealybugs, and red spider mites, yet many orchid growers may never encounter any problems at all. If spraying is needed, house plants are better taken to the basement in cold weather or outside in summer to keep the fumes out of the house.

Keeping Plants Clean

Cleanness is the best way known to keep plants healthy. Scrub the pots occasionally with a stiff brush. This removes any algae and accumulated fertilizer salts. At least twice

173

a month take time to wash the leaves with a soft cloth or sponge and warm water. This removes dust and dirt from them and helps keep the pores clean. Do not use oil on the leaves.

GREENHOUSE CULTURE

Having a greenhouse is the dream of just about every gardener, and thanks to the ingenuity of greenhouse manufacturers, it is now possible to own one in just about any size or price range desired. Modern technology and automatic devices have removed much, if not all, of the work of keeping the growing conditions the way you want them.

Figure 10-5. A greenhouse filled with many varieties of orchid is an unforgettable sight.

Courtesy Lord & Burnham, Irvington-on-Hudson, New York

Courtesy Faire Harbour Boats

Figure 10-6. One type of
emergency heater, fueled by
kerosene.

Temperature

Whatever heating system is used, there must never be any chance of fumes getting inside the greenhouse. Of these heater-caused fumes, ethylene gas, is especially toxic to orchids. (Ethylene gas, present in the fumes of oil, gas, and gasoline, is the result of incomplete combustion.) It can cause the sheaths to turn yellow, then brown, and eventually die. It also causes buds to drop.

The heater should be large enough to supply all the BTUs (British thermal units, the measure of heat) needed to keep the temperature at the desired level even during the coldest weather. It is one area where there should be no guesswork. Iron it out with your greenhouse manufacturer or local heating contractor.

175   Natural gas, electricity, or an extension of the house

Figure 10-7. A temperature alarm can be set for the desired high and low temperatures.

heating system are the most commonly used methods of heating. The thermostats should be ones made for greenhouses and able to withstand moisture.

Since there may be times when a power failure can bring heating systems to a halt, some provision must be made for this. Obviously, a generator large enough to take care of both heat and light both in the home and greenhouse would be ideal, but they are expensive. However, there are some kerosene or portable gas heaters available that are made specifically for boats and greenhouses that can be used temporarily to maintain some level of heat. The size of the greenhouse will determine whether you will need more than one. (The better ones have the BTU ratings right on them.) It is also helpful to have some type of alarm system that will register in the house when the temperature in the greenhouse becomes too hot or too cold. This same alarm can also be arranged to work in case of fire.

Courtesy S & G Exotic Plant Co.

Figure 10-8 (above and below). Where the winters are severe, these plastic bubble caps can provide welcome insulation to retain the necessary heat in a greenhouse.

Where winters are severe or the need for conserving energy is acute, the inside of the greenhouse can be lined with clear 6- or 8-mil polyethylene, which provides a barrier between the cold glass and the orchids. This can also save on the heating bill.

Ventilation

The ventilators are the chief means of exchanging the air in the greenhouse, regulating the temperature, and providing the necessary circulation of air. In the older greenhouses the ventilators had to be opened manually by gears or push rods. Now, however, they can be controlled automatically, and motors will open and close, them when you are not around to do it, if you wish. There are always days when the sun goes in and out a maddening number of times, making it necessary to keep opening and closing them. For situations like this, automatic vents are the most useful piece of equipment in the greenhouse, and if there is a power failure the ventilators instantly close to conserve whatever heat is in the greenhouse. The purpose of this automation is to take the work out of greenhouse growing. It should never replace a personal involvement with the plants.

Air conditioning units are also available from most greenhouse suppliers and are almost as necessary in hot and humid areas as heating systems are in the cold ones. Less expensive than air conditioners are evaporative coolers

Figure 10-9. An evaporative cooler unit placed like a heater on the outside of a greenhouse.

Meet the Orchids

PLATE 1.   Group of several varieties
of orchid
Courtesy Brighton Farms. Photo by Val Sarra and Walter Chubb

CATTLEYAS

PLATE 2 (above right). *Cattleya* (Encyclia) *citrina* 'Charlotte',
FCC–CCM / AOS
Courtesy American Orchid Society

PLATE 3 (below). *Cattleya aurantiaca* 'Kitty'
Courtesy American Orchid Society

PLATE 4 (right). *Cattleya amethystoglossa* 'King's Ransom',
AM / AOS
Courtesy American Orchid Society

PAPHIOPEDILUMS

PLATE 5 (left). *Paphiopedilums*
Courtesy Rod McLellan Company

PLATE 6 (below). Group of
twenty-five paphiopedilums
Courtesy Fred A. Stewart Orchids, Inc.

CYMBIDIUMS

PLATE 7 (left). *Cymbidium* Joan of Arc
var. 'Snowfall', AM/AOS
Courtesy Rod McLellan Company

PLATE 8 (lower left). *Cymbidium*
African Adventure 'Jungle Trails', HCC/AOS
Courtesy American Orchid Society

PLATE 9 (bottom left). *Cymbidium* Elliot
Rogers var. 'Red Beauty', HCC/AOS–ODC
Courtesy Rod McLellan Company

PLATE 10 (bottom). *Cymbidium* Dag
'Dorothy', HCC/AOS
Courtesy American Orchid Society

MINIATURE CYMBIDIUMS

PLATE 11 (below). Miniature cymbidiums
Courtesy Rod McLellan Company

PLATE 12 (top right). Miniature *Cymbidium* Orkney 'Pink Heather'
Courtesy Adelaide Orchids

PLATE 13 (upper right). Miniature *Cymbidium* Myponga 'Adelaide'
Courtesy Adelaide Orchids

PLATE 14 (lower right). Miniature *Cymbidium* Clarendon 'Shirley'
Courtesy Adelaide Orchids

PLATE 15 (bottom right). Miniature *Cymbidium* Amesbury 'Frank Slattery'
Courtesy Adelaide Orchids

PHALAENOPSIS

PLATE 16 (left). *Phalaenopsis*
Roswell 'Fireball'
Courtesy Shaffer's Tropical Gardens, Inc.

PLATE 17 (below). Phalaenopsis
Inspiration 'Lemon Drop'
Courtesy Shaffer's Tropical Gardens, Inc.

PLATE 18 (above). *Phalaenopsis*
Hymen
Courtesy Shaffer's Tropical Gardens, Inc.

PLATE 19 (above right).
Phalaenopsis Elisa 'Chang Lou'
Courtesy Shaffer's Tropical Gardens, Inc.

PLATE 20 (right). *Phalaenopsis*
violacea
Courtesy Shaffer's Tropical Gardens, Inc.

PLATE 21 (above left).
Phalaenopsis ambomanniana
Courtesy Shaffer's Tropical Gardens, Inc.

PLATE 22 (above right).
Phalaenopsis Inspiration
'Lemon Drop'
Courtesy Shaffer's Tropical Gardens, Inc.

PLATE 23 (left).   *Phalaenopsis*
Grace Palm 'Snowball'
Courtesy Shaffer's Tropical Gardens, Inc.

PLATE 24 (above right).   *Phalaenopsis*
Doris 'Fire Mountain'
Courtesy Shaffer's Tropical Gardens, Inc.

PLATE 25 (right).   *Phalaenopsis* Alice
Gloria 'Nancy', .SM / SWOC
Courtesy Shaffer's Tropical Gardens, Inc.

PLATE 26 (below).   Group of
Phalaenopsis Treasure Island
Courtesy Shaffer's Tropical Gardens, Inc.

DENDROBIUMS

PLATE 27 (above). *Dendrobium densiflorum* and *Dendrobium farmeri*
Courtesy Rod McLellan Company

PLATE 28 (below). *Rhynchostylis gigantea* 'Sagarik's Strain'
Courtesy American Orchid Society

RHYNCHOSTYLIS

VANDAS

PLATE 29. *Vanda sanderana*
'Hilo Prince', AM/AOS
Courtesy Jones and Scully, Inc.

PLATE 30. *Oncidium varicosum*
'Rogersii' (left) and *Oncidium*
Fall Delight 'Crary' (right)
Courtesy Rod McLellan Company

ONCIDIUMS

MILTONIAS

PLATE 31. Group of miltonias
Courtesy Rod McLellan Company

ODONTOGLOSSUMS

PLATE 32. Odontoglossums
Courtesy Rod McLellan Company

PLATE 33 (above left). *Epidendrum cochleatum* 'Courtney', AM/AOS
Courtesy American Orchid Society

PLATE 34 (left). *Epidendrum vitellinum* 'Jo Ann', HCC/AOS
Courtesy American Orchid Society
Photo by Lewis H. Tabor

PLATE 35 (below). *Epidendrum cochleatum* 'Spyhill', AM/AOS
Courtesy American Orchid Society

PLATE 36 (left). *Laeliocattleya*
Quadrille
Courtesy Rod McLellan Company

PLATE 37 (below). *Laeliocattleya*
Western Sunset
Courtesy Rod McLellan Company

PLATE 38 (right). *Potinara*
Tapestry Peak
Courtesy Jones and Scully, Inc.

PLATE 39 (below). *Ascocenda*
Bonanza 'Belle Tew'. AM/HOS
Courtesy Jones and Scully, Inc.

PLATE 40 (below right). *Aliceara*
Monte Cristo
Courtesy The Beall Company

INTERESTING
ODDITIES

PLATE 41 (right). *Masdevallia coccinea*
Courtesy Rod McLellan Company

PLATE 42 (below). *Stanhopea peruviana*
Courtesy Rod McLellan Company

PLATE 43 (below right). *Zygopetalum
blackii* 'Negress', AM/RHS
Courtesy Rod McLellan Company

Courtesy Automatic Sunblind Installations

Figure 10-10. Greenhouse shades can be controlled automatically, folding up when not in use.

for keeping the temperature down. These have the added advantage of also increasing the humidity as the air is passed through or over water-saturated pads before entering the greenhouse.

Where no special provision for cooling has been made, fans are always useful for cooling and air circulation. They do tend to reduce the humidity, but this situation can be alleviated somewhat by misting the plants.

Shade

One of the oldest methods of shading greenhouses is to paint the outside of the glass with a white compound available from greenhouse suppliers. Light green is sometimes available, but white is preferred because the green tends to cut down the light too much, especially on cloudy days. Today many people feel that paint is not only troublesome to put on, but may also need to be renewed during the year.

Somewhat more costly but also more effective are

Figure 10-11. Automatically controlled shading in place during the sunny hours of the day.

greenhouse roll-up shades of wood, alumimum, or vinyl. The space between the slats should be at least an inch or two so that when pulled down there will still be some dappled sunlight available, for on bright, sunny days the shades may have to be left down for 4 or 5 hours. For those who desire, these shades can also be controlled automatically. An English firm manufactures some mounted on runners that go over the top of the greenhouse, leaving room for the ventilators to open and close freely. Like the automatic vents, they are controlled by a thermostat inside the greenhouse.

Light green polyethylene cut to the size of the glass can be put on the inside of the ventilators. Moisten the glass with a fine spray and the plastic sheets will bond themselves to the glass as you smooth them on with a brush. These can be left on all year, if desired. They provide shading where the ordinary blinds do not reach and prevent the hot sun from streaming in through the ventilators. (This is an often-overlooked area that causes burned spots on the plants.)

To handle the thermostats, fans, and other electrical equipment without blowing the fuses, the electrical circuits,

Figure 10-12. A slatted shade covering the glass wall or roof of a conservatory or sun porch can be controlled automatically by a small motor.

Courtesy Automatic Sunblind Installations

of course, must be able to handle the load, and the whole electrical system must be water-resistant. Above all, when watering or misting, stay away from the electrical equipment. It is always better to be on the safe side.

Humidity

Damping down the greenhouse floor with a hose and misting the plants frequently are usually all that is needed to keep the humidity at the desired 50–60% level during the day. If you want to be exact, a greenhouse hygrometer will help you determine the level of humidity.

Because of the danger of water becoming lodged in the pseudobulbs or the axils of the leaves, automatic misting devices should not be used when growing orchids. Hand-watering and misting in a greenhouse are easy if one uses a hose just long enough to reach the farthest end of the greenhouse (but not long enough to become knotted or tangled) and a nozzle that can be adjusted from a coarse spray to a fine mist. Even fertilizing can be done easily with a hose-end attachment that carefully measures and distributes the fertilizer.

Microclimates

Fortunately, not every nook and cranny in a greenhouse has the same temperature nor the same intensity of light. Place thermometers in and around the plants and you will soon see how the temperature varies.

Near the inside glass and in the corners it is usually cooler, whereas the top of the greenhouse is warmer, because heat tends to rise. Thus, these special areas or *microclimates* are the places to grow those plants that need temperatures that are either cooler or warmer than the central thermometer shows. In this way you can have a greater variety of orchids than you might think possible if just the regular thermometer reading were considered. Further variation occurs in that these areas may change with the season. For example, due to the change in the sun's location, a previously cold spot can become a warm and sunny one, and vice versa. So by consulting thermometers in various places you can select spots that will give you just the right growing conditions for specific orchids and make all the difference in the way the plants will grow for you.

In the same way, check on the difference in light intensity throughout the greenhouse. All plants, even those of the same genus, may not need the same amount of light. If you find those places where the light is strongest and weakest, a plant that has had trouble flowering may find a change to one of these microclimates just what it needs.

Pests and Diseases

Daily attention makes keeping up with diseases and pests no great problem. A definite spraying schedule is an important part of culture. When you first spot trouble, apply the remedy suggested in Chapter 11 at once. If necessary, the insecticide can be applied and the greenhouse shut until the next day while the material works. Then, in the morning, opening the ventilators will air the place out, and the fumes will be dissipated before you have to work among the plants.

Keeping the Greenhouse Clean

Finally, of outstanding importance in greenhouse culture is keeping a clean environment, free from dead leaves, dead flowers, and debris. Keep a receptacle handy for this purpose. If decayed material is permitted to accumulate, it will provide a breeding place for all kinds of pests and diseases. If the greenhouse is kept clean every day, there will never be a need to spend valuable time cleaning up until the summer comes. Then one can give the greenhouse a really thorough cleaning and refurbishing when the plants are either summering outdoors or can be moved outside while it is being cleaned.

At this time, polyethylene linings can be removed, cleaned, and stored for use the following winter, and the glass behind the polyethylene cleaned if it has become covered with green algae. Wash the glass off with ammonia and water and then clean it with any good household window cleaner. A solution of Clorox and water and a brush will clean off any algae and dirt from the sills. When they dry, it is a good idea to paint these sills with a waterproof white paint.

With the plants out of the way, it is also a good time to fumigate. This should go a long way toward taking care of white fly and other insect problems.

183   This is a good time, too, to turn over and freshen up

or replace the gravel in the benches. At the same time, spraying the gravel with metaldehyde will eliminate any slugs.

Broken or cracked glass should be replaced in summer. The same holds true of any loose glazing compound. In other words, before any of the plants are put back in the greenhouse, it should be as clean as it was when it was new.

All plants should have their pots scrubbed with a wire brush to remove fertilizer salts or algae accumulated on them, and all empty used pots should be washed in a solution of Clorox and water (1 to 9) before putting them back. In this way there will always be a clean pot of the right size when you are looking for it.

Space Savers

As everyone who has ever owned one has found, no greenhouse is every large enough. No matter how much room there is, we all wish we had more space, but there are ways of getting around it. For example, glass shelves can be fastened with brackets to the frame of the greenhouse. Depending upon their length, these shelves can hold a varying number of plants and, being higher than the benches, are good for those plants that need more sunlight. Galvanized wire hangers can also be attached directly to the pots and can be used for many orchids.

GROWING ORCHIDS OUTDOORS

Although we have already touched upon the subject of growing orchids outdoors, we shall now discuss the matter more thoroughly. For those who can grow orchids in the garden year-round, it is a most satisfying and enjoyable experience. In the tropics, for instance, orchids grow wild in profusion.

But growing orchids outdoors does not have to be limited to the tropics. In fact, in those areas that have a Mediterranean-type climate, such as southern California, Florida, the Gulf Coast, the South of France, Italy, South Africa, and Australia, the growing of orchids outdoors year-round is enjoyed by many.

Temperatures govern not only the kinds of orchid that can be grown outdoors but whether they can be grown at all. In the Mediterranean area the days are usually mild and the nights cool. Away from the sea, orchid gardens can be located near swimming pools or fish ponds, both of which, to an extent, act like the ocean in providing a moister atmosphere. They also help keep the air warmer as the water stores the heat from the sun.

But swimming pools and fish ponds, although seemingly ideal, have some disadvantages. Extreme care must be taken at all times to prevent chlorinated water from being splashed on the orchids. Another precaution concerns the inhabitants of fish ponds. The insecticides used on orchids can be deadly to fish. Therefore, when orchids are grown near a fish pond, they should be grown in pots so they can be moved to another location when spraying is necessary.

The filtered sunlight that most orchids need can easily be arranged. If the orchids are planted in the ground, they should be placed where they will have the advantage of being shaded by a tree, particularly during the hottest part of the day. The plants can also be grown in pots or on slabs of tree fern in lath houses, where they then become an attractive addition to a garden setting.

The plants grown in pots have the advantage of being easily moved about—inside for protection when there is danger of a frost, or from areas which have too much sun. When orchids are planted directly in the garden the use of the orange growers' standby, the smudgepot, if permitted in your area, can save those plants from frost damage. Just do not place the smudgepots too close to the plants. For short periods the plants can also be covered with plastic or burlap, which is removed as soon as the temperature rises above freezing.

Unless there is a significant amount of rain, the plants will have to be watered just as they are indoors or in a greenhouse, only more frequently, for the winds and the heat cause the plants to dry out more quickly. The more rain the plants receive, the more fertilizer they need. Nothing leaches out fertilizer faster than a good rainstorm. On the other hand, orchids outdoors do not seem to have the problem of watersoaked potting material, because the more buoyant atmosphere and the winds outdoors dry it out faster.

Kinds to Grow Outdoors

Surprisingly, there is a good selection of orchids from which to choose for growing outdoors. Select only those whose temperature and other requirements most nearly match what you can provide, but do not hesitate to experiment.

Perhaps the orchids most frequently grown outdoors are the cymbidiums. They can be grown in the open soil or in pots in the garden, on patios, and in lath houses. They tolerate cool nights, even with the temperature dropping a bit below freezing once in a while.

Some species of laelia that come from Mexico, such as *Laelia autumnalis* and *Laelia anceps*, tolerate temperatures just above freezing. In fact, they need cool nights to flower.

Paphiopedilum insigne, a native of the Himalayas, actually flowers best when grown outdoors.

Some of the lycastes, the anguloas, and the bletillas like nights that are cool and do well as long as they do not freeze.

Although seldom planted in the garden itself, the odontoglossums do grow well outdoors in cool and shady places in pots or baskets. *Odontoglossums bictoniense, cirrhosum, grande,* and *pulchellum* all tolerate temperatures that get a bit below freezing.

For landscape effects there are a number of orchids that could be classified as beddng plants. Among these are the *Habenaria ciliaris, Orchis mascula,* and *Spiranthes cernua,* which when grown in clumps present an outstanding display of both foliage and flowers.

Phaius, which requires potting material containing loam, makes an excellent plant for the garden. It not only tolerates but actually needs cool temperatures to flower.

The reed-stem epidendrums, because of their long period of blooming, can also add as much color to a garden as any annual.

If orchids are to be grown in the garden itself, the top 2 feet of soil should be removed and replaced with a layer of broken bricks, stone, or crock several inches thick, over which should be put the growing mixture of loam, sand, bark, sphagnum moss, and leaves—all finely shredded. The need for windbreaks should not arise, since the growing site should be one that is sheltered from the wind.

It is noteworthy that orchids grown outdoors have surprisingly fewer insect problems than those in the average greenhouse. Slugs cause the most damage, but protection is easy. Merely keep the ground and tops of the pots treated with metaldehyde, either the pellet or the liquid form.

Once you have succeeded in making orchids an integral part of your garden, you will wonder how you ever gardened without them.

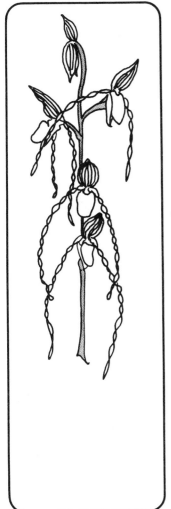

Coping with Insects, Diseases, & Other Problems

This chapter is not intended to scare off the would-be orchid grower. Nor is it intended to be a compendium of plant diseases, pests, and viruses. Rather, it is hoped that by knowing that these things do exist you can take appropriate steps to prevent such infestations and infections from occurring and, if they should occur, be aware of the best means of eliminating them.

The propagation of orchids by meristemming, for instance, eliminates the danger of direct passing of insects and diseases from one generation to another. In addition, good growing conditions with the proper amounts of light, temperature, water, humidity, and ventilation are highly conducive to healthy, pest-free plants.

CHAPTER 11

For the average grower, keeping the surroundings absolutely clean—be they greenhouse, lath house, screen porch, or indoors—is of major importance.

However, as we emphasized earlier, all newly acquired plants should be sprayed with malathion or a like substance and isolated until it is certain they harbor no insects. This is important, for even though the new plants may appear to be completely free of pests, some insects are so small that they are difficult to see with the naked eye. To keep your collection free of diseases and insects, there is no better way than to inspect them whenever you water. Go over each plant thoroughly. If this is done at least once every week, undesirable visitors will never be a problem.

This does not mean that orchids must be grown by themselves, but it does mean that when there is a mixed collection of plants, the chances of the orchids becoming infected will increase. Caladiums, crotons, gardenias, poinsettias, and anthuriums are just a few of the plants often grown with orchids in the house or greenhouse that unfortunately attract many insects.

Aphids, mealybugs, and scale insects are often brought in accidentally. Slugs may crawl up the walls of the greenhouse. Aphids and thrips can also fly in through open ventilators. One precaution is to avoid crowding the plants too closely together. This not only allows for a circulation of air that prevents many diseases from getting started, but it makes the passing of troubles from one plant to another less likely and makes caring for the plants a good deal easier.

Working with Pesticides

Although the majority of insecticides, fungicides, and miticides suggested here are among the safest to be found—and it is recommended that the plants always be treated according to the directions for the specific problems given on the package—it is also suggested that when using an all-purpose pesticide as a preventive the plants not be treated with it more often than once a month. It should also be borne in mind that the stronger, more toxic sprays do carry some risk to both the plants and the grower. Thus, it is clearly to the grower's advantage to keep his plants in a healthy atmosphere and one not conducive to diseases or pests.

Never use any pesticide that has not been specifically recommended for orchids, and always read the label carefully first. Furthermore, use only the amount recommended and at the intervals suggested. Make sure the material is fresh. Pesticides left lying around may have lost their potency, so once you have made up a batch of pesticide, use what you need and discard the rest. Do not try to store it.

No matter how harmless you feel any insecticide or fungicide may be, make a practice of wearing gloves when handling it. Then, if any suspicious symptoms arise, contact your physician at once and tell him the name of the pesticide. If possible, bring the package or bottle with you.

The use of herbicides to kill weeds in the pots is not recommended. Herbicides are powerful. Certainly, if the plants are taken care of properly and examined frequently, any weeds that get started can easily be pulled out. Then there will never be a need for a large weeding job.

Care should always be exercised before mixing one pesticide with another. A pesticide that is perfectly harmless by itself could conceivably turn into a lethal potion if mixed with another one. This is known as a synergistic reaction. One increases the potency of the other to a dangerous level or sets up a toxic reaction.

If you develop allergic reactions to any pesticide, get someone else to spray for you or wear a mask and rubber gloves. When finished, remove the clothes immediately and wash them thoroughly.

Identifying Problems

If disaster should strike any of your plants and you can find no other help in identifying the problem, send the affected portion of the plant, securely wrapped in polyethylene, to your State Agricultural Experiment Station. They may be able to provide an answer. You can also send a portion of the diseased plant, together with a fee of $1.50, to the Florida West Coast Scientific Laboratories, P.O. Box 11914, Tampa, Florida, 33680, and they will identify the cause of the problem for you.

INSECTS

Ants

There are numerous kinds of ants whose greatest nuisance is that they carry aphids and other pests to the plants. Obviously, they must be eliminated in and around the greenhouses. Many growers keep ant traps among the plants on the benches. Chlordane, if you can get it, and dieldrin, however, are the sprays most widely used for the control of ants; such sprays should be used with care, however, because in the concentration necessary to kill the ants they might damage the orchids. To be safe, keep the sprays away from the plants themselves, confining your treatments to the floors and the benches, as well as to the foundation of the greenhouse both inside and out.

If ants become established in the potting medium, a very dilute solution of the spray, such as 1 teaspoon of 50% wettable chlordane or 1 teaspoonful of 25% wettable dieldrin to 1 gallon of water, is usually the most potent strength that can be used with safety. Zectron, at the rate of 3 teaspoons to 1 gallon of water, has also been used with success. Whenever you use a new insecticide for the first time, try it out on only one plant. In this way, if there are any harmful effects, the damage will not be widespread.

Aphids

Aphids, or plant lice, can be green, black, red, brown, or yellow. Although they have no wings at most stages, they do acquire them periodically and can move about readily. They multiply by laying their eggs at frequent intervals and continue to produce generation upon generation of young aphids.

Aphids feed upon the buds and flowers of orchids by sucking the juices and are particularly attracted to cymbidiums. Cygon and Meta Systox are two effective systemic insecticides that will eliminate aphids. *Systemics* are insecticides that are absorbed through the leaves and the roots of plants and course around in the sap, effectively controlling infestations for up to a month or more. But they must be used with care because of their toxicity to man and the possibility that too strong a solution might be damaging to the orchids.

Among the conventional sprays, diazinon and malathion can be used successfully and are relatively safe. Any spraying with them will have to be repeated several times before all the aphids are eliminated, because the continued hatching of eggs will result in reinfestations for some time.

Cattleya Fly

The cattleya fly is not really a fly but rather a tiny wasp, *Eurytoma orchidearum.* The larvae feed inside the flower buds or on the pseudobulbs. DDT was instrumental in practically eliminating them, but since DDT has been banned,

occasional infestations do arise. At the moment, malathion
seems to be one of the best controls we have.

Mites

Mites are not really insects but minute creatures more like
spiders. (Mites have eight legs while insects have six.) Mites
are so small that they often are not noticed until a plant
has become badly infested. Like aphids, they suck the plant's
juices. Red spider mites, for instance, seem to occur worldwide and are probably the most common pests encountered
in greenhouses. They spin minute webs and thrive in hot,
dry climates. By spraying the undersides of the leaves with
a fine but forceful stream of water they can often be dislodged.
While almost microscopic, they can often be seen early in
the morning or late in the day when the angle of the sun
is low and the sun strikes the leaves in such a way that
the red spiders become visible.

Although all orchids can be attacked by this mite, it
does seem to have a great affinity for cymbidiums. Usually,
they feed on the underside of the leaves, which causes the
leaves to become minutely speckled or stippled. They can
also attack the buds and flowers, and when such a flower
opens it may have dark, mottled spots on it.

Since these mites cannot usually be seen with the naked
eye, it is wise to use a spray of diazinon according to the
manufacturer's instructions to prevent any damage from
becoming widespread. However, the spraying must be thorough or it is a waste of time. The undersides of the leaves
must be thoroughly wet. Wetting agents such as DuPont's
Wetter-Setter or B-1956 will help to keep the spray on the
plants. Although in an emergency a mild dishwashing
detergent can be used as a wetting agent, it's use over a
long period is not recommended, since some are known
to cause damage to orchids.

If spraying must be done when the plants are in flower,
extra care must be taken to prevent the spray from getting
on the flowers, which may be damaged.

For heavier infestations, sprays such as Kelthane, Ara-
mite, or chlorobenzolate may have to be used. Pentac has
also proved effective.

The use of the dithio smokes for small greenhouses,
whether the greenhouse is free-standing or attached to the
house, is subject to debate. It is far too easy for the pesticides
to get into the home. Thus, these smokes, although effective,
are best left for commercial greenhouse operators.

False Spider Mites

False spider mites can be white, yellow, or red and are also barely visible to the naked eye. They differ from red spider mites in that they do not spin webs. They are found on many orchids such as phalaenopsis, cattleyas, paphiopedilums, dendrobiums, and oncidiums. The so-called phalaenopsis mite, *Teniupalpus pacificus,* is mostly found on the upper surface of the leaves and causes them to look silvery and pitted. Other mites also cause discoloration of leaves and depressions on the surface, resulting in the leaves eventually falling off.

Kelthane and diazinon have proved effective in controlling these. As always, follow the directions on the package for the amount needed and the frequency with which it should be applied.

Mealybugs

Mealybugs are small, oval insects covered with a white, mealy wax, from which they derive their name. They, too, suck out the plant's juices. Mealybugs lay as many as 600 eggs at one time in masses of cotton sacs. Like aphids, they may also secrete a honey that attracts ants and encourages the development of a sooty mold fungus. The old-fashioned way of getting rid of mealybugs by using a swab dipped in alcohol to remove each one individually from the plant can still be used, if you have only a few plants and an abundance of time. It is probably still the best way to get rid of mealybugs on plants in the house, where spraying presents problems. When you spray plants in the house, it is always better to take them to a large area, like a cellar, where any obnoxious fumes will have a chance to dissipate before the plants are returned to their usual growing area.

For plants in a greenhouse, malathion and diazinon are both excellent. However, the spraying must be thorough, because only those mealybugs actually hit by the spray will be killed. Several sprayings at monthly intervals may be necessary to obtain complete control. Any of the wetting agents above will also help to keep the spray on the leaves.

Scale Insects

There are many different kinds of scale, some armored with shells and others soft or without shells. Scale insects cause injury to the plants by sticking to the stems or leaves and sucking the sap from the plant as do the pests above. Scale insects may also secrete a "honeydew" on which sooty mold fungus grows, sometimes seriously disfiguring the plants.

Among the common scales are the brown scale, *Coccus hesperidium;* orchid soft scale, *Coccus pseudohesperidium;* a hemispherical scale, *Saissetia hemisphaerica;* and black scale, *Saissetia oleoe.* Dendrobiums, odontoglossums, phalaenopsis, paphiopedilums, and cymbidiums are among the orchids most often infested with these scales.

The armored scales have hard shields that cover their bodies. These scales do not usually secrete "honeydew," but like the soft scales they suck the juices from the plant. The ivy or oleander scale is the most commonly found armored scale on orchids in the greenhouse. The hard covering protects them from sprays, making them more difficult to control than the soft scales.

Both types, however, may be found on leaves, stems, sheaths, tips of pseudobulbs, rhizomes, and roots. As of this writing malathion and diazinon seem to be the most effective against these scales, particularly against the soft scales.

Dipping a soft toothbrush into a solution of malathion and gently scrubbing the infected parts can be effective in getting rid of scales. Unfortunately, toothbrushes cannot always get into the hard-to-reach areas such as down in the pseudobulbs. Where the infestation is severe, the whole plant can be dipped into the solution for a few minutes.

Shell No-Pest Strips, which contain Vapona, have also been used with success. Just be certain that you use enough of them to provide adequate protection in the greenhouse. To prevent your breathing the fumes, you can hang the strips in the greenhouse at .night and put them away in jars during the day when you are working in the greenhouse.

Finally, since diseases thrive best where the surroundings are damp, keeping the atmosphere around the plants a little drier for a time helps them as they convalesce from the damage done by the scales.

Thrips

Thrips are minute pests. They can be black, red, or dark brown. They are about $\frac{1}{25}$ inch long and cause great damage by sucking the plant's juices. They absolutely love tender little seedlings. Often the only evidence that thrips are around is the presence of tiny black spots of excrement that they have left behind. Spraying with malathion is a good means of both control and prevention.

SLUGS AND SNAILS

Slugs and snails are among the most insidious and serious of orchid pests. Slugs are like snails without shells and feed mostly at night when it is damp and dark, although they can also feed during the day when the weather is dull. Slugs travel by crawling, leaving behind a silvery trail of mucus. Snails, too, have become a widespread problem in recent years, and the damage they do is often erroneously blamed upon poor cultural practices such as overwatering and the like. When the roots of a plant have been destroyed, never overlook the possibility that snails or slugs are the culprits.

Snails make their homes in damp soil, and some 60 eggs hatch out in about two weeks. They have a great affinity for the spaces between the pieces of bark deep down in the pots where it is dark and moist.

Both snails and slugs can particularly damage pots of tender seedlings, chewing holes in the leaves and the tips of the roots. Seeing an otherwise beautiful flower on a mature plant disfigured by a hole in one of its petals is a disheartening experience.

To date, metaldehyde is the most effective control for both snails and slugs. It comes in both dust and pellet forms that can be sprinkled on top of the pots, on the benches, and on the floor of the greenhouse. It can also be sprinkled

Figure 11-1. Petal damage caused by slugs.

Figure 11-2. A flower petal
that has been eaten by slugs.

Photo. Ralph Collins

in the pots of plants outside for the summer. Metaldeyhde also comes in a liquid form known as Slug-Kill and can be used as a spray on the same areas where dry forms are used.

Unfortunately, slugs and snails are persistent creatures. It does no good to spray or dust once. Keeping them at bay requires constant effort, and the use of metaldehyde at monthly intervals should be as much a part of greenhouse culture as watering.

Because ground covers provide cool, shady places for the pests to hide, it is always better to have the greenhouse floor made of crushed stone or patio blocks.

NEMATODES

Nematodes are near-microscopic creatures that look like but are not worms. The damage occurs when they invade the roots, leaves, or flowers of a plant. Nematodes cause the roots to rot, and this generally undermines the health of the whole plant.

Vandas and cymbidiums seem to be the most prone to nematode attack, possibly because they sometimes have soil mixed into their potting medium. The best control is always to use a soil that has been sterilized before it is added to an orchid mix.

DISEASES

Orchid diseases may be caused by bacteria, fungi, or viruses. If not controlled they can cause a plant's death. Bacterial and fungal diseases are spread by spores that are all around us in the air but that need a moist environment in which to grow. Nevertheless, a greenhouse that is kept clean will go a long way toward preventing diseases from becoming rampant. Well-grown plants are always less vulnerable to diseases. All waste should be disposed of each day.

However, should a plant become infected, all is by no means lost. Although there are many excellent pesticides that will control diseases, it is up to you to see that the diseases do not get started in the first place, or, if they do, to take steps immediately to eradicate them and from then on take preventive measures to preclude reinfection.

In any case, there are some routine things that can be done to cut down on the chances of plants becoming diseased. One is, when cutting out any diseased part of a plant or dividing a plant at potting time, being sure that all the tools used are sterilized. Never use a tool that has

Figure 11-3. This disfiguration, which is nonrepeating and can be either yellow or black, is caused by a fungus.

Photo, Ralph Collins

been used on one plant on another plant until both your hands and the tool have been sterilized again by rinsing them in alcohol.

Temperatures that are too low while at the same time the humidity is too high present ideal conditions for the start of bacterial and fungal infections. The same holds true when temperatures and humidity are both too high.

Misting and watering plants early in the day, so that they have a chance to dry off before night, also helps in preventing infections. As we have emphasized before, there must always be good circulation of air around orchids. Therefore, they should never be crowded together.

Again, adequate ventilation is important. All plants continuously lose water through the pores in their leaves. Consequently, in a moist atmosphere, unless there is adequate ventilation and good circulation of air, water vapor may condense into a film on the surfaces of the leaves, thus affording an ideal place for diseases to start.

Insects, too, must be controlled, because wherever they have damaged a plant the way is open for an infection at the point of the damage.

Most important, any plant that shows any signs of disease should be isolated immediately where there is less humidity and more ventilation and sprayed with a control recommended for that specific disease. A diseased plant is a threat to every other plant around it.

It is often possible to cut off diseased portions, cutting to a point below the diseased tissue. If a diseased plant needs to be repotted, be sure that all the old potting medium is removed and that the roots are dipped into a recommended solution before the plant is repotted in a clean pot and fresh potting material.

Diseased parts removed from plants should always be burned and your hands thoroughly washed before you touch any other plants.

Usually bacterial and fungal diseases are first noticed as watersoaked, partly transparent spots on leaves, which if allowed to spread may in time cover the leaves then spread into the pseudobulbs or other growths. Some diseases start at the roots and in no time cause them to rot. In any case, the treatment needed will depend upon the disease.

The so-called rots, for example, are diseases that cause the decay and death of plant tissues. The affected parts become black or brown and look and feel wet and mushy.

197 These rots are, for the most part, caused by bacteria or fungi.

Their control depends upon changing the unfavorable
conditions that allowed the rot to develop. The affected
parts of the plant should be cut and the rest of the plant
sprayed with a fungicide such as Natriphene (according
to the directions on the package) or with a fungicide

Orchid Black Rot

Orchid black rot is probably the most destructive disease
to hit any orchid plant, particularly the cattleya. Usually
it starts on a new leaf or new lead and progresses downward
until it reaches the roots of the plant. The leaves appear
purplish or show some brown areas, while other areas are
slightly yellow in marked contrast to the green of the rest
of the leaf. These diseased areas become very soft and when
squeezed exude water. Once it starts, decay is rapid.

When such an infection reaches the roots, it continues
through the root system and then spreads back upward from
the roots to the pseudobulbs.

On mature plants all the diseased areas must be cut
off down into healthy tissue with a sterile knife. If the
pseudobulbs are badly infected, it may be necessary to cut
down to the rhizome until you come to the place where
the tissue is free of the disease. After the diseased areas
have been removed, the plant should be dipped into a
fungicide and allowed to dry off before it is repotted.

Black rot is best prevented by not having either the
plants or the atmosphere too wet. Tersan and Fermate provide
excellent control on mature plants. Seedlings can be treated
with an Anti-Damp solution according to the directions on
the package.

Brown Rot

Brown rot particularly affects paphiopedilums. It starts as
small, round water spots wherever water has become lodged
in the leaves for any length of time, and it spreads rapidly,
turning the leaves a dark brown. This often happens when
plants are hanging in pots over paphiopedilums, so that
the water drips down and settles in the axils of the leaves.
When both the temperature and the humidity are high, the
conditions are ideal for brown rot. Any parts of a paphiopedilum that are broken or bruised also offer places
where brown rot can get started.

The cure is twofold. First, cut away diseased leaves
with sterile shears or scissors. If the disease has gone too

198

Photo, Ralph Collins

Figure 11-4. The brown,
darkened areas on the leaf are
caused by brown rot.

far, an entire section of the plant may have to be severed
and destroyed. Second, dip the plant into a solution of
Anti-Damp or Natriphene for about an hour. This may need
to be repeated every few days to be sure that the disease
has really been controlled. A Tersan spray is also good
as a preventive.

Basal Rot

Basal rot is a deadly malady resulting from moisture remaining in the axils of the leaves. It is a form of brown rot
caused by the bacillus *Erwinia cypripedii*. Also, it is frequently seen in plants that have become root-bound. It is
interesting, however, to note that this disease does not seem
to attack unflowered seedlings, giving rise to a theory held
by some that old flower stems, if left on the plants, rot
at the base and have much to do with causing the problem.

Root Rot   Root rot, *Pellicularia filamentosa*, affects both seedlings and
mature plants. It usually occurs when the potting medium
has become severely broken down and/or when the plants
have poor drainage causing the roots to rot. As its name
implies, it is a brown rotting of the plant tissues; it can
also attack the rhizomes and pseudobulbs. In fact, the small
beginning leaves of seedlings can also become affected once
199   this disease has attacked their roots.

Fortunately, this difficulty does not come unannounced. The fungus works its havoc over an extended period. The leaves and pseudobulbs become yellow and shrivel, and both appear thin. Also, the plant's new growth is not as large as was the old growth, because of the loss of roots.

If this is allowed to progress and serious damage is done, it will be necessary to discard the plant. If it is recognized in time, however, the rotted areas can be cut out with a sterile knife or scissors, and the plants dipped into a solution of 1 tablespoon of 75% Terrachlor in 1 gallon of water for 4 or 5 minutes. Tersan and Natriphene are also helpful.

The plants should then be repotted in clean, sterilized pots that have adequate provision for drainage. Only fresh potting material should be used. The plants should also be set off by themselves for several weeks until it is certain that all the rot has been eradicated.

Soft Rot

Soft rot is caused by bacteria that get into wounds that result from improperly sterilized cuts or areas damaged by insects. It gives off an unmistakable offensive odor, spreads rapidly, and can be very serious if it gets a head start. Cattleyas, phalaenopsis, oncidiums, odontoglossums, paphiopedilums, and cymbidiums are all subject to infection with soft rot.

The only cure is to cut off and destroy all infected parts of the plant. Then the traditional treatment is to coat the cut surfaces with Bordeau Mixture (see below), although newer fungicides will also work. The pot in which the plant was growing should be thoroughly disinfected and cleaned with Clorox before it is used again. Furthermore, the benches and the surrounding areas where the infected plant grew should be cleaned with Clorox and water. By using only sterilized tools with the plant, incidence of soft rot can be cut down considerably.

Bordeau Mixture

This is an old remedy consisting of copper sulphate, hydrated lime, and water. To make a small quantity, dissolve $\frac{1}{2}$ pint of copper sulphate and $\frac{3}{4}$ pint of hydrated lime in $6\frac{1}{2}$ pints of water. Mix the two together, making certain to stir them well. The mixture should be light blue in color. You should use it within a few hours of mixing. Bordeau Mixture can also be obtained commercially in either paste or dry form; you simply add water according to the instructions on the package.

Crown Rot

Crown rot affects phalaenopsis. Another name for it is southern blight. It causes the collapse and rotting in quick succession of the roots, pseudobulbs, and leaves. The first symptom is likely to be the yellowing of the leaves. Then very small brown sclerotia (miniscule, hard bodies) form on the diseased tissues. Any plants infected with crown rot should immediately be removed from the vicinity of other orchids. If the disease is allowed to spread, it could wipe out a whole section of plants. Dipping the plants into a solution of Natriphene according to the directions should, however, solve the problem.

Figure 11-5. Crown rot results in black and watery areas at the apex of the leaves.

Photo. Ralph Collins

Orchid Wilt

Orchid or collar wilt is caused by a fungus, *Sclerotium rolfsii*, and seems to affect cymbidiums and paphiopedilums more than other orchids. The infection at first causes the stems to become yellow, later to turn dark brown as the disease progresses. It spreads down from the stems to the roots and from there up into the leaves. At times, when it first becomes noticeable, a white fungus appears on the stem. This is followed by the appearance of near-microscopic, hard yellow bodies called *sclerotia*.

This disease is most prevalent when temperature and humidity are too high. The diseased parts of the plant can be cut out and the plant dipped into Natriphene for about an hour or dipped into a solution of $\frac{1}{10}$ of 1% of Ceresan for 5 or 10 minutes.

Athracnose, or Leafspot

Athracnose, (leafspot), is found in many greenhouses. Temperatures that are too warm, too high, humidity and too much shade favor its development. The leaves of the plants are most frequently affected, and it usually occurs only when the leaves have been weakened or injured by unfavorable growing conditions or by chemicals.

It first becomes noticeable as a sharply defined and sunken brown discoloration that is either round or irregular. As the disease spreads, the organisms continue to develop in the areas that have already died. Flowers show signs of athracnose when small, round black or brown spots develop on their sepals or petals. The use of long-lasting fungicides, not just on the plants but throughout the greenhouse, is necessary to eradicate it completely. In any case, the complete drenching of the plants, with particular attention given to seeing that the undersides of the leaves are completely wet with a fungicide such as Captan, Ferbam, or Zineb, should get rid of leafspot.

Petal Blight

Petal blight affects many orchids, causing the flowers to become disfigured; the old flowers still on the plant and those that show signs of fading are susceptible to petal blight. It occurs mostly when the weather is damp and cold and there is not enough circulation of the air around the plants. The blight begins as a small circular spot on the sepals or petals of the flower. The spots become brown, with a slightly pinkish line around them. At times a grayish mold grows on the petals.

Photo, Ralph Collins

Figure 11-6.   Petal blight (botrytis infection) shows up as black dots on the flowers of an infected plant.

The solution is to cut off and destroy any flowers that show signs of infection. This prevents the fungus from infecting later flowers.

Black Sheaths, or Sheath Rot

Sheaths should normally be green, but when they have been attacked by a fungus, particularly during humid weather and when water has been left standing between the leaf and the sheath, they may turn black. Such sheaths should be cut off just above the buds that are inside. This will usually be enough to prevent the fungus from spreading to the buds. This rot first appears as a discoloration at the base of the sheath as the latter is developing, but it can also appear at the tip of a full-grown sheath. This particular rot sometimes causes sheaths that do not contain buds to appear as though they were bulging out with air.

Rust Diseases

Rust diseases are caused by fungi that first become noticeable when one sees powdery masses of yellow spores. Rust is easily carried from plant to plant, and although it seldom kills the plants, it does weaken them sufficiently so that they may not be able to flower properly.

203

Tersan, or a copper sulfate fungicide, usually provides adequate treatment. By cutting off the rust-infected leaves, the appearance of the plants is greatly improved. Infected leaves should always be burned.

Leaf Dieback and Leaf Blight

Leaf dieback is caused by a water mold called *Pythium splendens* and leaf blight by a fungus, *Glomerella cincta*. In leaf dieback there is usually a clear line between the healthy part of the leaf and that which has become diseased. It is during periods of high temperatures and light intensity, such as occur during the late spring and summer, that these diseases are most prevalent. Besides a fungus, leaf dieback, particularly in cattleyas, is often attributed to fertilizer salts that have accumulated in the potting material, rotted plant roots resulting from overwatering, and too high a concentration of phosphorous in the fertilizer. There are some growers who attribute leaf dieback to a deficiency in calcium. It is also true that some plants are just naturally more susceptible to it than others, possibly because of genetic factors.

The diseased leaves should be cut off with a sterile knife. Cattleyas, cymbidiums, and many other genera seem prone to this infection. Any fungicides safe for use on orchids will help control leaf dieback.

Botrytis

Botrytis is another fungus disease that can cause the leaf tip to become spotted with powdery spores. This fungus can also cause flower blight, which makes the developing flowers speckled. Flowers so infected should be cut off immediately to prevent the spread of the fungus. Botrytis thrives when the environment is both damp and cold, but good air circulation and humidity that is not so high help keep this fungus under control.

Molds

Various kinds of mold can become troublesome. Sooty mold, for instance, grows on the excreta left by scales and aphids. It is also found where the plant has been wounded either by cutting off a diseased portion from a leaf that has been broken or on one of the new growths that has been damaged. The "honeydew" that the insects secrete is where sooty mold is found. A cotton swab dipped in a solution of Ivory soap and water will remove this mold about as well as anything else.

Snow Mold Snow mold is so called because it looks thick and white. It is often found on the top of bark potting mediums. Sometimes it resembles small, round granular heads. The principal harm it does is to weaken plants through suffocation, because the mold prevents the roots from getting enough air.

The best way to eliminate snow mold is to take the plant out of the pot, remove the old potting medium, and wash the roots with a solution of 1 ounce of Shield in 1 gallon of water. Then repot the plant in a clean pot with fresh potting material.

Bacterial Bulb Rot Bacterial bulb rot, *Erwinia corotonona*, is found especially on cymbidiums. The bulbs become soft and ooze a foul-smelling liquid. The infected bulbs should be cut out with a sterile knife or shears and destroyed, then the remaining bulbs sprayed with a solution of Agri-Strep or a similar product. However, one must bear in mind that these substances, although excellent, have been known to damage plants if misused. So be careful.

A better way to handle the problem is to remove all the diseased bulbs and, if there is any part of the plant left that has not become infected, to pot that and watch it carefully. If the disease reappears, destroy the plant altogether.

VIRUSES Now we come to the most baffling of all diseases, the viruses. The word comes directly from the Latin *virus*, which means "Poison." As far as is known, the first scientist to show that a mosaic disease in plants was not caused by a microbe but rather by a contagious living fluid and to use the term virus to describe this was Beijernich in 1898.

Some viruses seem to have an affinity for certain orchids and are accordingly identified with the plants with which they were first associated, as for example cymbidium necrotic ringspot and cymbidium mosaic virus. This does not mean that these viruses affect only cymbidiums. They may also affect other orchids. In fact, the same virus may cause ringspot on one species and a mosaic pattern on another. In some cases, plants that have become infected do not show any marked change, while in others the damage is clearly visible. Again, the symptoms, especially in the

Figure 11-7.   The first sign that an orchid has become infected by a virus is the yellow bleaching and disfiguration of a leaf.

Figure 11-8.   Blackened, sunken areas on the surface of a leaf caused by a fungus.

beginning, may be confused with a bacterial disease or insect injury. Finally, any plant in a weakened condition will always be more susceptible to viruses than a healthy one.

Viruses can be spread by aphids or infected tools. All tools should be sterilized after being used on one plant and before being used on another. This holds true not only when dividing a plant or cutting out diseased parts, but also when cutting off flowers. The tools should not be used again until they have been sterilized. The few minutes' extra it takes to do this can save months or years of trying to get rid of a virus.

Viruses can also spread if plants are put into old pots that have not been thoroughly cleaned and scrubbed in Clorox and water.

Furthermore, there is no part of a plant that is immune to viruses. They can even affect pollen and seed.

Although orchids in their native habitat may be, and sometimes are, completely free of viruses, unless the collector takes every precaution to keep his hands and tools clean and the containers in which he places the plants clean, the once-virus-free plants may be virus-free no longer. Obviously, any plants known to be virus-infected should be destroyed, for if such a plant were to be divided, each section would be infected. This is what happened for many years before the advent of meristemming, particularly with the Westonbirt cymbidiums.

Now, however, conscientious professional growers, by using only meristemmed plants as the foundation of their collections, begin with virus-free plants; with good culture they keep them that way. Then, if those who buy their plants give them the proper culture and pest and disease prevention, a huge step in halting the spread of virus-infected plants will have been taken and a reservoir of virus-free plants created.

If you suspect that a plant does have a virus, isolate it at once, making sure you provide it with the same culture it has been getting. It used to be felt by some growers that the plant would eventually outgrow the virus. Unhappily, this is just not true. Furthermore, there is no chemical control at this time for viruses on orchids, and orchids have so far proved unresponsive to antibiotics.

Consequently, when plants are purchased, make every effort to be sure they are virus-free. If mericlones (meristemmed plants) are bought, the problem is taken care of—up until the time you bought the plants. However, it does not necessarily follow that they cannot become infected through improper culture.

Cymbidium Mosaic Virus

Cymbidium mosaic virus is probably the most common of all the viruses of orchids. It affects not just cymbidiums but also cattleyas and just about any orchid, greatly diminishing the vitality of any plant infected.

The first signs that a cymbidium has the mosaic virus are usually small chlorotic areas; these are abnormally yellowed areas resulting from the breaking down of the chlorophyll. These spots and streaks become more sharply defined as time passes, and the tissues so infected become darker. Within six months both the upper and undersides of the leaves will have developed huge black spots and streaks. Eventually these leaves will drop off the plant.

On cattleyas the areas are brown, black, and deep purple and the leaves develop a roughened appearance. Again, as with the cymbidiums, the cattleya leaves eventually fall off. Infected flowers are always smaller and last a much shorter time than they normally would. Ironically, the flowers open with no sign whatsoever of having anything wrong with them, and it is not until a week or so later that the first brown streaks and spots appear on the petals and sepals. Sometimes the spots grow and cover the entire flower; at other times they remain restricted to the few original spots.

Cattleya Flower Break and Color Break

Flower break and color break are perhaps the two most common viruses to affect cattleyas. In flower break the flowers do not develop as they normally would. In color break small parts of the flower are irregularly darker than the surrounding area, and the color may be in the wrong place. The flowers themselves are usually distorted, with twisted and puckered places, breaks in the color pattern, or blotches of color. Color break may also be noticeable as lack of color. At the same time, the leaves may show the mosaic pattern of light and dark areas and may be deformed.

Ringspot

There are many types of ringspot, some named after the orchids on which they were first found, others after those on which they are most prevalent. The symptoms usually become apparent as rings on the surface of a leaf. This ringspot at first turns yellow, but as the spots get older they tend to turn purplish black. Needless to say, they are easily recognized and are quite deforming to plants.

OTHER DANGERS

Fertilizer Injuries

Plants should not be overfertilized. Besides causing the growths to become overly lush and weak, other, even more serious problems can occur from overfeeding. If a plant is given too much food, the food, instead of improving its growth, can actually inhibit it. This is partly because of the concentration of the fertilizer salts that remain around the roots and burn them. Fertilizer salts tend to cling to clay pots in particular, giving them a grayish appearance. This can be prevented by flushing the pots with water whenever watering. Having its roots burned, the plant then becomes further weakened. A fertilizer higher in nitrogen than the plant needs can also cause in the leaves, particularly those of cattleyas, a condition where they can actually be rolled around a finger without breaking them. Finally, too high a concentration of salts around the roots can even cause a reversal of osmosis, with the result that the sap flows out of the plant.

The water-soluble fertilizers that leach out with heavy watering have always been considered the safest for orchids, because no particles of fertilizer càn remain around the roots,

Figure 11-9. Overfeeding results in many small growths, which often do not flower.

Photo, Ralph Collins

which is possible with the dry fertilizers. Usually, when the roots near the top of the potting medium have died while those at the bottom are still in fairly good condition, excessive fertilizer salts can be considered a contributing factor. When a plant has sustained such damage, it usually shows up first on the new leaves as tip scorch. The tender new growths are the most susceptible to damage.

Usually, when a plant has been overwatered, the leaves and pseudobulbs shrivel. When a plant has been overfertilized, there is a definite dieback of leaves and pseudobulbs.

Of course, not every orchid requires the same amount of food at the same intervals. Some orchids, such as paphiopedilums, are light feeders, while others like cymbidiums are heavy feeders. Give each plant only the amount of food it needs for optimum growth.

Incorrect Potting

You can never expect a plant that has been potted incorrectly to grow well. For example, a cattleya whose back portion was placed way down into the pot while the front part was left way up in the air, with no potting material beneath it to support new growth, has no way to get the food and water it needs.

Paphiopedilums, in particular, if potted too deeply become easy prey to basal decay. The new growths on such plants tend to decay before they have a chance to emerge.

The time to repot a plant is after it has finished flowering and has started to develop new eyes and new roots. Potted at this time, when the eyes are still small, there is far less chance of breaking off any of these eyes. Furthermore, plants that desperately need repotting and are not repotted cannot be expected to develop good growths in a potting medium that is decayed or if the new growths have no place in which to grow. Under these conditions it will not be long before the leaves and pseudobulbs begin to shrink and the roots become injured as they grow over the outside of the pot.

Overpotting a plant—putting it into a container too large for it—makes it all too easy to overwater it. The plant has more potting material than it actually needs, and the excess does not dry out as rapidly as it should. Orchids also like to attach their roots to the insides of the pots and should not, therefore, be too far from the sides.

Toxic Substances

Other than on the floor of a greenhouse, it is strongly recommended that you bypass the use of weed killers, not only in the pots but also on the benches, where it is easy for weed killers to come into contact with the plant roots. Rather than using chemicals, pull the weeds out by hand as they grow, every day if necessary, and it will never become a huge undertaking.

Pesticides

Though they may be highly recommended for other plants, not all pesticides have been found safe for use on orchids, and you must make sure of any pesticide before using it. The types of injury range from stunted growth to leaf spot, abnormal leaf coloring, and the death (necrosis) of the plant's tissues where the pesticide has been sprayed or blown.

There is nothing much that can be done with this type of injury. If the entire plant has not been killed, good culture will help it recover. Then when new growth develops, the damaged portions may be cut off. If you suspect a plant has been damaged by a pesticide, washing the leaves off with a hose nozzle may help—if done soon enough—although there is no guarantee as to its efficiency.

Along with the directions on the pesticide package regarding the amount and frequency of its use, there is often also a warning against using the material when the temperature is high. With orchids, do not apply any pesticide during that part of the day when the sun is hottest and the temperature highest. If you do, the plants may be burned.

Toxic Paints and Preservatives

Although aluminum greenhouses have come into common use in recent years, there are many wooden ones in use, as well as wooden benches. In this connection, one substance that should never be used as a wood preservative is creosote. It is highly toxic to plants. In fact, to be safe, many growers do not use any wood preservative inside a greenhouse, particularly not on the baskets in which orchids are grown.

Of course, the paint used on the outside of a wooden greenhouse can be any good exterior paint, for it has no effects on the plants. Inside, wooden benches should be of cypress or redwood, which resist rotting and do not need paint.

Cultural Factors

Water is necessary for plant growth, but if it has been treated with a water softener, it can cause a buildup of sodium salts in the potting medium. Water splashed on flowers can cause brown spots, and as we have mentioned before, water lodged in the axils of a leaf can lead to rot. This

211

is why overhead watering and misting are not generally used when growing orchids.

Sunlight is another important factor. If excessive, it can burn the plant's tissues. Fortunately, however, such injuries only affect that part of the plant that has been directly exposed to the hot rays. For example, the yellowing of the leaves is often a result of the bleaching out of the chlorophyll by too strong sunlight. In cymbidiums, deformed buds and flowers have resulted from the plants having been grown in too cold a temperature at night and having had exceptionally intense early morning sunlight.

High temperature, particularly at night, will cause growths to become weak, thin, and often blind (they do not produce flowers).

On the other hand, too much shading may cause the

Figure 11-10. The tissues of a plant can be badly burned by exposure to excessive sunlight.

Photo, Ralph Collins

leaves to become too lush and soft. This, too, contributes to the overall weakening of the plant. At the same time, the number of hours of daylight a plant receives also affects it. If the plant is one that blooms when the days are short, increased hours of sunlight mean it will not flower. Conversely, a plant that needs long days will not flower if grown where the shade is too dense and thus the hours of good light too few.

Another problem is too low humidity. It results in leaves, particularly on thin-leaved orchids, becoming not only wrinkled and pleated but also stuck together. The cure for this is to increase the amount of moisture in the air and to separate the leaves gently so that they can unfold and develop properly.

Air Pollution

Although great strides have been made in the control of air pollution, as long as we are dependent upon fossil fuels we will continue to have some air pollution. The conditions in your immediate area are not the only ones to be considered. Winds travel usually from west to east worldwide. Yesterday's pollution in one area can be the next day's pollution miles away. Because of pollution, some commercial orchid growers have been forced to move their places of business to areas where the air pollution is less and the damage to their orchids also less.

The leaves of orchids should always be kept clean, free of dust and dirt. The daily misting of plants usually does this. But should air pollution result in dust particles and a large amount of dirt being deposited on these leaves, they will then need to be washed off with a hose nozzle.

Besides clogging the pores of the plants so that they cannot breathe properly, this dust and dirt may contain contaminants that could harm the plants. At the same time, there are other pollutants like ethylene gas and carbon monoxide from automobiles. It takes just a minute quanitity of ethylene gas to damage a flower or cause injury to the plant itself. Gas burners used in greenhouses should always be completely vented outside, and if oil burners are used, they should be checked every year before the heating season begins.

In some areas butane or bottled gas is used for heating. This is quite safe for orchids provided the bottled gas heaters are properly vented outside. In fact, no heater should be used that does not have venting to the outside.

213

Photo, Ralph Collins

Figure 11-11.   Sepal wilt caused by ethylene gas or other pollutants.

There are times during power outages when the use of emergency heat is necessary to prevent the plants from freezing. In such a case, be sure before you use any heater that it is one that has proved safe for use in greenhouses, and particularly with orchids.

The tips of the sepals on cattleya flowers are exceptionally sensitive to ethylene gas and are usually the first part of the plant to show effects. When exposed to this gas, the flowers age rapidly and instead of remaining in excellent condition for weeks or months will die within two or three days.

If the amount of ethylene gas is great and the exposure lasts for any length of time, the petals and sepals may completely collapse. If there are buds on the plant, the ethylene gas may turn them a pinkish, leathery brown and cause them to drop off. High concentrations of ethylene gas also turn white flowers to a creamy yellow and at times turn colored flowers pinkish orange. On cymbidiums it can cause the flowers to turn a sickly pink and the leaves to become yellow and drop off. It can also cause flower sheaths to yellow, but it is the older parts of the plants that are most affected. The newer growths that are just starting seem to escape much of the damage.

Although there is no cure for such damage once it has occurred, it can be prevented. Use fans when the atmosphere is heavy and laden with pollution: the air may still be contaminated, but at least it will not be stagnant. This, in itself, might lessen some of the damage.

MISCELLANEOUS PROBLEMS

Although in reality orchids are tough plants, particularly those that have leathery leaves (such as cattleyas), leaves, pseudobulbs, and growths can still be injured by rough handling or accidentally bent or broken. Whenever any part of a plant has been damaged, if the injury is severe, that part should be cut off with a sterile knife and the remaining portion of the plant dipped into a fungicide recommended for use on orchids.

Sometimes a tender growth or an eye is inadvertently broken off. Nature takes care of such contingencies by making provision for the development of another eye almost at once. Still, this should serve as a reminder to handle the orchids with more care in the future. The aerial roots that grow out over the sides of a pot, in particular, can be broken off by careless watering or by brushing against them.

The pseudobulbs are the tough parts of the orchids and are usually able to withstand physical injuries, but they can be ruined by diseases and fungi. Once in a great while a pseudobulb will split leaving a crack in the bulb. This may be due either to an inherited factor or to the plant's lack of boron. Applying a solution of 1 teaspoon of boric acid in 1 gallon of water four or five times a year will correct this deficiency, if present.

Leaves that are too near the glass of a window or greenhouse can become frostbitten on cold nights. The areas thus affected turn black. Orchid flowers chilled by being too near cold glass may also turn black and quickly wither. So be careful.

Too dry an atmosphere invariably brings on sticking. This happens when a large amount of nectar gets on the buds and causes them to remain closed. Although buds should not be wet when the plants are watered, an exception should be made when buds are stuck. Spraying them lightly with water early in the day will help them to open.

Extremely hot weather also takes its toll of flowers. They never last as long during the hot summer months as during the cooler weather. The plant uses up all the moisture available, and so there is just not enough left for the flowers. Sickly plants that still try to flower may suffer from bud drop. The cure is to strengthen the plants through better care.

At times the stems may not be strong enough to hold the flowers up properly. This necessitates propping them up and tying them to stakes. Weak stems may result from genetic factors, but are more probably a result of the plants being grown in too much shade.

Some buds develop at the tops of pseudobulbs without the protection of a sheath, which failed to develop. The flower stems in such cases need to be staked much earlier.

Sometimes flowers are deformed. They may have too many or too few sepals or petals, or other parts of the flower may be missing or maybe duplicated. The reason for this has never been fully determined. These flowers are called "freaks," but all subsequent flowers on the plant may be normal. If a plant should continue to produce "freak" flowers, discard it.

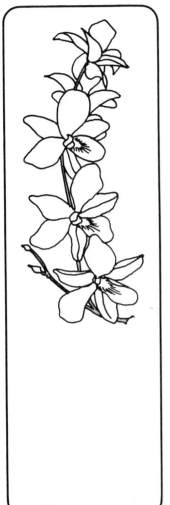

Warm-Climate Orchids

Although it is every orchid grower's desire to have as many plants of as many different genera as possible, because of their different environmental needs not all orchids can be grown side by side.

Those orchids whose native habitats are in the tropical areas of the world—South America, Southeast Asia, Africa, the islands of the Pacific, etc.—and who therefore require a night temperature of never less than 60–65°F (15–18°C) and an overall warm yet buoyant daytime atmosphere have been grouped together for ease of culture and classified as warm growing. They comprise by far the largest group of orchids and, therefore, give you an opportunity to grow quite a variety of plants under more or less similar conditions.

CHAPTER 12

217

CATTLEYAS Of all the thousands of orchids it is the cattleyas that are most familiar to the greatest number of people. Their flowers are the ones most often used in corsages and the ones that have come to represent the elegance, luxury, and beauty of the orchid clan.

It was noted in the first chapter how with an inauspicious start—as wrapping material for some so-called exotic plants—today's queen of orchids first came to the attention of plant lovers. Without William Cattley's curiosity it might have been much longer before it was discovered, and it would have taken many more years for orchids to attain the popularity they now have if it had not been for that fortunate accident.

As indicated earlier, cattleyas are epiphytic and closely related to epidendrums, laelias, and brassavolas, with which they have been crossed many times to produce some of the most outstanding orchids. Their native habitat is the high slopes of Central and South America, including Venezuela, Brazil, Peru, Mexico, Guyana, and Argentina.

The more-than-50 different species and untold number of hybrids have been divided into two separate groups. One, the unifoliate or labiate group, so named because of their large lips, have but one large leaf that emerges from each pseudobulb. It is also in this group that the largest flowers are found.

The plants range from 12 to 18 inches high, and their sheaths may contain from one to six or more buds, while the flowers come in just about every color from white to yellow, pink, blue, green, lavender, and red.

The second group is known as the bifoliates, and have two leaves emerging from each tall pseudobulb. The flowers, borne in clusters, are somewhat smaller but have a wide range of color and shape. In contrast to the labiates, their petals and sepals sometimes have distinctive markings.

Cattleyas also have what is known as *sympodial growth*. They have a rhizome from which a new growth or shoot emerges and from which develop both the leaves and the flower sheath. At the end of the growth cycle, after the plant has flowered, a new cycle starts again with another new growth.

If you examine a cattleya closely, you will see that is has large, thick pseudobulbs that nature has provided for the storage of water against times when water is unavail-

able. Cattleya leaves also are tough and leathery to retain

Figure 12-1. *Brassavola digbyana*

moisture. In their native habitats the rhizome, which is actually a stem, grows along on the trunks of trees or even on rocks. Instead of a network of fine, fibrous roots like other plants, orchids have spongy roots that can grow out to quite a length along the sides of the trees or up in the air, and when the plants are grown in pots the roots grow both inside and outside the pot. At the same time, the thick layer of white material, velamen, absorbs many times its own weight in moisture from rain, dew, or water vapor, and at the very tip is a light green growing point containing chlorophyll. This distinctive root system is the reason cattleyas cannot grow in ordinary potting materials like soil.

New roots on cattleyas develop from the base of one of the older, mature pseudobulbs, usually during or right after the plant has flowered. Thus, the appearance of new roots is a sign that a new cycle of growth is beginning.

Following the appearance of new roots, new growth begins, covered with a paper-thin substance, and at the base of the pseudobulb underneath this sheathing material is the new eye, which eventually breaks through it as it grows. If you strip this covering from the pseudobulb, there is a danger that this new eye as well as some of the roots might be broken.

Both sunlight and insecticides can also damage the pseudobulb when this protective sheathing is removed too soon. However, as the growth gets older, this covering often becomes dry and a haven for scale. Only then should it be removed gently and after first being moistened.

Some cattleyas develop only one new lead each year. Others develop multiple leads, making them still more desirable, because the more leads a plant develops, the more flowers it is able to produce.

There is a trick that is often used by commercial growers to force a plant into developing more than one lead. This consists of cutting the rhizome about halfway through near the backbulb. When the new lead appears, the plant may be repotted, if necessary, keeping the entire plant intact, or after the new growth and roots have developed on one of the backbulbs behind the cut the severing can be completed and there will be two plants instead of one, each with a new active growth.

Often you will notice that at the base of a pseudobulb there is one live eye developing nicely and a sort of bump or undeveloped eye. This is nature's way of assuring that if the eye should be broken off the second eye will immediately replace it.

Because cattleyas grow in trees where their roots are constantly exposed to the air and to heavy showers interspersed with warm, drying sunshine, the potting material must be porous enough to provide good drainage so the roots may dry between waterings. In the wild they also survive daytime drying not only because their pseudobulbs hold a reserve supply of moisture, as do their velamen-covered roots, but, perhaps most important of all, the night air is filled with mist, which is absorbed by the roots. This is one reason why misting orchids is such an important part of their culture.

Flowers

Most cattleya flowers have a delicate fragrance that is truly delightful. It takes anywhere from one to two months for the buds to reach the top of the sheath, emerge, and finally open. (If you hold the plant up to the light, you can see the buds developing within the sheath.) If they appear cramped or too large for the sheath, which often happens, slit the top and sides of the sheath to let the buds develop freely.

When the buds emerge from the sheath they will be green if the flowers are to be white, but if the flowers are to be colored, the buds may begin to show a slight pigmentation. For example, they will often have a lavender tint if the flowers are lavender-colored. Also, when the flower first opens it is always pale and limp, but as it unflods it shows more substance and the color deepens. Even the whites become more intense. This usually takes two or three days.

Temperature

Since cattleyas love warmth and sunshine, they grow best in a sunny location where the daytime temperature ranges from 65°–86°F (17–29°C). If there is a good movement of air and the humidity is sufficiently high, the temperature can go higher, but as was indicated earlier, cattleyas must have lower night temperature so that they do not use up all of the food made during the daylight hours.

221

Light and Shading

Cattleyas need all the light they can get short of burning their leaves. This is apparent when the first warm days of spring arrive and the sun is climbing higher in the sky, for then they really begin to grow rapidly, their pseudobulbs become plump and healthy once again, and their roots strong and firm.

Often blind growths occur on otherwise healthy, well-grown plants, because they did not receive sufficient light to initiate flower buds. Insufficient light can cause the pseudobulbs that are farthest back on the plant and normally do not have very good root action anyway to shrivel and fall off.

Cattleyas also react to the number of hours of daylight. Some do not initiate flower buds when the days are long; others *only* initiate their buds when the days are long. Thus, if a plant consistently refuses to flower, try moving it to a darkened room before night actually arrives to give it fewer hours of daylight. If this does not work, try the reverse. Extend the daylight hours by use of artificial light. Once the buds are formed, the plant can be returned to its usual place to grow along with the other cattleyas. The longer day will not cause the buds to stop growing.

In any case, always leave enough space between the plants so that each receives sufficient light and sunshine. Hanging them up in the greenhouse or growing them in hanging baskets usually provides them with more light than growing them on a bench.

If possible, shading should be gradually increased in late winter and early spring and then reduced in later summer and autumn to give the plants a chance to harden up. During November, December, and January there is little need of shading. In any event, the shading material used must always be such that it allows some filtered sunlight at all times. When flowering, cattleyas should be placed in a shady place to prolong the life of the flowers. For further information on light turn to Chapter 3.

Humidity and Ventilation

Cattleyas need a moderate to high humidity. Without it their pseudobulbs and leaves become wrinkled and dry.

Humidity also helps temper the heat and higher light intensity. Normally the humidity should be around 50%, but as the temperatures rise, it can go to 70% or even higher.

However, high humidity without sufficient air circulation is the road to disaster. Ventilation helps control temperatures and keeps the atmosphere fresh and buoyant, which aids in preventing diseases and fungi from getting started. On the other hand, cattleyas should never be grown where there is any chance of cool or hot blasts of air blowing on them.

Watering and Misting

One of the most important points to remember is that cattleyas must be allowed to become almost dry between waterings. Although there is no hard-and-fast rule regarding frequency, the plants usually need water about once every week or 10 days during the winter and perhaps as often as twice a week during the summer.

Since cattleyas usually have a short rest period when there is no active growth after flowering the need for water then is less. Frequent misting of the leaves and pseudobulbs—but not the potting material—will keep the plants plump and allow new roots time to develop without rotting from too much water. (Misting also helps cool the plants when they become too hot.) Then when the new eyes and roots emerge, the plants will again need the regular watering.

Sometimes after a plant has been repotted you will notice some of the pseudobulbs shrivel and the leaves become yellow. Don't panic and decide they are dying. Continue misting the foliage rather than pot-watering until the roots have had a chance to start growing again. The yellowed leaves may fall off. Since they are old leaves, this is nothing unusual.

Of course, when the flower buds are developing, the plants need more water at the roots. Providing extra water at this time is the best way to insure the plant will have long stems. A plant with many roots in good condition, especially one whose roots are growing out all over the sides of the pot, can utilize more water than a plant that only has a few. Finally, all plants in a collection do not need watering at the same time. Check each plant individually.

Feeding

As noted in Chapter 7, plants potted in osmunda do not need additional food, except perhaps an occasional foliar feeding. But if plants are potted in bark, a fertilizer high in nitrogen is needed to offset the nitrogen the bark uses in breaking down. In any case, small amounts at weekly or biweekly intervals are preferrable to large amounts at one time, and the pots should be thoroughly flushed with water, preferably with a hose, once a month to prevent a buildup of fertilizer salts.

Potting

It has been often said that more growers come to grief with improper potting than with any other aspect of growing, for if a cattleya is improperly potted, the chances of its ever being able to grow well are almost nil, regardless of the care it is given. Because of this need for drying, clay rather than plastic pots are favored by most growers.

Although there is no definite rule regarding the time of year when cattleyas can be potted, the winter months are generally considered the least desirable. Rather, the warmer months, when the days are longer, sunshine is increased, and there are more favorable growing conditions to help the plant become reestablished, are to be preferred.

Although some roots appear on the top of the potting material, the majority, and by far the most important for the development of the plant, grow below the surface of the potting material and are attached to the sides and bottom of the pot. For the details of potting, from seedling to mature plant, turn to Chapter 5.

However, if the cattleya seems determined to grow horizontally instead of up straight, this situation can be corrected by gently tying the growth to a stake firmly set into the potting material. Then gradually it can be straightened up as it grows, but care must be taken to prevent breaking off the new growth.

Propagation

Cattleyas are propagated by seeds and increased by division. See Chapter 9 for details.

EPIDENDRUMS   The name *epidendrum* comes from two Greek words, *epi* meaning "upon" and *dendron* meaning a "tree," thus signifying the manner in which these orchids grow. The early botanists, who were not familiar with epiphytic plants, called all orchids they found on trees epidendrums. Even Linnaeus, in 1753, improperly included some others in this genus, such as *Arachnis* and *Brassavola,* which have since been reclassified into separate genera.

Epidendrums comprise an extremely large genus, with well over 1000 species, and in the wild are spread over a larger area than any other genus with the possible exception of the dendrobiums. They are found all over South America, in great numbers in Central America, and in the West Indies and Mexico. In fact, epidendrums frequently grown in greenhouses—*Epidendrum cochleatum, tampense,* and

Figure 12-2. *Epidendrum difforme* 'Seminole,' AM/AOS

Courtesy American Orchid Society

conopseum—have as their native habitats Louisiana and South Carolina. Of all the tropical and subtropical orchids, the epidendrum is the one that grows the farthest north in the Western Hemisphere.

In the wild, most are found at moderate elevations along with the cattleyas. Some grow in enormous tufts on the trunks of trees, which they have been known to strangle. There are also a few that grow on rocks and a still smaller number that grow in soil.

Epidendrum cochleatum, whose species name provides us with a good description of the plant's flowers (it means "spiral" or "shell-like"), was the first epiphytic orchid to grow in England, in the Royal Botanic Gardens at Kew in 1787, where it became known as the "cockleshell orchid." Going farther back in history, we find the plant depicted in the carvings on ancient Aztec temples. Although there is no such thing as a black orchid—despite the myths about it that have grown up through the years—this species comes close to being one, with its dark purple flowers, which look almost black.

Horticulturally, epidendrums have never been of great importance, although some of the smaller species have been grown for their fragrance and delicate flowers. The main interest growers have had in them has been in using them for hybridizing. They have been crossed with cattleyas to produce epicattleyas and with many other genera to produce some intriguing bigeneric and multigeneric hybrids. The hybrids usually combine the growing habits of the epidendrum with the colorings of the flowers with which they are crossed.

The first epicattleya was registered by the firm of J. Veitel in 1897. From then until the 1960s there were less than two dozen crosses registered, but in the 1960s hybridists began to show greater interest in creating epidendrum hybrids, and from that time on some of the loveliest hybrids in the orchid family have been created.

Those epidendrums that have pseudobulbs have a *sympodial* type of growth similar to cattleyas. Sympodial growth is a form in which each new shoot develops from the rhizome of the previous growth and is complete in itself, terminating in a flower. The reed-stem type has a *monopodial* growth. This latter type has no rhizomes or pseudobulbs.

It is characterized by a single shoot or stem that culminates in the flowers that rise from the axils of the leaves when the growth of the stem has been completed. However, the single stem may have many branches, and the roots develop not only at the base of the plant but also along the stem itself.

General Culture

Because there are so many epidendrum species and they come from so many different areas with such varied climates, the cultural requirements depend to a great extent upon the epidendrum being grown. But they all need cattleyalike conditions, temperatures of 80–85°F (27–29°C) by day, a low of 65°F (18°C) at night, and humidity of 50% or higher.

The first (sympodial) type needs to dry out between watering like cattleyas, and when the plants are watered they should be given copious amounts. With both leaves and pseudobulbs thick, they can take both hot sun and drought in stride.

At the same time, they need a decided rest during the winter at a temperature of about 50–55°F (10–13°C), which is quite a bit cooler than they need when they are actively growing. While resting, they also need little water but should never be permitted to shrivel to nothing. After the rest period they can once again be grown in a warm place and gradually exposed to an increasing amount of light.

Included in this first group are also those epidendrums whose leaves are thinner and have much softer, stemlike pseudobulbs. These need more shade and more moisture than those with stouter pseudobulbs and thicker, more leathery leaves.

The second type of epidendrum, the reed-stem type, has no pseudobulbs in which to store water. Because their leaves are thin, they always need some shading and a moister atmosphere. They also require watering all year round, for they have no resting period.

In warm climates where outdoor gardening is year-round, these can be incorporated into garden plantings, perhaps in pots to help hide a tall fence. These reed-stem epidendrums also have long aerial roots that grow out all over the place and must be protected from breakage.

Epidendrums, however, are easy to grow. Perhaps this

is why they have been neglected in favor of those that present more challenge. Although some are just too large for the average grower to find room for, there are many small ones, such as *Epidendrum fragrans, difforme,* and *tampense,* that should be in every collection of orchids.

Flowers

Epidendrum flowers are small and clustered and have a wide range of colors, including yellow, white, rose, red, and a light green and tan. They all have a characteristic wide-spreading, three-lobed lip and are long-lasting, usually remaining in good condition on the plant for several months.

Potting

Like cattleyas, epidendrums must have good drainage, so all pots should be well crocked. The potting medium may be bark, osmunda, *hapuu,* or tree fern. The smaller epidendrums can also be grown on tree-fern logs or in hanging baskets, where they make very decorative accents. The reed-stem epidendrums, however, can be grown in light, porous mixtures containing some soil as well as in the usual osmunda or bark.

Repotting is done when new growth begins, usually from late winter until some time in May, and they usually can be repotted every year without a setback. Instead of repotting them it is also possible—if they have not outgrown their container—to scrape off the top of the old potting material and replace it with some fresh medium. This allows the plant to grow for a while longer before it is necessary to disturb it.

However, if the plants do need to be repotted, all the old material should be removed, and any roots that have died or decayed should be cut off. The potting material should always be moistened, soaked overnight, and the surplus water squeezed out before it is used.

Epidendrums should always be firmly potted with the bases of the growths even and level with the rim of the pot. Also, they should not be overpotted, which can lead to soggy conditions and decay. Water sparingly until the new growth develops, then increase the amount of water. When misting, try not to let any of the water remain in the new growths. Epidendrums also benefit greatly from a bimonthly feeding, either with a balanced water-soluble fertilizer or a foliar feeding.

One word of warning, however; before you decide to buy any epidendrum, find out the maximum height of the plant. Five-foot reed-stem types might be ideal in large greenhouses, but small, 12-inch plants make better epidendrums for a windowsill.

Propagation

Although epidendrums are usually bought as mature plants, it is fun to grow them from seed. After the pod has ripened, which takes about six months, the seed can be sown thinly on top of moist sphagnum and placed in a frame where they will be kept warm and constantly moist. The seeds germinate rapidly, and as soon as they are large enough to handle can be transplanted into small pots kept in a frame where they will still be able to be kept warm and moist.

Growth is rapid, and it is not at all unusual for an epidendrum to flower within three years. When the plants approach the flowering stage, they, too, should be grown under the same conditions as cattleyas. In fact, they can be grown right alongside them.

Reed-stem epidendrums can be propagated from little growths called *keikis* (The Hawaiian word for "babies"), which grow out from the sides of the stem. These *keikis* can easily be removed with a knife and placed in a pot filled with bark. They bloom within six months. Should an epidendrum seem to often produce too many *keikis* and no flowers, remember that *keikis* are vegetative growths and develop best when there is more shade than otherwise necessary, increased temperature, and high humidity.

Epidendrums can also be propagated by cutting up stems into 4-inch sections. These pieces can then be placed on top of a pot or a flat filled with vermiculite. The epidendrums with pseudobulbs can be divided in the same manner as cattleyas.

If an epidendrum doesn't seem to grow well—and this is indeed a rarity—try to find out about its native habitat and strive, so far as possible, to duplicate the growing conditions it was accustomed to. *Epidendrum elegans*, for example, needs cooler conditions than *Epidendrum fragrans*. It is just this little difference in temperature that spells success or failure.

ONCIDIUMS The lovely oncidiums are often called the "dancing ladies" or "butterfly orchids," because of their graceful, dainty, doll-like flowers. They require little attention and will grow under many different conditions, and their blooming season stretches throughout the year.

Oncidiums were introduced into England in 1793 and since then have been grown and loved by orchidists everywhere. The sixth Duke of Devonshire, William George Spencer Cavendish, who did so much to make orchids popular, was so captivated by an *Oncidium papilio* he saw at a Royal Horticultural Society exhibit in 1823 that he resolved there and then to acquire one of them. This purchase began a lifelong interest in orchids and sparked the beginning of what was considered the foremost collection of orchids in the world.

Oncidiums are a distinctly New World species, native from Florida to the West Indies, Mexico, and as far south as Brazil. Their habitats range from high elevations in the Andes to swamplands at sea level. As with all orchids, the conditions under which they grow in their native habitat determine their cultural needs.

Types

There are four different types of growth: those with leaves shaped like fans; those with thin leaves; those with large, thick, leathery leaves; and those with thin, terete (cylindrical) leaves that twist and turn in such a way that they are often referred to as "rat-tailed oncidiums."

Oncidium leaves also vary in size from $\frac{1}{2}$ inch to over 2 feet in length. Some oncidiums have prominent pseudobulbs, while others have none at all. Those that have no pseudobulbs have thin leaves and, therefore, no place in which to store moisture and food. Consequently, they must never be permitted to dry out.

Flowers

Oncidiums are also an extremely large group, including 750 species and many beautiful hybrids. Some grow to be quite large, while others are truly miniature gems, but regardless of size, the flower characteristics are the same. The lip is the most prominent part of the flower, at times even dwarfing the sepals and petals. Both the color of the

Figure 12-3. *Oncidium boissyense*, CCM/AOS

flowers and the myriad designs on each cover a wide range. Although yellow is the predominating color, there are also browns, reds, pinks, lavenders, a greenish yellow, and even some reds and whites; the markings include splashes, bars, and even polka dots.

Although they usually blossom only once a year, after pseudobulbs have matured the flowers are so long-lasting and so beautiful they are well worth waiting for. For example, almost every orchid collection has in it *oncidium splendidum* for its masses of buttercup-yellow flowers; it is known as the "tiger orchid" because of the distinctive tigerlike markings on its sepals and petals.

Oncidium flowering habits are quite variable. Some plants produce only a single flower on a stem, yet this stem, as it elongates, goes on to produce still more flowers; the blooming period is thus extended for months. Others develop long sprays bearing hundreds of tiny, dancing flowers. The flowers vary in size from $\frac{1}{2}$ inch to over 3 inches in diameter. However, the one thing that distinguishes the flowers of the oncidium from those of their close relations, the odontoglossums, is that the base of the oncidium's lip is short, resembles a butterfly's wings, and is always at right angles to the central column.

Temperature and Humidity

Since their temperature and light requirements are similar to those of cattleyas and epidendrums, oncidiums can be grown right alongside them. The only exceptions might be those oncidium species that come from the high altitudes of Colombia, Peru, and Ecuador and their hybrids. Obviously, you should grow them in a cooler temperature. Those with thick, leathery leaves grow in a warmer one.

Ideally, the night temperature should be 55–60°F (13–16°C), with the day temperature rising to 75°F (24°C).

The humidity should, again, be similar to that for cattleyas, from about 50% to a high of 70%, and there should be good air circulation. While the plants relish misting during the warm summer months, they do not need as much during the winter.

Light

Oncidiums require good light—2000–4000 footcandles— and therefore do their best with a southern or western exposure. The plants that have the thick, leathery leaves can stand full sunlight, except during the middle of the day, while the thin-leaved oncidiums need filtered sunlight.

Watering

When the leaves become crinkled, it is a sign the plant has not been getting sufficient water. When watering, do so copiously especially during the growing and flowering seasons, but give them a chance to dry out somewhat between waterings in order to prevent the potting material from becoming soggy and also to keep the roots in a healthy condition, for, as always, healthy roots are the key to abundant flowering.

On the other hand, the dryness between waterings should never be carried to extremes. The warm-growing oncidiums have a large number of aerial roots and therefore need more water than the cooler-growing ones.

Feeding

If the plants are potted in osmunda, they will not need to be fertilized, but in bark or in one of the mixes they should be fed once a month with a balanced fertilizer. In fact, fertilizers high in nitrogen seem to impede flowering. Also, oncidiums should be fed when they are flowering—a departure from the usual cultural directions for orchids in bloom.

Potting

Contrary to what one might think, even though these plants have an abundance of roots, they grow best when kept in small pots or containers. In fact, shallow pans or pots are preferable to the conventional deep ones, because oncidium roots generally grow close together in the upper portion of the potting material. The small types and those that have drooping flower sprays do especially well in baskets, while the climbing types can be grown on slaps of cork.

Oncidiums do not seem to require repotting as often as most other orchids. Repotting only becomes necessary when the old potting material is worn out or has turned sour, and the best time to do this is between February and April, just as the new growths and roots make their appear-
233 ance. On the other hand, if the plant only flowers during

the spring and summer, repotting must be delayed until the plant has finished flowering and started growing new roots again. In any case, try not to schedule any repotting in cold, damp, cloudy weather.

The so-called cool-growing oncidiums sometimes have a short rest period, but the majority tend to grow continuously throughout the year. The roots are extremely brittle and may break off in potting, so handle them gently.

Osmunda and bark are the usual potting materials, although some growers have successfully used a mix containing bark and sphagnum moss. If any of the newer pseudobulbs have grown out over the edge of the pot, they can be separated from the older ones by cutting through the rhizomes. The new front divisions can then be potted as separate plants. The older pseudobulbs that are left can then be placed loosely in a flat containing osmunda or bark until they have had a chance to develop new roots, after which they can be potted. While in the flat they should be misted frequently. New eyes and new growths develop in a short time, but before putting the older sections into pots, trim off any roots that have become diseased or rotted. As with all oncidiums, pot moderately firmly.

Care after Potting

All newly potted oncidium plants should be kept somewhat shaded until new roots and growths begin to appear. They should also be kept somewhat drier than actively growing plants. Furthermore, young growths have a tendency to rot off. So care must be exercised when watering to be certain that the plant drains well and that there is always ample time for the leaves to dry off before night.

Tender new leaves are also susceptible to burning and should not be subjected to the direct rays of the sun. In fact, during the growing season oncidiums always need some shade, particularly during the middle of the day.

After the pseudobulbs have matured, the flower spikes begin to develop, taking as long as three or four months before there is any sign of buds. The spikes may also grow as long as 2 or 3 feet.

Old leaves and dry flower spikes should always be removed, particularly from the old pseudobulbs, not only to keep the plant tidy but also to eliminate places where scale might start. Never crowd oncidiums. They need plenty of space around them for good air circulation. Also, the tall, erect sprays must have sufficient room overhead to grow unrestrictedly.

Propagation

Mature oncidiums can be divided in the same manner as cattleyas. Each division should consist of three or four pseudobulbs or growths. Of course, as with all orchids, oncidiums can be grown from seed, but that is too complicated for nearly all but professionals.

VANDAS

Vandas always bring to mind the soft breezes, blue skies, and warm sunlight of Hawaii, where they have long been used in those lovely leis that, when bestowed with a fond "Aloha," convey so much better than mere words the graciousness, hospitality, and kindness of the Islanders. In fact, the vanda 'Miss Joaquin' has become known as the "lei flower" because it is used so frequently in those lovely garlands.

In 1920, so the story goes, Lester Bryon, a prominent resident of Hilo, received some vanda cuttings as a gift while on a visit to Singapore. The cuttings multiplied so extensively and Mr. Bryon was so generous in sharing them that it was not long before the vanda replaced the hibiscus as the traditional flower of the Islands, and thus began Hawaii's orchid industry, which has become such an important part of its economy.

There are more than 70 species of vandas growing in the tropical and subtropical areas of China, Burma, India, Thailand, the Malay Archipelago, the Philippines, New Guinea, Sri Lanka (Ceylon), and Java, where they are grown as garden plants not only for the beauty of their many-colored flowers but also for the attractiveness of the plants themselves.

The genus *Vanda* was established by Dr. Robert Brown when a plant, later named *Vanda roxbourghii* in honor of Dr. William Roxbourgh, director of the Calcutta Botanic Garden, first flowered for him in England in 1819. The name *vanda* comes from the Sanskirt word for "epiphyte," which is most appropriate since vandas do grow on trees.

Figure 12-4.   *Vanda onomea* 'Walcrest, CCM

Types

There are three distinct types of vandas, distinguished by the shapes of their leaves: the strap-leaved type, whose leaves grow anywhere from 2 inches to 1 foot in length; the terete-leaved vanda, which has long, cylindrical leaves; and the semiterete type produced by crossing the terete-leaved and the strap-leaved vandas.

Vandas have what is known as monopodial growth—a single vegetative shoot that grows out from the terminal bud year after year. Since vandas have no pseudobulbs in which to store water, moisture is retained in their thick, leathery leaves, their large main stem, and their fleshy roots.

There are also many aerial roots that help keep the plant supplied with moisture, and, of course, the roots are covered with velamen, the white, spongy substance that soaks up water. Furthermore, these roots grow out anywhere along the stem, and in their native habitat these roots cling to the trees. At times they even try to attach themselves to nearby plants in cultivation. This is quite all right provided the roots do not become so entangled in the other plant that they damage it, but try not to let them attach themselves to the bench in the greenhouse, because they would be broken every time the plants are moved. In the wild they take full advantage of any rain that falls, which means that when grown indoors they need frequent misting.

The main stem of a vanda grows taller each year and can reach a height of 6 or 7 feet. The new leaves, which grow quite close together, give the plant a neat, symmetrical appearance. In addition, branches keep growing out from the stem. In their manner of growth they do not exactly follow the other epiphytic orchids.

Flowers

The flowers are produced on racemes that develop from the axils of the leaves. (A raceme is a long stem from which the flowers, on short stems, develop at intervals—somewhat in the manner of a hyacinth.) The flowers are usually flat, 2 to 4 inches in diameter, and the lips have short spurs, the distinctive characteristic of all vandas. The colors range from pure white to brown, green, pink, and lavender-blue. The flowers also have dots and etchings one on top of the other in happy profusion. Unlike most orchids, they have no distinct blooming season but usually reach their peak in late spring and early summer.

Vandas may take a while to acclimate themselves to new surroundings, but once adjusted they richly reward the grower with an abundance of flowers over a long period. As one spray finishes, another spray develops. However, vandas have individual idiosyncrasies, much as we do. While some readily adapt to living indoors, others, even though they grow and flower, seem to lack the vigor and robustness they have outdoors. Furthermore, they have no resting period, but grow continuously throughout the year.

Temperature

Since vandas are tropical plants, they need a tropical atmosphere. This is particularly true during the summer, when the minimum night temperature should never be less than 60–65°F (15–18°C). They can tolerate long periods of heat, but cold only for very short periods.

Ventilation

Because vandas need warmth and a great deal of light, good air circulation is essential. Good ventilation also helps prevent the lower leaves from dropping and causing the plant to look leggy. Therefore, never crowd the plants.

Light

In order to flower, vandas require more light than cattleyas. The semiterete hybrids need almost full sunlight. If they are shaded at all, it should only be during the hottest part of the day. The strap-leaved kinds, too, need an enormous amount of light and should be grown where they get full morning sunlight, shade during the middle part of the day, and full sunlight again in the afternoon. The true terete type, however, seems to grow well only where the sunlight is the strongest and brightest, as in the tropics. They can stand as much as 8000 footcandles of light. Therefore, this group does not do as well in northern areas where the light is much less intense.

It is light more than any other cultural factor that determines whether or not vandas will flower. Leaf burn can be avoided by keeping the humidity high.

Watering and Misting

When vandas are grown outdoors in the summer in northern areas or year-round in the tropics, they need to be watered and misted every day to keep the aerial roots in good condition. In greenhouses they need somewhat less water, but the potting material must never become completely dry.

Much of the active root system of vandas grows outside the pot. During the winter, after repotting, and during prolonged periods of damp, cloudy weather, watering should be done sparingly. But when the plants are actively growing they need plenty of water. At the same time, keep the water off the leaves to prevent crown rot.

Feeding

Vandas require a great deal of food, and foliar feeding is an ideal way to give them the needed nourishment, but fertilizers with a high nitrogen content should not be used even when the plants are potted in bark, for it impedes or reduces flowering.

On the other hand, a dilute solution of a balanced fertilizer such as 10–10–10, 18–18–18, or fish emulsion gives excellent results if applied every 10 days; the pots should be thoroughly flushed out at least once a month to prevent a buildup of fertilizer salts. Also, it is never wise to force a plant into producing more and more flowers by extra feedings when it is at the end of its blooming period.

Potting

Potting should always be done during the warm weather, preferably in the spring. Vandas can grow in osmunda, *hapuu*, bark, or tree-fern fiber as long as the potting material is porous yet able to retain moisture. They also grow extremely well on large cypress logs.

If bark is used, select the largest chunks. This gives the roots something solid to cling to. Since the roots must always have room to breathe, they should never be squeezed into pots too small for them. Aerial roots, particularly, will stop growing if forced too tightly into pots. This is one reason why baskets are preferred by many vanda growers. If pots are used, they should be crocked at least one-third of the way up.

239   When potting parts that have been topped off, the bases

of the stems should be placed deep in the pot. This way, most of the aerial roots can be tucked inside the pot and the potting material worked around them. The long roots should be twisted around their new axils so that they can be placed in the pots with the least breaking. Since these roots have until now been exposed to the light and air, they must have good drainage. If some of the roots break, branch roots will develop, and if any of the roots are too long to put in the pot or are growing too far out into the air, they should be left as is.

The plants should be placed in the center of the pots with the stems tied to stakes. When the pots are full, shake them once or twice to settle the potting material. Fill to within $\frac{1}{4}$ inch of the top.

Newly potted vandas should be kept shaded for a few days, watered just enough to keep the potting material moist, and misted frequently with tepid water. Then they can gradually be returned to places where they will receive plenty of sun. Should the potting material ever get soggy, the roots in the pot will rot.

As the flower spikes develop they should always face the same direction. Otherwise, the flowers will twist toward the light and the plant will be unattractive. If the plants persist in growing lush, green leaves and no flowers, give them more light. During the summer, vandas can be moved outdoors. The increased light will have them showing spikes in no time.

Propagation

Air layering is one propagation method often used with vandas when the stems and branches cannot be placed directly in the potting material around the plant. When a new stem begins to develop, make a cut partway through it a couple of inches below the apex. Then wrap sphagnum moss or osmunda around the cut and tie it securely with a piece of wire or a twist tie. This ball of sphagnum moss or osmunda should be kept moist at all times. When the roots begin to show through the moss, the stem may be cut completely and the top potted as a separate plant.

As vandas develop they send out basal growths, which in turn send out other growths. At the same time, the plants grow extremely tall and lose their lower leaves, giving the plants a leggy appearance. When this happens, the plant

should be shortened.

The stem is cut off just below the remaining leaves, with some of the aerial roots left on the plant above the cut. These aerial roots then become extremely important to the survival of the cut-off section, for they enable it to be potted as a separate plant. The rest of the plant can remain in the pot and continue growing until such time as it needs to be topped again.

A third way of increasing vandas is to cut off the little offshoots, or *keikis*, that grow out from the main stem as soon as they develop roots of their own. They can then be put into small pots, where they will grow quickly into additional plants.

ASCOCENDAS

Smaller versions of the strap-leaved vandas are the delightful, colorful ascocendas. First appearing in recent years, ascocendas are bigeneric hybrids, the result of a cross between

Figure 12-5. *Ascocenda* Anjo Mitterer 'Bloom's Orchids,' HCC

Courtesy American Orchid Society

an ascocentrum and a vanda. Because of their petite size they have become popularly known as "little vandas."

The genus *Ascocentrum,* which includes less than 10 species, belongs to the *Vandeae* tribe of orchids, like the vandas. Asocentrums are found in Java, South China, Borneo, Malaysia, and the Himalayas. The tiny flowers come in shades of yellow, rose, and red and are borne on dense spikes. Although this genus was discovered in the 1840s, it did not create much impression in the orchid world until recent years.

The ascocenda was created by Dr. C. P. Sideris in Hawaii as the result of a cross between *Ascoscentrum curvifolium* and *Vanda lamellata* and was registered in 1949 as *Ascocenda* Portia Doolittle.

The purpose in making this cross between the large vanda and the miniature ascocentrum was to produce a small plant with large vanda-type flowers. It succeeded wonderfully. These little hybrids seldom exceed 4 to 10 inches in height and are covered with bright flowers in all the lovely tones found in both the vanda and the ascocentrum. Ascocendas are rapid growers and often flower several times a year.

One of the most famous of all ascocendas is the colorful *Ascocenda* Yip Sum Wah, registered in 1965, which came into being as the result of a cross between *Vanda pumila,* whose flowers are creamy to pink, and *Ascocentrum curvifolium,* whose flowers range from a peach through orange to red.

Another beautiful ascocenda is *Ascocenda* 'Meda Arnold,' which came into being in 1950 from a cross between *Ascocentrum curvifolium* and *Vanda rothschildiana.* It is this hybrid that has been the basis of much of the breeding of present-day ascocendas.

Temperature, Ventilation, and Humidity

Temperature should not get any lower than 65°F (18°C) at night. Like the vandas, ascocendas can tolerate a great deal of heat during the day provided there is good air circulation and a humidity between 40 and 65%.

Light

Ascocendas can be grown beside the strap-leaved vandas or with cattleyas. They need full sunlight—up to 7000 footcandles—in order to flower. They also need some shade during the hottest part of the day to prevent burning.

Watering and Misting

Since ascocendas are small and are grown in small pots, they tend to dry out more quickly than the larger vandas. Ascocendas should be kept moist at all times, but the potting material should never be soggy. Misting the plants frequently not only keeps them fresh and helps cool them off but also aids in increasing the humidity.

Feeding

A balanced water-soluble fertilizer or fish emulsion applied every three weeks keeps ascocendas growing and flowering vigorously. They also respond favorably to foliar feeding between the pot feedings. Remember that the more light the plants get, the more food they are able to use.

Potting

Ascocendas need a potting material that is reasonably retentive but also quick-draining. Osmunda, bark, or one of the mixes is the usual choice. The potting material should be placed around the plant in the same manner as it is for vandas. Many growers have a decided preference for redwood slat baskets in which to grow their ascocendas, since they provide excellent drainage and give the roots plenty of air.

Propagation

Ascocendas can easily be propagated by division—by removing the little *keikis*, the new vegetative growths that grow out from the sides of the main stem, and potting them in bark.

PHALAENOPSIS

The name *phalaenopsis* is derived from the Greek words *phalaina*, which means "moth," and *apsis*, which means "appearance." Also known as "moth orchids" because of the mothlike appearance of their flowers, phalaenopsis are easy to grow, for they need no wide variation between night

243

Courtesy Shaffer's Tropical Gardens, Inc.

Figure 12-6. *Phalaenopsis* Bridesmaid purity

and day temperature and their general care is simple.

An interesting story is told about how the phalaenopsis received its name. Although the plant itself was first scientifically described by G. E. Rumphies in 1653 and was called *Angraecum album magis,* it remained in obscurity until 1825, when Dr. Karl Ludwig Blume rediscovered it in a tropical forest in Java toward the end of a long and busy day. When he first saw the plant he thought it was a large flight of white tropical moths, but upon closer examination he found it was an orchid. Because the plant's snowy white flowers so resembled moths, Blume renamed it *Phalaenopsis amabilis.*

There are few orchids that can surpass phalaenopsis for sheer beauty, and none for the long-lasting qualities of its flowers. They can remain in excellent condition on the plant as long as five to nine months.

Phalaenopsis are found primarily in low-altitude regions in some of the hottest and most humid parts of the world: the Philippines, Java, the Malay Archipelago, New Guinea, Burma, Formosa, and on down into Queensland, Australia. They grew about two-thirds of the way up on the trunks of trees, with their lower leaves hanging down so that any rainwater can drain off. Thus, they, too, are epiphytes. The leaves are evergreen, large, flat, and leathery. Normally they grow from 6 to 14 inches long and 2 to 4 inches wide, but some exist with leaves up to 2 feet long and 6 to 7 inches wide.

The leaves develop one at a time on opposite sides of the plant, and when mature several sets of leaves are present, one above the other. Sometimes the lower leaves turn brown and drop off, but as long as new leaves are developing this can be considered a natural occurrence. Phalaenopsis are also monopodial.

Flowers

Over 40 species are known to exist, as well as an ever-increasing number of hybrids, whose 4- or 5-inch flat flowers with broad, usually plain petals develop on graceful arching sprays. Their colors range from pure white to pink, lavender, rose, and yellow—and the new peppermint-striped hybrids.

The flower spikes develop from a short stem just below the leaves, and each successive spike comes out from the next higher leaf axil. There is no definite blooming season: they can and do flower in any month of the year. This leaves the time between April and October for the plant to develop its vegetative growth. The buds, incidentally, may all open up at once or just a few at a time, but when all are opened they present a truly spectacular sight.

Flower stems that remain on the plants when the flowers are cut off will often send out new side shoots and give the plants a second round of flowers. This is fine if the plants are vigorous, but if they are weak or have outgrown their containers, these second spikes are better removed to prevent weakening the plants.

It is this constant development of flowers that assures a display that can last so many months. It usually takes only about a month-and-a-half for a new spike to make its appearance, with the flowers opening in another two months.

245   It takes strong stems to produce the large flowers. Too much water and too little light during the growing period may push the spikes up too rapidly before they are sufficiently hardened to support the weight of the flowers. Once a stem has become bent there is nothing that can be done to straighten it without breaking it. So see that it always has some support. This should be done before the buds have had a chance to develop to any great extent.

Temperature

Phalaenopsis plants need a fairly constant temperature, without the wide fluctuations between day and night that other orchids must have. The lowest the temperature should fall at night is about 65°F (18°C). During the day it can rise to around 80°F (28°C). However, if night temperatures are consistently too high, the plants may not be able to initiate flower spikes. Consequently, if phalaenopsis refuse to flower, try reducing the night temperature to about 60°F (15°C) for two or three weeks. Once the buds have opened, low night temperature should be avoided, for it can cause sepal wilt and botrytis. You can also lower the temperature to get a plant to grow an extra stem when it has completed its flowering.

Ventilation

Since phalaenopsis grow high on the trunks of trees, where there is always good circulation of air, they grow more vigorously when they have a constant gentle movement around them. At times this may require the use of a fan. This is particularly true when they are blossoming, in order to prevent spotting of the flowers from condensed water vapor. For the same reason, they should never be grown too close together.

Light

Light intensity should preferably be fairly low. It can vary from 1000 footcandles in the greenhouse to 600 indoors, since phalaenopsis require less light than most other orchids. Although they are warm-growing orchids, phalaenopsis do not like their warmth from the hot rays of the sun. In fact, too much sunlight tends to burn the leaves. It is the atmosphere around them that must be warm.

Some shading is always needed. However, during their active growing season, which comes during the summer, they can stand a bit more light, although nowhere near the amount cattleyas can stand.

In any case, phalaenopsis leaves should always be firm. If they are too soft, give them a little more light from time to time—but be careful.

Humidity

Because phalaenopsis grow where the humidity is high, for best results they should have at least 70% humidity, and even higher as the temperature rises, when grown in greenhouses.

On the other hand, excessive humidity—that is, humidity approaching 90%—if coupled with a sudden drop in temperature, can cause both bud drop and crown rot. By misting the plants frequently in the greenhouse or placing dishes of water among them or even growing them above (but never on) wet pebbles in the house, they do fairly well.

Watering

Since phalaenopsis have no pseudobulbs in which to store water or food, they need to be watered and fed frequently. Fortunately, there is not as great a risk of killing a phalaenopsis with too much water as there is a cattleya as long as there is good drainage in the container and the potting material is sufficiently porous. Soggy potting material always causes root rot.

As with most orchids, phalaenopsis should never be watered so late in the day that water remains on the leaves overnight or collects in the leaf axils, where it can lead to black mold or crown rot. Try to schedule your watering so that it will not have to be done on cold, cloudy, damp days, and always let the plant dry out just a bit between waterings.

The feeding roots of phalaenopsis grow mostly on top of the potting material. These roots are quite thick and are covered with velamen. Not only do the feeding roots need a plentiful supply of moisture, but so do the aerial roots, which often grow right out between the leaves and into the air.

Feeding

A dilute water-soluble fertilizer every third week is usually sufficient for phalaenopsis in flower, but during their growing period feeding can be increased to every 2 weeks or even every 10 days. Also bear in mind that a fertilizer too high in nitrogen encourages lush, weak growth. Should this occur, decrease the amount of nitrogen and increase the percentage of phosphorous and potash. This is important, for soft, lush growth is susceptible to bacterial and fungal infections and should be guarded against.

Potting

Generally, repotting is necessary only when the potting material has started to break down, when water is not able to drain freely through it, or when the plant has lost so many of its lower leaves and roots that it is growing way out above the potting material. If at all possible, however, phalaenopsis should not be repotted during the winter.

There are times when it is necessary to repot a plant every year, but usually a plant can grow for several years before being disturbed.

Remember, though, that since phalaenopsis require frequent watering and feeding, the potting material breaks down more rapidly than it does with many other orchids.

When phalaenopsis have completed their flowering, they take a short rest. This may not be too apparent, as they otherwise grow all year. To repot before the new roots develop is hazardous, since the plant can get its water and nutrients only from actively growing roots.

The plant should always be taken out of its pot gently. Run a sharp knife around the inside of the pot. This usually helps loosen the roots that are clinging to the inside of the pot. Then before the plant is repotted, it should be given a thorough cleaning. Remove all the old, decayed potting material from around the roots and cut off any roots that have become rotted. If necessary, live roots can be shortened to about 3 inches. Branch roots will usually develop from the stubs.

Some of the long aerial roots can also be shortened so that they can fit into the potting material and thus help anchor the plant. This is important, for phalaenopsis have only a few roots that will go down into the pot itself but many growing outside it.

Figure 12-7. A phalaenopsis should be taken out of the pot gently to leave as many of the roots intact as possible.

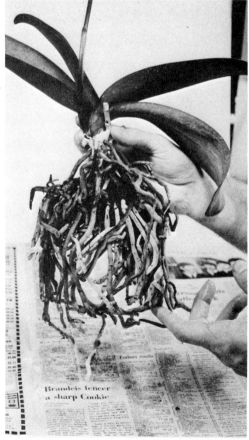

Figure 12-8. These long roots will need to be shortened to about 3 inches before the plant is put in a new pot.

Figure 12-9. Phalaenopsis are always placed in the center of the pot, with the potting material pushed in firmly around the roots.

Phalaenopsis can be grown in clay or plastic pots, in baskets or on blocks of tree fern, in osmunda or bark, but they do not like growing in pots that are either too small or too large. Phalaenopsis are fast-growing plants, so watch them closely.

Pots should be well crocked and baskets lined with sphagnum moss before any potting material is added. The plant should then be placed in the center of the pot and pinned down with pieces of wire. The new potting material can then be pushed into the pot around the plant until it is firmly settled, with the crown of the plant resting just above the potting material and the base of the plant level with the top of the pot.

Care after Potting

After potting, phalaenopsis should be kept shaded, moist, and free from drafts. Misting at this time helps keep the plants moist and raises the humidity, but do not feed them until the new roots have started to grow. Any spikes that still have live bud tips may be left on the plants to produce additional flowers.

When a plant loses all or most of its leaves, it can still be saved by placing it where the atmosphere is somewhat drier and watering it sparingly until it shows signs of developing new roots and leaves. Finally, when you find a location where phalaenopsis grow well, leave them there. Moving can bring about a drastic change in the growing conditions and a subsequent decrease in flower production.

Propagation

Large phalaenopsis can be divided by cutting off the top portion of a plant slightly below the leaves. If it has some good roots, this portion can then be potted and will grow just as well as if the whole plant had been repotted. In the meantime, the bottom part, which now has no leaves, can be left undisturbed in the pot, and if it is placed in a shady location where there is high humidity and not watered, new plantlets may begin to emerge. Within several weeks, when these plantlets have developed their own roots, they can be cut from the plant and placed in small pots.

Just as with vandas, sometimes a phalaenopsis will develop *keikis* either from the stem or from between the leaves. These, too, can be removed and potted.

DENDROBIUMS

Two Greek words, *dendron*, meaning "tree," and *bios*, meaning "life," were combined by Olaf Swartz in 1799 to give the genus *Dendrobium* its name, which refers to the epiphytic habits of the plants. The dendrobium is one of the largest and most complex genus of orchids, containing over 1500 species and many lovely hybrids.

Dendrobiums are sympodial, yet vary tremendously in their vegetative characteristics. Some have pseudobulbs that are round and rather small. Others have canelike pseudobulbs that can grow as tall as 5 feet. Also, their leaves are the most varied of any genus of orchids, some being flat and thin while others are thick and leathery.

They are found throughout the Far East—in India, Burma, Sri Lanka (Ceylon), Korea, the Philippines, and Australia and on the slopes of snow-capped mountains in

Japan and China. The most northern one is *Dendrobium moniliforme*, from Japan; the most southern *Dendrobium striolatum*, from Tasmania.

Types

In all there are three principal groups of dendrobium: the evergreen, the semideciduous, or nobile; and the deciduous. Each group should be grown according to its own basic requirements for light, temperature, humidity, and watering, but generally speaking, all dendrobiums are extremely easy to grow and flower.

The evergreen type needs warm days and nights that are somewhat cooler but with the temperature not going below 60°F (21°C). They require as much light as cattleyas and should be shaded only enough to prevent the leaves from becoming burned and the plants dehydrated.

A humidity between 50 and 70% is needed to ensure maximum growth and flowering for evergreen dendrobiums. The plants should be kept moist at all times and never permitted to dry out. Use copious amounts of water during their growing cycle and less when they begin to flower.

The deciduous dendrobiums shed their leaves. They require cooler temperatures than the evergreen types both day and night. The temperature at night can safely go down to 55°F (13°C), the same as that for odontoglossums. Some plants in the deciduous group have pseudobulbs similar to cattleyas, while others have canelike stems.

Deciduous dendrobiums need the same amount of light as cattleyas but require more shade during the brightest hours of the day. They do not need as high humidity as the evergreen types, but require copious amounts of water before they begin to flower. However, before they begin to develop flower buds, the growths must be allowed to dry off. This means giving the plant little if any water at this time. Without this drying-off period, the plants continue to grow and do not produce flowers.

Many of the semideciduous or cane-type dendrobiums can be grown beside the cattleyas. Their long, slender pseudobulbs, which grow like canes, can grow 3 or more feet tall. At the end of their growing cycle, when they are being dried off to force them into flower, they tend to lose some of their leaves. Although this drying-off period is essential, it does not have to be as drastic as that needed

by the deciduous type. The plants should be given some

water, but less than the usual amount and not as frequently.

In addition, these nobile dendrobiums require a period of much cooler nights to initiate their flower buds than do the other types. They should be kept cool when budding. Temperatures as low as 55°F (18°C) at night for about three weeks will do wonders for producing a good supply of blooms. The resting period occurs when they are dried off.

Flowers

Dendrobiums have an extended period of flowering that runs throughout the year. As the last leaf develops, the flower spike becomes visible at the top of a cane and in some cases grows into a graceful spray. In others, the flowers are borne on racemes or in dense clusters, and it is always possible for a cane that grew the previous year still to produce some flower spikes.

Dendrobium flowers come in just about every color imaginable and vary in size from $\frac{1}{2}$ inch to 4 inches in diameter. Some have sprays with a dozen or so blooms, while others are literally covered with flowers. Like phalaenopsis, their lasting qualities are fantastic, the majority staying in excellent condition for many months.

In size the plants range from miniatures to some over 6 feet tall. So when you select a plant, bear in mind the size of the space available.

Light and Ventilation

Depending upon the type of dendrobium, the light intensity should range from 2400 to 3600 footcandles. Usually, dendrobiums require little, if any, shade from the middle of October to the middle of February, except when the sun is especially bright. At most, they benefit from a slight amount of shade during the middle of the day. Then, during the summer, they need a greater amount; as autumn approaches, the amount of shade should be lessened gradually.

The atmosphere should always be buoyant, meaning the plants need good air circulation at all times.

Watering

Dendrobiums should never be overwatered. This is even more important than with cattleyas. Let them become almost dry before replenishing the supply of water. The periods right after repotting and just before the flower spikes are formed are when they must be kept the driest.

If a plant receives too much water when its spikes are developing, development may be halted and the plant forced into more vegetative growth in the form of plantlets. With a little experience, you will be able to judge just how much each plant needs and when it needs it. For the most part, treat dendrobiums as you do cattleyas and you cannot go very far wrong.

When a dendrobium is resting, it needs only enough water to keep the potting material moist and to prevent the newest pseudobulbs or canes from shriveling and the roots from drying out.

When the young shoots begin to grow, the amount of water can gradually be increased. The plants then need a liberal amount of water until their growth has been completed. Once the flower spikes begin to appear, it is again time to increase the amount of water until just before the buds begin to open. Should the plants have a tendency to drop their buds, decrease the amount of water.

Feeding

Evergreen dendrobiums are heavy feeders and benefit from a dilute solution of fertilizer twice a month—fertilizer that is too strong will invariably damage the roots.

The cane and deciduous dendrobiums benefit from a balanced fertilizer if potted in an orchid mix, or a high-nitrogen fertilizer if potted in bark.

When the buds appear, or if it is necessary to stimulate a plant that seems reluctant to set flower buds, the use of a high-nitrogen fertilizer should be discontinued and one higher in phosphorous substituted.

Potting

Repotting should only be done when the plants show signs of developing new growths. The new roots that grow out from the bases of the plants should be only a few inches long when the plant is repotted. Remember, dendrobiums have small root systems composed of rather slender roots.

The cane type does not need to be repotted very frequently. This is fortunate, because they dislike being disturbed. In the case of the evergreen type, potting should be done so that the bases of the plants are above the rims of the pots. No portion of the stem should ever be buried in potting material. Before potting, all old, decayed potting material should be shaken from the roots. Similarly, dried or decayed roots should be cut back at this time, and any pseudobulbs not needed can be cut off. However, if a plant is a vigorous grower and flowers profusely, it might be well to keep all the growths intact so that the plant can grow to specimen size.

Backbulbs can be saved and laid on moist sphagnum moss or on osmunda. Then, when they show signs of developing roots and the once-dormant eyes have grown several inches, they can be potted as separate plants.

The smallest pot that will comfortably hold a dendrobium is the size to use. Later, when the root systems develop, the plants can be transferred, if necessary, to larger pots, but dendrobiums must never be overpotted. They need to be pot-bound in order to flower. It may look strange to see a 3-foot plant in a 3-inch pot, but this is what these plants like. If the roots are unable to fit inside the pot, they can be trimmed back several inches. Aerial roots can be left to drape themselves over the sides of the pots; they should be misted each day to keep them white and healthy. The pots should be heavily crocked and the drainage holes not blocked.

Osmunda, bark, prepared orchid mixes, and tree-fern logs may be used. The loose material should be pushed in and around the roots. The thickened stem, like a pseudobulb, should always rest on the surface of the potting material, not be buried in it. Dendrobiums should be potted firmly. Should any of the old canes remaining on the plant look unattractive, they can always be removed.

After potting, the plants should be watered thoroughly and placed in a cool and shaded place until the new growths appear. It is better at this time to rely upon frequent misting rather than pot-watering to keep the plants fresh and plump. If the newly potted plants start to lose their leaves, do not become upset. The plants may only be going into a rest period, and new growths will not begin until the resting cycle has been completed. It may take many months for these new growths to appear, but do not despair. When they do start to grow, gradually increase the amounts of both light and water.

255   Once the plants are growing vigorously, they can be

watered thoroughly and then allowed to become almost—but never completely—dry before being watered again. This gives the pseudobulbs a chance to store up moisture. In late autumn or early winter, when the new growth has matured, the drying off and lowering of temperature can be started once again. This is the way to force a plant into flowering.

Finally, all the growths should be loosely tied to stakes to prevent their flapping around and to support the plant when it begins to flower. Otherwise, the weight of the flowers could break the stems.

Propagation

Dendrobiums can be increased by separating the old pseudobulbs from the newer ones and leaving both sections to continue growing in the pot. These eventually develop new growths at the base of the pseudobulbs or canes, at which time the plants can be separated and repotted as individual plants.

The nobile, or semideciduous, type develops lateral plantlets from the pseudobulbs. These can be helped along by keeping the plants moist at all times instead of letting them dry out completely during their rest period. Then, instead of producing flowers, the plant will keep on making vegetative growths. This type can also be increased by cutting some of the old canes into pieces 7 or 8 inches long and laying them loosely on damp sphagnum moss or osmunda until they develop roots. The pieces should be kept damp and shaded, for moisture from watering and misting is essential to keep the cuttings alive and to help them grow. In time, they develop plantlets that can be cut off and potted.

The cane type, which has no well-defined resting period, can be divided whenever not in full growth. Because of its vigorous growth, this type needs a fairly large pot.

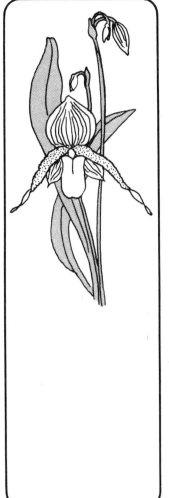

Cool-Climate Orchids

The native habitats of the orchids that are considered to be cool growing cover a vast geographical area from the moderate temperature regions of China, the islands of the Pacific, South America, etc., to the cool regions of the Colombian Andes and the Himalayas.

Among this group are orchids ranging from those whose night temperature requirements may be only a few degrees cooler than those of some of the warm-growing, more tropical types of orchid to types such as the odontoglossum, which can only be grown well when the night temperature is close to 45–50°F (7–13°C) and the daytime atmosphere is kept as cool as possible. Many of the terrestrial orchids are found in this group as well as some of the most beautiful orchids known.

CHAPTER 13

PAPHIOPEDILUMS

For a long time the lady's slipper orchids were called cypripediums (or "cyps"), a name derived from the Greek *kypris*, meaning "Venus," and *podilon*, meaning "slipper";

Figure 13-1 (opposite).
Paphiopedilum Martha
Torrance 'Tyoh,' AM

the old-time growers still refer to them by this name. But this term now properly refers only to those plants native to the temperate regions, such as our hardy American woods orchids.

The tropical and subtropical slipper orchids, with which we are concerned in this book, should now be referred to as paphiopedilums, another word of Greek origin derived from *paphos,* meaning "sandal." These, by way of contrast, come from the warmer areas of China, the Himalayas, and throughout Southeast Asia, including Indonesia, New Guinea, and the Philippines. They grow from sea level to elevations of 5000 feet. It is interesting to note that no species are found in Africa or Australia. A third related group, called phragmopedilums or phragmipediums, are native to South America, and in recent years these South American slipper orchids have become of increasing interest to growers and hybridists alike.

Although paphiopedilums have been known from the days of Linnaeus, who was the first botanist to describe them in detail, the first paphiopedium hybrid was not made until 1869. This was the result of a cross between *Paphiopedilum barbatum* and *Paphiopedilum villosum.* In all, there are over 500 species in this genus and a large number of many-colored, beautiful hybrids.

Charles Darwin considered the paphiopedilum "to be a grandfather, in a sense, of the present day exotics." For the most part, the slipper orchids are terrestrial plants, which means that they grow on the forest floor beneath large trees, which provide them with shade. Very few are epiphytic.

Types

There are two distinct types of slipper orchid: the cool-growing ones and those that require greater warmth. It is easy to tell the difference between them. The plants that have plain leaves are the ones that need cool growing conditions; those with mottled leaves need the warmer temperatures.

Flowers

Unlike the orchids we have discussed so far, paphiopedilums have neither reedlike stems nor pseudobulbs. Their leaves are stiff and may be either green or a mottled green and white, but it is their flowers that are both unusual and truly delightful; they have a waxy look that gives them an artificial appearance and are borne singly on flower *scapes* (stalks), which are often purlish and covered with short, fine hairs. These scapes are usually less than 12 inches tall.

The most unusual feature of the flower is, of course, its lip, which is shaped like a boot or a pouch—and this is what has given the plant its common name. The colors range from white to yellow, pink, deep mahogany, and a soft green and white. Frequently, there are many dots and markings on both sepals and petals. Their lasting quality is exceptional. Three or four months is not at all unusual. Thus, with just a few plants it is possible to have flowers all through the year.

Temperature

It is possible to grow both kinds together, but the cool-growing paphiopedilums need a daytime temperature of 65°F (18°C) and a cooler one at night. (The temperature should always be lower than that needed by cattleyas.) In fact, the failure of plants to flower is often the result of the night temperature being too high, particularly from March through June, for night temperature is the key factor in getting paphiopedilums to flower.

Ventilation

Paphiopedilums need good air circulation to keep them cool, help dry up water that might remain on the leaves, and help reduce the incidence of diseases.

Light

For best results paphiopedilums should receive only early morning sunlight, and even that should be filtered. Being terrestrial forest plants, they are not used to, and consequently do not tolerate, too much light. The amount should be somewhere between 600 and 700 footcandles from spring until autumn and no more than 800–1000 footcandles during the winter. If the leaves turn yellow, it is an indication that they have been exposed to too much light. Actually, they need less than half the amount cattleyas do. Sunlight not only burns the leaves but also causes the plants to be lanky, and, most important, it can keep the plants from

Figure 13-2. *Paphiopedilum* Alma Gavaert 'Merle Pennock,' CCM

flowering. Consequently, paphiopedilums always require some shading, which has the added benefit of helping keep them cool.

Humidity

Paphiopedilums require only a moderate amount of humidity, between 40 and 50% during the day. Humidity that is too high may allow moisture to remain on the leaves, and this leads to disease.

Watering and Misting

These plants have no pseudobulbs in which to store water. Therefore, the potting material can never be allowed to dry out. On the other hand, they will not grow if their roots are constantly wet. During very warm weather they may need to be watered two or three times a week. The leaves should be misted daily—often several times a day during warm weather—but it is equally important that any moisture on the leaves evaporate before nightfall. Above all, no water should remain in the leaf axils after watering or misting. Water left on the leaves encourages bacterial rot, which in turn results in both basal decay and the leaves turning black.

After the roots have developed and the plants are growing actively, they require more water. Also, the quality of the water is important. Chlorinated water is harmful to all orchids, but more so to paphiopedilums than to any other genus. It kills the natural fungi on the roots, without which growth is retarded. If chlorinated water is constantly used, the plants may even die.

To be safe, put all newly potted plants together in one place. In this way you will not run the risk of overwatering plants whose root systems have not had a chance to develop. Placing a red marker in each pot can serve as a reminder not to water too frequently. Always bear in mind that newly potted plants tend to dry out more rapidly and, therefore, must always have some moisture available. It may take several months for newly potted plants to return to normal growing conditions and require again a regular schedule of watering. Obviously, during periods of bright, warm weather they need more water than during cloudy, damp weather.

Feeding

These orchids do not require much food. In fact, under the cool, shady conditions in which they grow, they need less food than just about any other orchid. If fertilized too heavily or too often, they tend to die back at the tips of the new growths. Plants absorb the salts in fertilizers, and when there is too much, these salts may then become lodged in some of the cells of the leaves, which then become so clogged that the moisture cannot get up as far as the tips of the leaves—and without moisture the leaf tips die. Too much fertilizer may also cause the roots to die.

Plants potted in osmunda will not need to be fertilized at all. However, if they have been potted in bark or one of the mixes, they should be lightly fertilized with a balanced water-soluble fertilizer at half the recommended strength or with fish emulsion about once a month; the pots should also be flushed out thoroughly with plain water at least once a month.

Potting

Paphiopedilums are terrestrial orchids growing on the jungle floor, and jungle soil is a fragile thing composed of decayed matter—leaves along with occasional droppings of jungle birds and animals. Nature does not pack this compost. It always remains fluffy and friable. Thus, the potting material must, above all else, be light and allow plenty of air to reach the roots so that water can drain through it easily. It can be the seedling-size bark, cut-up osmunda, or one of the orchid mixes containing shredded oak leaves. The latter has the disadvantage of breaking down rather rapidly, and this necessitates repotting much sooner. There is yet another mix often used by the commercial growers composed of $\frac{2}{5}$ osmunda or bark, $\frac{2}{5}$ loam, and $\frac{1}{5}$ sphagnum moss.

Either clay or plastic pots can be used, and a good layer of crock or pebbles should be placed in the bottom of the pot, for drainage is even more important with paphiopedilums than with many other orchids, and ample provision must be made for it.

Slipper orchids should be repotted when the foliage shows signs of starvation, when the leaves turn yellowish and the plants look wilted, or when the old potting material has decayed. Generally speaking, they need to be repotted about every two years. So try to anticipate the time when the plant will need to be repotted and do it before the roots have a chance to rot or die off.

The best time to repot is always right after the plant has finished flowering. However, any time a plant looks unhealthy and the potting material is not in good condition, it is better to repot than to risk waiting and losing the plant. Nevertheless, when a paphiopedilum becomes root-bound, it is never wise just to shift it to a larger pot. Such a plant might become susceptible to disease if overwatered. This is a common problem when large pots are used. It is far better to disentangle the roots and shake off all the old potting material—but be careful. The tips of the roots are tender and can break off easily when handled. The plant should be rinsed with clean water, and all dead or diseased roots and any portion of the plant that has died should be cut off. What remains may then be potted.

To remove the plant from its present pot, hold it upside down, insert a stick into the drainage hole, and push gently

Figure 13-3. Paphiopedilums should be pulled apart gently to separate, not severed with shears.

Figure 13-4. The original plant can be potted in a large pot, while the newer separated growths, which will flower within one year, can go into a smaller pot. Do not overpot the slipper orchids.

but firmly. The plant should then slip out of the pot. It also helps to have the plant moderately damp before attempting to unpot it. When it is too dry, the roots tend to stick to the inside of the pot. A 4- or 5-inch pot is the usual size. A pot that will take about an inch of new material beyond what the plant previously had is about right and will allow room for the plant to grow for several years.

Only pots that have been thoroughly cleaned and sterilized should be used. Clay ones should be soaked overnight to fill the pores so that they will not take water from the plant. While you have the plant out of the pot, notice the hairlike appendages on the roots. These fine hair roots should always be kept moist, which is why paphiopedilum roots need more water than the velamen-coated roots of the cattleyas.

Care after Potting

Paphiopedilum plants should be watered only enough to prevent the potting material from drying out. Both the leaves and the top of the potting material should be misted once or twice a day until the new roots have had a chance to develop. When they begin to grow, the plant will need more water. For a while keep the plant shaded a bit more than usual. During the winter, when artificial heat can be quite drying, the plants need to be checked daily to see that the potting material has not dried out.

If the plant has not flowered, it may be the result of too much light, not enough water, or, more rarely, not enough food. To remedy this, change the watering schedule or move the pots to a shadier location or a combination of both and increase slightly the amount of fertilizer.

As the flowers develop, they will need to be staked. Metal stakes with little rings at the top to encircle the flower stems are ideal. Staking should be started when the flowers have reached half their final height and adjusted as the flower stems grow, although there are some growers who wait until the flowers are fully developed before staking. The danger with this is that the stems may grow bent as the flowers reach toward the light, and the slipper flowers always look best when held erect.

The quality of paphiopedilum flowers varies from year to year. A plant should not be discarded just because it has not flowered or even because it looks half-dead, for proper care will return it to a healthy state. Sometimes a flower will have a missing sepal, or one part may be a different color than the rest of the flower. Give the plant another year, and invariably the next time the flowers will develop normally, for abnormalities are usually the result of the plant's being weakened by drastic division.

There are some paphiopedilums that have two flower buds on a single stem. If the first bud shows signs of being disfigured, cut it off at once. The second bud will usually develop normally.

Many beginning orchid growers wonder which type of orchid is the easiest to grow. Without a doubt, the answer is the lady's slipper, particularly in the home. It is also the favorite of those who grow orchids under lights.

Within recent years there has been developed a miniature or pygmy paphiopedilum. Careful hybridizing has resulted in plants that, although small in size, yet have flowers of about $2\frac{1}{2}$ inches in diameter.

Propagation

Unless you want to grow a plant to specimen size, in which case you would just place the plant in a larger pot, you should divide it at repotting time. Dividing is always an easy way to get more plants. The plant should be broken apart at the rhizome with your fingers rather than cut with a knife or shears. A quick twist is all that is needed, but try to leave some of the old growths behind with the newer ones. Any small extra pieces that are left can be potted, too, and in no time they will be blooming.

Sometimes, when a plant is being separated, there are more roots on the back portion than on the front or lead section, but this is to be expected. In any case, the roots should be spread out gently in the pot. They should not be crammed into a ball, and the base of the plant should be set about $\frac{1}{2}$ inch deep in the potting material. If this is not done, the plant may never grow well. The plant should not be placed too deeply in the pot. By putting the crock into the pot after the roots have been put into position, it is much easier to anchor the roots.

If osmunda is used, it should be dampened first. Then it should be put in the pot in horizontal layers, rather than vertically, while you hold the plant steady in the center of the pot. Continue adding osmunda until it is flush with the rim of the pot. Then check to be certain that the base of the plant is still $\frac{1}{2}$ inch below the top of the osmunda. By potting toward the center of the pot, the plant is better able to develop its roots. This method also allows better aeration.

When using either bark or one of the mixes, the material should be packed moderately, for paphiopedilums do not need to be potted quite as firmly as cattleyas. The way slipper orchids are potted has a great deal to do with their future health and well-being. Stunted, stubby plants are generally the result of improper potting. The whole idea is to let the plant develop its roots freely and to allow both air and water to pass easily through the potting material.

MILTONIAS

The names of most orchids have, almost invariably, been derived from Greek words that describe an outstanding characteristic of either the plant or its flowers. Not so the miltonia. The "pansy orchid," as it is popularly known, received its name in the early 1800s from John Lindley as a tribute to a renowned horticulturist of the time, Earl Fitzwilliam, the Viscount Milton, who had one of the finest collections of orchids at the time.

Figure 13-5. *Miltonia* Bert Field 'Riopelle,' CCM/AOS

Although there are only about 20 species of *Miltonia*, many delightful and beautiful hybrids have been developed. The first was made in 1889 as the result of a cross between *Miltonia roezlii* and *Miltonia vexillaria* and was called *Miltonia bleuana* in honor of its originator, Monsieur Bleu of Paris.

As far as manner of growth goes, miltonias resemble oncidiums, odontoglossums, and brassias. Before John Lindley's time, taxonomists included the Colombian species in the genus *Odontoglossum*. These orchids are all so close in appearance that often it is not possible to identify them correctly unless they are in flower. Miltonias are epiphytic, with sympodial growth. The pseudobulbs are flat and grow about 4 inches tall. They grow closely together in a dense clump, and the leaves that develop from them are extremely thin.

Types

The native habitats of miltonias range from high elevations, where the plants have cool-growing conditions, to the warmer climates of Brazil, Costa Rica, Colombia, and Peru. This difference in temperature needs has resulted in the genus being divided into two groups: the warmer-growing Brazilians and the cool-growing Colombians. However, both are still classified as cool-growing orchids.

Flowers

The flowers resemble pansies, which is what gave the plant its popular name. (There are a few miltonias, however, whose flowers more closely resemble those of the odontoglossums.) The flower spikes develop from the base of the pseudobulbs, and each spike bears at least several flowers, which range from $\frac{1}{2}$ inch to 3 inches in diameter. They are fairly long-lasting, usually staying in excellent condition for six weeks or so.

Figure 13-6. *Miltonia* Currie Marr

Miltonias often flower more than once a year, and there are times when the spikes appear a long time before the flowers show any signs of developing, sometimes as much as three or four months. The flower sprays are not always short and compact. In fact, there are some whose sprays grow to 2 or 3 feet in length. In the Colombian group, several new leads often emerge as soon as the plant has finished flowering, and these also go on to blossom, thus providing a long flowering period.

Miltonia flowers come in many colors, including yellow, brown, pink, white, and red or rose, and all are truly gorgeous. Fortunately, too, the plants have the happy faculty of being able to produce many flowers, with comparatively little exhaustion of the plant. Also, they are able to flower at various seasons of the year. Interestingly, though, they are about the only orchid that does not seem to last when cut and put into water.

Temperature

Since these are all cool-growing plants, even though the Brazilian group is referred to as warmer-growing, they need a temperature kept below 80°F (27°C) during the day. In those areas where summer temperatures rise above this and shading alone does not hold it down, an evaporation cooler or an air conditioner may be needed. Night temperatures should be kept between 55 and 60°F (13–15°C).

Light

One of the biggest differences between the two groups of miltonias is their light requirements. The cool Colombian group should not be grown where the light is too strong. They require about the same amount of light as paphiopedilums, 1000–1500 footcandles during the summer and a bit more in the winter. If the light intensity is too great, they may develop a reddish pigmentation in their leaves. The warmer Brazilian miltonias, however, do much better when grown with more light. Nevertheless, both groups should always be shaded from bright sunlight, since their leaves are thin, easily burned, and turn yellow from exposure to light too strong for them. They prefer a light intensity of 2000–3500 footcandles.

Since both types of miltonia are shade-loving, when the time comes in the autumn to harden them to bring on maturity and the ability to produce flowers, great care must be exercised to make certain that any increase in the amount of light they receive is gradual. Too much light hardens them too quickly and adversely affects the plants' ability to produce flowers.

Ventilation and Humidity

Since miltonias need moderate humidity when the temperature is low and more when the temperature rises, good air circulation will help to keep the atmosphere buoyant and thus help prevent disease.

Watering and Misting

Miltonias need to be kept slightly moist at all times. When the temperature is high, it may be necessary to water and mist the plants every day. Nevertheless, even if miltonias have been neglected and have shriveled, they can still be brought back to good health with a good watering, which will plump up the pseudobulbs. It is important to be sure that the newest or front pseudobulbs do not shrivel, since this has an adverse effect upon flowering. One common cause of failure is not enough moisture when their root action is at its height.

The leaves on any plant that has had insufficient water will become crinkled. If, on the other hand, the plant has had too much water and the potting material remains saturated, the sheathing at the base of the growths decays, the tips of the foliage become spotted, and the entire plant eventually succumbs. It is particularly important that the plant not become too dry when the spikes have developed, for this might cause the pseudobulbs themselves to become wrinkled. Preventing such shriveling is always a lot easier than trying to cure it. There is only one period in the growing cycle when a miltonia may be kept somewhat drier: when it is flowering. This helps to keep the flowers from becoming spotted.

Once in a while an inside leaf appears to adhere to the one next to it. When this happens, insert a thin knife between the leaves to release them.

Feeding

Miltonias are not heavy feeders. If the plants are potted in osmunda, they need no additional fertilizer other than a foliar feeding with a balanced water-soluble fertilizer once every six weeks during the winter. If potted in bark or an orchid mix, they will benefit from a high-nitrogen fertilizer once a month.

Potting

The best time to repot miltonias is after flowering, when the new roots first make their appearance and the new growths are just a few inches high. If potted at this time, the plant receives the least possible setback. Miltonias have no real resting period but grow continuously through the year, generally making two new growths each year from the most recent pseudobulb. Consequently, in two or three years the plants can grow to quite some size.

Most growers prefer clay pots. These should be just large enough to accommodate the plant and allow for the new growths.

Overpotting is always a deterrent to good growth, as is potting too loosely. Large miltonias can be allowed to grow into handsome specimen plants or they can be divided into several smaller plants, but bear in mind that miltonias should not be divided frequently. It is better to allow them to develop many new leads and to increase the size of the pot each time they are repotted.

The potting material can be bark mixed with tree-fern fiber, but above all, the potting material should be loose and porous, because the roots of miltonias are fine. When the plant is taken out of the pot, it should be examined carefully. Then cut away old backbulbs and remove all the decaying potting material from the center of the plant, all the while handling the plant gently. Never pull a miltonia apart.

The bottom of the pot should be crocked about one-third of the way up. The plant should be then placed in the center and the potting material in and around the roots, which have been gently spread apart. The potting material should be pressed into the pot by working it toward the center of the pot. The plant should be potted moderately firmly—but not quite so firmly as cattleyas—and the base of the plant should be just below the rim.

If for any reason a plant cannot be potted when the new roots first begin to grow, and even if the roots have grown longer than one would like and the new growths are half-developed, if the plant needs repotting, go ahead and repot it. In this case, however, remove any flower spikes that may develop later so the plant has a full year in which to become established before it tries to blossom again.

Care after Potting

Newly potted plants should have just enough water to keep the potting material from drying out completely until the new roots have had a chance to develop. It is better at this time to rely upon misting several times a day, if necessary, in order to keep the plants moist, but at no time should miltonias be made to grow in potting material saturated with water.

When the new roots have developed, the plant can be returned to a normal misting and watering schedule. Then, as the plant approaches its flowering period, the atmosphere around it should be kept somewhat drier and pot watering done less frequently. At all times, unless all watering and misting can be done carefully, moisture can collect in the growths and cause the leaves to rot.

When the flowers have died, the flower stems should be cut back to just below the bottom flower and the stem pulled away from the leaves. Miltonias also have a tendency to bruise easily, so they must be handled carefully. If a dead flower should fall on a leaf and remain there, the leaf might rot at that spot and the rot rapidly spread to the entire plant.

Miltonias are also unusual in that at times they produce vertical roots that are not true aerial roots. Some growers recommend cutting off the basal leaves so that these roots can get into the potting material. But it is never really wise to cut off green leaves from any orchid. These vertical roots will grow right through the leaf and then down into the potting material in time.

I hope all the above instructions have not frightened you, for like paphiopedilums, miltonias make fine house plants. They are rather easy to grow, flower freely, and add so much beauty to their surroundings. An east window is an ideal location for them, for there they are able to get the early morning sun plus light all day long with no danger from the hot burning rays. As a parting reminder, when you purchase a miltonia, be sure you find out whether it is a cool-growing Colombian or one of the warmer-growing Brazilian ones.

ODONTOGLOSSUMS The genus *Odontoglossum* was established in 1815 by Humboldt, Bonpland, and Kunth. Although ondontoglossums are classified as cool growing and many do require the coolest growing conditions of all the orchids, there are also some that need somewhat warmer temperatures.

Types

The most familiar odontoglossums come from an elevation of 13,000 feet in the Colombian Andes and require such cool growing conditions that there are many parts of the world where, without air conditioning or evaporative coolers, it is impossible to grow them.

Then there are other species native to much lower

Figure 13-7. *Odontoglossum* Hyrastro 'Mr. Christmas,' AM

altitudes in Mexico and Central America. These are known as the Central American group and do not require such cool growing conditions as the Andes group. These Central American odontoglossums can be grown the same way as those oncidiums that have pseudobulbs, but even though these particular plants do grow in a warmer climate, the nights are cool and there is always a brisk movement of air. Consequently, they are not able to withstand consistently hot summer days and nights unless aided by cooling devices. They, too, will grow best if treated as cool-climate orchids.

There is an intermediate group, known as the Grande group (after Admiral Grande), that come from Central America, particularly the lower highlands. Their growing conditions fall in between those of the Andean and Central American groups. In fact, these are the most spectacular of the odontoglossums.

All have prominent pseudobulbs, each one topped by a pair of thin leaves, and it cannot be stressed too strongly that, while odontoglossums require cool growing conditions, their thin leaves make them highly susceptible to freezing. Although they may be covered with snow at times in their native habitat, they will not survive freezing temperatures when grown elsewhere, for their hard pseudobulbs do not contain a high content of sugar and freeze easily, particularly since they seldom get sufficiently hardened by a higher light intensity in the autumn. Sometimes a shipment consisting of a variety of orchids including, along with odontoglossums, some cattleyas, cymbidiums, miltonias, and so on, is inadvertently left lying around in freezing temperatures, and surprisingly it is the odontoglossums that are damaged most.

Flowers

The flowers of odontoglossums vary in size, shape, and color. Some are rather small, while others, like those of *Odontoglossum grande,* are a good 4 inches in diameter. They have fantastic patterns, consisting of spots, blotches, and dots on petals and sepals, which contrast nicely with the basic flower colors of white, yellow, green, and a truly magnificent red. Although the flower spikes take a long time to develop, when the flowers do come they remain on the plant in good condition for several months—if the plants are kept cool.

The main flowering season is spring, although many do flower at other times and also flower more than once a year. In all, there are over 300 species of this strikingly beautiful epiphytic. From these have come hundreds of superb hybrids. In fact, in addition to the man-made hybrids there are more natural ones in this genus than in any other.

The year 1890 saw the flowering of the first man-made odontoglossum hybrid. Many crosses had been made prior to this, but although they grew, they never flowered. Monsieur Leroy, a gardener at the Paris estate of Baron Edmond de Rothschild, deserves the credit for this triumph. The cross was appropriately registered as an *Odontoglossum leroyaneum* and was made between *Odontoglossum crispum* and *Odontoglossum luteo-purpureum.* Odontoglossums have subsequently also been crossed with oncidiums, miltonias, brassias, and other related genera to produce some outstanding multigeneric hybrids.

The name *odontoglossum,* incidentally, is derived from the Greek words *odontos,* meaning "truth," and *glossia,* meaning "tongue," and alludes to the shape of the lip and the toothlike hairs on the flower crest near the base of the lip.

Fortunately, these orchids are not difficult to grow once their needs are understood and met, and the beauty of their flowers is ample reward for any extra effort expended in growing them.

Temperature

The cool-growing Andean group needs a night temperature around 45°–55°F (7–10°C) and a daytime one of 60–70°F (15–21°C). The Central American group can tolerate a somewhat higher temperature, up to 80°F (27°C), but still needs a nighttime temperature of about 50–55°F (10–13°C). The Grande group prefers an intermediate range, 50°F (10°C) at night and up to a high of 75°F (23°C) during the day.

Light

Odontoglossums need more light than the paphiopedilums and cymbidiums. The Andean group need 1200–1500 footcandles, while the warmer growing Central American group requires 2000–3000 footcandles. The Grande group does best at 2000–3500 footcandles. The odontoglossum leaves should be a medium green, which may necessitate adjusting the amount of light to keep them so. Shading tends to darken the leaves, and so leaves turning light bronze or purple is a sign that the plant is receiving too much light.

Since odontoglossums have relatively thin leaves, they always need some shade, not only to reduce the intensity of the sunlight but also to prevent the leaves from becoming scorched. Sunlit days bring with them increases in temperature, and odontoglossums like neither bright light nor high temperatures.

Humidity

Odontoglossums require a moderately high humidity, somewhere around 70%. However, during the winter, when the temperature can be kept low, the air must be kept free of excess moisture, for low temperature and excessive moisture are the ingredients for the start of many diseases.

Watering

Watering requirements are simple. Although the Andes group need an abundance of water, the potting material should be kept moist—although never allowed to remain soaking-wet for any length of time. Using plenty of crock and a potting material that drains easily are the keys to keeping a good root system.

The warm-growing Central American odontoglossums should be just a bit drier than the Andes group between waterings. Any excess water that accumulates at the tops of the growths should be removed. The Grande group must dry out between waterings, especially during the winter. All odontoglossums need more water during the summer than during the cloudy days of winter.

Feeding

Since odontoglossums grow in a cool, shaded atmosphere, their need for fertilizer is slight. If potted in osmunda, they will not need any fertilizer other than a foliar feeding once a month. Those potted in bark benefit from a dilute fertilizer once every three weeks. At all times when fertilizing, use only half the strength recommended for cattleyas. Even
though odontoglossums are light feeders, the pots must be

Cool-Climate Orchids   thoroughly flushed out with water once a month to prevent any buildup of fertilizer salts, which can greatly damage the thin-leaved types.

Potting

The best time to repot odontoglossums is about a month after the plants have had their last flower spikes removed and when the new growth is about an inch long. If potting is delayed beyond this and the new growth gets much longer, the new roots will also have begun to grow, and any disturbance at this time gives them a decided setback. The most noticeable result is shriveling of the pseudobulbs.

To delay repotting once it is necessary is to court disaster, for the potting material continues to decay and the roots continue to rot. However, repotting should never be done during the summer. The plants have enough to contend with just surviving in the heat without adding to their miseries by disturbing them. Autumn, with its coolness and shorter days, is the time odontoglossums respond best to repotting. The roots recover quickly from being disturbed, and the plants regain the fresh, green appearance that is the sign of good health.

Odontoglossum pseudobulbs should never be allowed to grow out over the side of the pot, because there they are unable to get sufficient water to keep growing.

The Grande group should be repotted each year for best results. On the other hand, since repotting does give the Andean and Central American odontoglossums a setback, an annual shifting is not desirable. One year is too short a time for the plants to regain their vigor before again being subjected to the shock of repotting.

The preferred potting materials are osmunda or a fine- to medium-grade fir bark or tree fern. Above all, the growing medium must be porous, which is why the orchid mixes do not work as well. For even better aeration, if using tree fern, add an equal amount of perlite. Any material that lacks porosity will become a sodden mass in no time because of the frequency with which these plants need water, and you end up with a plant dead from rotting roots. When repotting, choose a size of pot that will allow for two years of new growth and no more. Most growers prefer clay pots, because the evaporation of moisture through their walls

278   helps keep the roots cool.

Ease the plants out of their pots by gently pushing a stick through the drainage hole. Then remove all the old potting material from the plant, for it would only go on decaying and possibly cause the center of the plant to rot. Cut away unwanted pseudobulbs, such as lifeless or shriveled ones, by cutting through the rhizome with a sharp knife. Usually, two or three pseudobulbs, plus the new leads, are sufficient for the plant.

Next press the plant down into the pot, making certain that the back pseudobulbs are close to the edge of the pot and that there is room enough for the new growth to develop toward the front. The potting material should then be worked in and around the plant while it is continually pressed down and in toward the center of the pot. When the potting has been completed, the potting material should be about 1 inch from the top of the pot. Remember, odontoglossums should be potted moderately firmly.

If any of the backbulbs you removed still have some sign of life and you want to try to keep them, place them loosely on some damp osmunda or sphaghum moss, and when new roots and growths have developed, pot and care for them for as you would any plant.

Care after Potting

The plants should be watered for a few days after they have been potted, and then the potting material should be kept just barely moist. This can be done by misting it lightly, along with the leaves. Daily misting helps to keep the pseudobulbs from shriveling. The plants should be well shaded for several weeks until new root action has begun. Keep the plants as cool as possible. Once the new roots and growths have begun to develop, the plants will then have to be kept moist at all times. The only exception is *Odontoglossum grande,* which should be allowed to become dry between waterings during the winter.

Far too many plants are allowed to flower before they have had a chance to become really established. This is the reason many commercial growers recommend removing the first flower spikes at an early stage the first year. Although this is not absolutely essential, such flowering, or too-frequent flowering, does tend to shrivel the pseudobulbs, deplete the plants' vitality, and make the development of new roots more difficult.

279

One common problem is the rotting of the backbulbs after repotting. Cutting the rhizomes halfway through while the plants are still in the pots and then leaving the plants in the pots until the new growth begins on the severed portions often helps overcome this.

Resting

Odontoglossum grande and its hybrids require a decided rest period during the winter. At that time they are given less water and allowed to become dry between waterings, yet they should never be permitted to become completely dried up. When the plants do not flower, the cause can invariably be traced to not having had a sufficiently long rest period. The warmer-growing Central American group, however, need only a slight resting period, while the Andean group need no rest period at all. Those species with the softer pseudobulbs come from Colombia, Venezuela, and Ecuador, while the hard-pseudobulb species come from Mexico, Guatemala, and Honduras. This is the one way to tell the difference in their cultural requirements—the harder the pseudobulbs, the more rest the plant needs.

Summer Care

During the hot days of summer these cool-growing orchids have a hard time. Sometimes they practically stop growing, but once the cool days and nights return, it is wonderful to see how they revive. Unless grown in an air conditioned home or a greenhouse equipped with a cooler, they may not be able to survive. If there is no air conditioning in the house, close the windows and shutters during the hottest part of the day and open them again only in late afternoon, leaving them open all night. This will give them at least some of the cool, moist atmosphere they need. In a greenhouse, unless an evaporative cooler or air conditioner is used, a combination of fans and frequent misting to keep the plants cool may get them through. In fact, sufficient moisture during the hot weather is most important, because dryness combined with summer heat quickly leads to leafless pseudobulbs. Adequate moisture does not mean just high humidity; odontoglossums should also have a strong movement of air around them.

Propagation

As with all orchids that have pseudobulbs, odontoglossums can easily be increased by dividing them. They can, of course, also be grown from seed, and although seedlings require very cool growing conditions, they do grow rapidly and reach maturity in about half the time it takes cattleyas, often within two or three years. If you want good, healthy plants that will bloom freely, do not let the seedlings flower the first year, since this results in a setback for the plants.

CYMBIDIUMS

Cymbidiums are a joy to behold at any time of the year. Even when not in flower they are handsome plants, with long, beautifully proportioned and graceful foliage. Cymbidiums are evergreen and do not drop their leaves. As a plant grows older, a leaf or two will die, and these can be cut off.

Their native habitat ranges from Australia to Japan, from the Philippines to northern India, Burma, Malaya, Thailand, Vietnam, and the Himalayas, where they grow at elevations of 5000 to 8000 feet, assuring them the bright light and cool nights so necessary for their flowering.

The cymbidium gets its name from the Greek word *cymbid,* meaning "boat," which undoubtedly refers to the shape of many of the flowers. The Swedish botanist Olaf Swartz seems to have been addicted to making typographical errors, because there are those who strongly believe he meant to use the Greek word *cymbium,* which refers to a slender drinking cup and more aptly describes the flowers of the majority of cymbidiums.

In any case, the genus *Cymbidium* was differentiated in 1799 by Swartz, although the plants themselves were well known much earlier in China and Japan. The first cymbidium hybrid was registered by J. Veitch and Sons of England in 1889 and was developed from a cross between *Cymbidium eburneum* and *Cymbidium lowianum.*

Cymbidiums are both terrestrial and epiphytic, having about 70 species and several thousand hybrids, but it is the hybrids that are mostly grown today and these are terrestrial. Their roots are large and fleshy, and the pseudobulbs vary from the very large to what would appear to be a small thickening of the stem. The new growths develop out from the side of the base of the older pseudobulbs.

Figure 13-8. *Cymbidium* Rusper 'Mem. Percy Ellings'

Types

There are two kinds of cymbidium: the standard, which is taller and has longer leaves and larger flowers and which requires cool growing conditions; and the miniatures, about one-third the size, delightfully smaller versions that require somewhat warmer conditions.

The most famous orchid of all time is a standard cymbidium Alexanderi 'Westonbirt,' which received an award in 1922 and which has a prominent place in the ancestry of the majority of the standard cymbidiums seen today. The first miniature cymbidium, named 'Minuet,' was introduced in 1942 by the well-known English firm of H. G. Alexander and was the first miniature cymbidium to receive an award from the Royal Horticultural Society in England. But, as with the standard cymbidiums, 'Minuet' was not the first miniature known. Over 1000 years ago a dwarf species was described by the Chinese scholar Kin Sho. Yet it was really not until the 1950s that miniature cymbidiums became popular. *Cymbidium simulans*, a miniature from China and Japan, and *Cymbidium devonianum*, from Assam in northern India, are included in the ancestry of most of the hybrid miniature cymbidiums grown today.

Miniature cymbidiums can be further classified as first-generation miniatures resulting from the crossing of a miniature species with another miniature species or with a standard or a miniature hybrid cymbidium. Then there are second-generation miniatures, which result from a cross of this first-generation miniature with a standard hybrid or species. Further along in size is the intermediate or medium size cymbidium, which is a hybrid, larger than the miniature, that results from a cross between a cymbidium species of a first- or second-generation miniature with a standard cymbidium. This will perhaps explain why some miniatures are tiny, while others, though still classified as miniatures, are as large as some of the smaller standards.

The Cymbidium Society of America has designated that a cymbidium is considered a miniature not by the size of its foliage, but rather by the size of its flowers—specifically, if the flowers are not over 2 inches in diameter. On the other hand, the American Orchid Society classifies a cymbidium as a miniature if the plant has a dwarf species in its ancestry.

In the 1950s hybridists began in earnest to create smaller size cymbidiums that would possess the qualities of ease of culture and profuseness in flowering. They crossed a short-spiked miniature cymbidium with a standard *Cymbidium insigne.* The result was a plant that blossomed freely and could be grown under warmer conditions than were hitherto possible. They continued to breed the species *Cymbidium pumilum, ensifolium,* and *tigrinum* with standard hybrids and produced compact plants with much the same flowers as the standards, but in miniature. One great advantage of the miniatures is their early season flowering. For those who cannot provide the cool conditions required for the standards, the miniatures have proved ideal. They can be grown just about anywhere.

Flowers

The flower spikes also emerge from the bottom of the pseudobulb into either an arching spray or an erect stem with many medium to large size flowers of just about every conceivable color, from pastel pink, light green, and white to the darker shades of red, brown, and yellow and green, some with delightfully arranged dots of a contrasting color on the sepals and petals. At times the spikes may grow out from a previous year's growth, but seldom if ever do they grow from a backbulb.

It is not difficult to tell whether a new growth is another vegetative one or whether it is a flower spike, because the spike is blunter all around than the vegetative shoot. When the buds first begin to show color, the plant should be placed in a cool, somewhat shaded location and kept there until it has finished flowering, for during the time the spikes are forming, too much sunlight can cause the spikes to burst.

The flower spike is almost as interesting as the flower itself. It has many layers of sheaths, which enfold the tiny buds. As the spike grows, the flower stem inside the sheaths also grows in length until it reaches the top of the outer sheath and finally emerges into the air. Cymbidium spikes have quite a bit of "honey" on them that, unfortunately, also attracts ants. (See Chapter 11.)

The spikes have three basic habits of growth: they grow straight up, arch into lovely sprays, or grow somewhere between. Staking should be started as soon as the spike has grown about 3 inches. A long, thin stake or a fairly flexible piece of wire can be pushed down into the potting material behind the spike and slightly bent towards the plant. A loose tie should be placed around the spike in such a way that the tie can easily be slid up the stake. As the spike grows, additional ties can be added. Never tie a spike too tightly to a stake, because the spikes are easily broken. When the spike reaches the place where it can be arched away from the stake do not do any more tying but let the spike continue to grow freely and form its natural arch.

While the spike is growing and arching, the buds continue to develop and get larger and heavier. The upper part of the stake that is not being used can be cut off; at its new top you can make a hole, insert flexible wire, and bend it to follow the natural arching of the spike. The other end of the wire can be put into the potting mix. Then, as the spike continues to arch along the wire, a tie can be placed loosely around both spike and wire every few inches.

Some cymbidium spikes grow horizontally and are difficult to get to grow erect. If a tie made from a loose loop of yarn is wrapped around the spike and each day the loop is tightened, it is possible to coax it into an upright position. Miniature cymbidiums, because their spikes are short, look best tied to upright stakes.

Do not leave the flowers on the plants until they die. This depletes the plants' energy. Either cut them off after they have been on the plant for several months and enjoy them in the house, or cut them off when they show signs of looking withered.

Each flower spike produces from two to as many as 30 or more flowers, averaging 4 inches in diameter, that last two or three months, usually from late autumn to early summer, with the peak period in winter and spring. The flowers are favorites of florists, who use them in cut flower arrangements and for corsages. However, it does not follow that the earlier a spike appears, the earlier the flowers will be, for this depends upon the inherited qualities of each plant.

Among the chief causes of unhealthiness in cymbidiums are podding and overflowering. No plant should ever be permitted to make seed pods unless it is in robust health. In fact, sickly plants should not be allowed to bear flower spikes. It is far better to remove the spike and let the plant concentrate its efforts upon building its strength. Unless cymbidiums are given less water from mid-August to the time the first flower spikes appear, they will continue to send up only vegetative growths and no flowers.

Temperature

Cymbidiums need just enough warmth to keep them comfortable. The daytime temperature should not go higher than 75°–80°F (24°–27°C), although an occasional 90°F (32°C) can be tolerated. At night a temperature around 45–50°F (7–10°) is ideal. Too much heat at night contributes to bud drop. The standard cymbidiums often need an even lower night temperature to initiate flower buds. This is why it is advisable whenever possible to put indoor cymbidiums outside during the summer and keep them outdoors until they have had several weeks at a night temperature of 40–45°F (4–7°C). Growing them outdoors during the summer beneath large trees or in lath houses usually produces hardier growth, sturdier foliage, and rounder and fuller pseudobulbs. Not summering outdoors, where the air is fresh, the days warm, and the nights cool, is often the reason the plants do not flower. Where the nights do not get as cool as desirable, some growers put ice cubes around the plants early each evening in the autumn.

The miniatures, however, do not seem to need this hardening. They tolerate a greater variation in temperature than the standards, in large measure because of characteristics inherited from their ancestors. As a general rule, miniature cymbidiums like the night temperature to be cool, but not quite as cool as that needed for the standard cymbidiums.

Ventilation

Fresh air is one of the most important requirements for growing cymbidiums successfully. They need good air circulation, not only while they are growing but also while flowering. As often as possible, let them have some fresh air, even in winter, but no drafts. When outdoors in the summer, it readily becomes apparent how much the plants are improved when they have an abundance of fresh air.

Light

Light is an important factor. In fact, it is only in recent years and after much experimentation that the importance of light to growing cymbidiums has been fully recognized.

For years, growers tended to keep their cymbidiums heavily shaded. But while the plants need an abundance of light to flower, too strong sunlight tends to increase the overall temperature to a higher point than they like. Light of 4000 to 8000 footcandles in summer is ideal, provided the plants can be kept cool, and any increase in light should always be gradual. From late autumn through winter they can tolerate more sunlight, but only if it is filtered. (After the warm summer days during which the plants were grown in more shade, the increased light helps to ripen the pseudobulbs.)

If cymbidiums are grown in fairly bright light while buds are forming, the color in the reds, bronzes, and yellows will be intensified. On the other hand, plants with green or white flowers should be shaded as soon as the buds begin to develop in order to assure clear color. Then, once the buds begin to swell, the amount of light should be gradually decreased on all cymbidiums to help prevent bud drop, and after the plants have finished their flowering they can once more be given more light.

Cymbidium leaves should be greenish yellow. If too green, it is an indication they have been receiving too little light. Early morning sunlight, filtered mid-day sunlight, and full sunlight from mid-afternoon on is a good schedule to follow. When cymbidiums consistently refuse to flower and everything else seems favorable, moving them to a place where they get more light usually brings out the buds.

Humidity

Cymbidiums need moderate humidity, usually between 40 and 50%, but somewhat higher on a warm day. On the other hand, it should be less at night and when the plants are flowering.

Watering and Misting

Cymbidiums must have a steady supply of moisture while growing. This means that if they are outdoors in summer and there is not sufficient rain, moisture must be supplied by pot-watering, sometimes as often as twice a day, for if moisture is lacking the pseudobulbs will be small and the plant not strong enough to produce flower spikes. This is also true of cymbidiums kept indoors. When cymbidiums have completed their growth, usually in late summer or early fall, and when flowering, they do not need as much water as when actively growing. Not only does this help them ripen their pseudobulbs, but, if regular watering were continued at this time, they would just go on making vegetative growth at the expense of flowering. In any case, when the plants are watered they should be watered thoroughly, then allowed to dry out a bit before being watered thoroughly again. Once again, remember that consistent overwatering leads to root decay. A monthly flushing-out is needed to prevent fertilizer buildup. Misting is important in supplying moisture, and at no time is this more important than when growing cymbidiums. It helps keep the plants cool in hot weather and in the winter when the sun has raised the temperature around them. Those who grow cymbidiums outdoors in warm climates will have to choose those varieties that can tolerate more heat.

On the other hand, avoid misting the plants when the sun is shining directly on the foliage. Wait until the plants have been shaded or the sun has gone by the plants, and then they will appreciate a misting to help freshen them up after the heat of the day, but do not leave them wet for the night as this invites disease.

Feeding

Since cymbidiums are large plants and grow quickly, they are heavy feeders. No cymbidium can grow without adequate food. If the plants are growing in bark, they require a greater amount of fertilizer and at more frequent intervals than those in osmunda or a mix containing loam, oak leaves, sphagnum moss and sand.

A good schedule for fertilizing is to use a water-soluble formula such as 30–10–10, which is high in nitrogen, from March to the end of August, and from September to December to use a fertilizer low in nitrogen but high in phosphorous, such as 10–30–20, to increase the number of flowers. Then from December to March a balanced fertilizer, such as 10–10–10 or 20–20–20, can be used. The plants should be fertilized every week or 10 days and foliar-fed in between. They always use more food during the spring and summer, when the days are longer and they are growing rapidly, than during the shorter, cooler days of winter.

When plants are potted in a cymbidium mix, slow-release fertilizers such as Osmocote or MagAmp can be used with good results. Cymbidiums are also one of the very few orchids that can utilize dry fertilizers to advantage, but be careful with them.

The food available to a plant is divided between its leaves and roots. If there is not enough food to take care of all the plant's needs, the leaves will get more than the roots. In turn, this results in poor leaf growth and soft foliage that becomes susceptible to disease.

Miniature cymbidiums should not be fertilized as frequently as standards. They should be fed only every third week. Too much fertilizer causes the tips of the leaves to be burned.

Potting

There are probably as many formulas for potting mixes for cymbidiums as there are growers. Besides bark or osmunda, the basic mix for cymbidiums often contains some loam, peat, sphagnum moss, osmunda, finely shredded bark, and possibly some leaf mold, all finely ground and well mixed. Some also add perlite, for any mix used must provide good drainage. The pH (acidity rating) for cymbidiums should be 6.

Actually, cymbidiums, unlike many other orchids, can be repotted each year. But practically, if a plant is growing well, appears healthy, and has not outgrown its pot, a few inches of the old potting material may be scraped from the top and replaced with new material. If you make your own potting mix for this, add a bit more sphagnum moss or osmunda than you ordinarily would. Then press the mix firmly into the pot. This will allow water to pass through all the potting material, both old and new, much more readily than if too much loam were used, for the latter would tend to pack and become hard.

Obviously, all plants should be repotted when they have outgrown their pots and the pseudobulbs are crowded along the edges of the pots. They also need to be repotted when their roots have become so abundant that there is very little, if any, potting material left in the pots to nourish the plants or if at any time during the growing cycle they appear not to be doing well.

Again, never overpot cymbidiums. Overly large pots tend to retain too much water at the center and never get a chance to dry out. Rather, choose pots that will allow for two or three years' growth. Each year you can count on one to two new growths from each pseudobulb. Thus, 8- or 10-inch pots are about right for the average-sized cymbidiums.

The best time for repotting is after the plants have

finished flowering, just when the new roots have started to grow, and before the older roots begin to break out into new growth. However, cymbidiums often produce their flower spikes and new growth at the same time. When this occurs, potting should be done as soon as the plants have finished flowering. If it were done before this, the shock of repotting would lead to the loss of the flower spikes.

Remove each plant from its pot, then shake off and wash away the old potting material. Diseased or rotted roots should be cut off with sterile scissors. Unless you find that the roots are too long to go easily into the new pot without being broken, there is no need to cut any of them back. If there are lifeless backbulbs, now is the time to cut these off. Sometimes there is a circle of lifeless bulbs at the center of the plant and cutting them out would leave a hole. In this case, the time has come to divide the plant.

Care after Potting

Until the new roots begin to grow once again, the plant needs less water than usual. Frequent misting will help supply both the needed moisture and humidity. The plants should be kept out of bright sunlight but never completely shaded. Plants that have been divided will need to be kept somewhat dry for a time to aid healing where they were cut and where the roots were shortened.

When the plants have recovered from the shock of being repotted or divided, the regular watering schedule can be resumed. The plants should be spaced far enough apart so the air can circulate around them. Both the standard and miniature cymbidiums are among the strongest of all the orchids. They have great stamina.

Red spider mites, the nemesis of all cymbidiums, thrive in dry conditions. This is another good reason for keeping the foliage and atmosphere moist when pot-watering is reduced.

Resting

Cymbidiums have no real resting period. The new growths make their appearance right after the plant has finished flowering, at the same time that the plant is flowering, or at any time during the growing period. They must never be allowed to remain dry for any length of time in the mistaken belief that these orchids, like some others, need a rest period.

Outdoor Care

What could be more delightful than orchids in the garden? Wherever outdoor gardening is a year-long possibility, cymbidiums are the most frequently grown orchids, either in the garden or in tubs and pots on patios. This is so because regular, garden-type growing conditions are ideal for them. While cymbidiums need copious amounts of water, the problem of too much water is seldom encountered, because garden plots drain more readily than pots. Cymbidiums revel in the cool night air, and those who grow cymbidiums outdoors in the warm climates must choose varieties that tolerate more heat. That is where the miniatures come in. There is one climate, however, that despite its mildness, is not conducive to cymbidium culture. That is the desert, which has both extremes of temperature and low humidity.

Of course, in some areas there is the danger of an occasional killing frost. Obviously, it is not convenient to dig up plants growing in the garden soil and bring them in for protection, but they can be grown in locations protected by the house or other buildings and where they receive warmth from the building. The plants also can be covered with plastic or tents of burlap during critical periods. Fortunately, cymbidiums can tolerate light frosts, but temperatures that go below 28°F (12°C) are likely to cause some damage and may kill both buds and foliage.

Cymbidiums growing in tubs can be rolled into a sheltered place when frost is forecast. However, even if some of the leaves are lost, the plant most likely will still survive, although it may take some time, even up to five years, to regain sufficient strength to flower again.

When considering growing cymbidiums in the garden, select a location that, along with ample sunshine, also has periods of partial shade. The sunny location will be especially important during the winter, but if there is no provision for shade during the warm parts of the year, the foliage is likely to be burned by the sun. If cymbidiums are planted in the open soil, the roots should be spread out much as one would spread the roots of a rosebush, and the soil should contain plenty of bark or one of the mixes recommended for cymbidiums, and the material should be hilled up around the base of the plant.

Some growers like to add northern oak leaves that have been finely shredded and some perlite. The latter helps the soil retain its porosity and aeration, yet also holds moisture. Many growers like to use the slow-release fertilizers. They work well and cut down on the amount of care needed. Cymbidiums have an extensive root system, particularly when grown in ground beds, and benefit from a mulch of bark or peat moss placed around them to conserve the moisture and keep the roots cool.

Propagation

Pseudobulbs grow close together, and cutting them apart requires care so that the tiny, fragile, new vegetative growths are not broken. Dividing is not as difficult as it may seem and should be done immediately after flowering. Waiting too long means the plants will not flower the next year.

When the potting material has been washed off the plants, the rhizomes that connect all bulbs can then be seen. Press the pseudobulbs gently apart. Then cut through the woody rhizomes and gently pull or cut the growths apart, but do not use force. Each severed division should then be dipped into a fungicide. A good cymbidium division consists of two pseudobulbs and their leads. There are usually two leads on each pseudobulb. As many as five or six bulbs can be kept together, thus assuring a better flower display. If a division is too small, it probably will not flower the first year. It takes a well-established, healthy plant to produce an abundance of flowers.

Although it is not necessary to cut back the roots in repotting, when the plants are divided it is a good idea to cut them back to about 4 inches. Some of the pseudobulbs may be completely rotted inside. These should be discarded and the plants cut back to clean and healthy tissue, for bulb rot can spread throughout the plant if all of it is not removed. Even after the plants have been divided and repotted, some pseudobulbs may continue to lose their leaves and to have a watery look. The only solution for this is to unpot such plants and cut back even further until every bit of disease has been eradicated.

Any backbulbs that appear sound and healthy and have a dormant eye may be placed in—not on—some damp sand, sphagnum moss, osmunda, or cymbidium mix deep enough so that they will stay in place; they should then be kept shaded and misted frequently. The dormant eyes should swell and grow within several months. Then they can be potted to make additional plants.

Omnium Gatherum

If variety is the spice of life, then diversity in the selection of plants should be the aim of every orchid grower. The more varied your collection, the more you will learn about the whole large family of orchids and the greater will be the chance of your having orchids continuously in bloom.

From the miniatures, both hybrids and species; to the botanicals, among which are to be found some of the rarest of orchids; to the interesting and sometimes flamboyant oddities; to those hardy enough to be grown as part of the outdoor garden wherever climate permits; through the fascinating realm of hybridization, where crossbreeding is giving us the orchids of the future—there is something for everyone. This is what makes orchid growing so satisfying and such a source of never-ending pleasure.

CHAPTER 14

MINIATURES

We have seen that it was not until the late 1700s and early 1800s that the first orchid species were discovered. Then, half a century later, the first hybrids were created. Many of these were quite large and none really small, but when the large estates were broken up, the huge greenhouses dismantled, and the owners had moved to smaller quarters, there came a need for smaller orchids. For once a person has been bitten by the orchid bug, he never loses his love for them.

We have seen how, for example, the dwarf cymbidiums that grew in Japan and South China were crossed with the large ones to create the miniatures suitable for windowsill culture and for growing under lights.

Then the hybridists set to work to see what could be done about miniaturizing other kinds, and collectors scoured the earth in search of tiny orchids, which they knew would be in great demand. Many of these fascinating little plants, both species and hybrids, seldom grow over 6 to 8 inches high, and some are as small as 3 inches, with flowers from near-microscopic to some that appear to be larger than the plants themselves. These miniatures are available from most commercial orchid growers and from amateur growers who are only too willing to share plants if it means introducing someone else to the delight of growing miniature orchids.

In the following list are sure to be many orchids that will bring delight to any grower. All need to be kept moist

Figure 14-1. Small orchids grow well in a lighted terrarium

and out of drafts, and although they benefit from a dilute solution of balanced water-soluble fertilizer, they also respond well to foliar feeding, or both, at 10-day intervals. The miniatures show some variation in their temperature requirements; if they do not respond at the temperatures advised for the large plants of the same genus, try growing them at slightly warmer ones.

Aeranthes. A native of Madagascar, whose name comes from the Greek word for "flower." It needs the same amount of light as cattleyas. The flowers are light green, summer-blooming, and fragrant.

Angraecum chloranthum. A native of Madagascar. Its name has been latinized from the Malayan word *Angrek,* or *Angurek,* which refers to its epiphytic habit. It has small green flowers in summer.

Brassavola glauca. A small plant native to Central America. The genus was named in honor of a Venetian nobleman, Professor Brassavola, and has been much used in hybridizing. Its springtime flowers are greenish white.

Brassavola nodosa. From Central America; known as the "lady of the night" because its white flowers are fragrant during the evening. It is also long-lived.

Broughtonia sanguinea. From Jamaica; often called the "orchid of Jamaica." Its flowers resemble the cattleyas and are red. This plant blossoms at any time of year and needs to be grown in a warm atmosphere.

Cattleya luteola. Native to Brazil and Peru; it has pale yellow 2-inch flowers during the late winter and early spring.

Dendrobium aracenites. From Laos; it blossoms during the summer. Its orange flowers look like spiders.

Dendrobium trinervum. From Laos; flowers in summer and has small white blossoms.

Epidendrum fragrans. From Mexico and the West Indies; it has 2-inch white to pale green flowers during the summer. It is particularly noted for its fragrance.

Epidendrum tampense. A native of southern Florida, the Bahamas, and Cuba. It has small, 1-inch pseudobulbs and slender leaves. The flowers are either reddish orange or reddish green and bloom in late spring and early summer.

295

Laelia pumila. From Brazil. Its flowers are white with a rose-colored lip and appear in late summer. It likes plenty of sun and rather high humidity and should never be allowed to dry out.

Masdevallia lilliputiana. One of the smallest of the masdevallias, its leaves are only $\frac{3}{4}$ inch long. The flowers are about $\frac{1}{2}$ inch wide and are cream-colored with red spots.

Masdevallia muscosa. This orchid has a slender, 6-inch stem and yellow flowers and is one of the most intriguing miniatures. Even the slightest breath on the lip of the flower causes the lip to shut, at first slowly and then with an accelerated and decided click that is audible. Woe betide the poor insect trapped inside the boat-shaped compartment. He stays there for a half-hour, after which time the lip opens and the insect, which by this time is covered with pollen, is released.

Oncidium bifolium. A native of Argentina; it has bright yellow flowers during the summer.

Oncidium puchellum. From Jamaica; it flowers in spring and has delightful white, pink, and lavender flowers.

Oncidium pumilum. Called the "burro ear"; it comes from Brazil. It flowers in late winter or early spring. The blossoms are waxy yellow, spotted with red.

Ornithocephalus inflexus. This orchid is just as attractive when not in bloom as when displaying its white flowers.

Paphiopedilum bellatum. A native of Thailand. Its 2-inch flowers are creamy with maroon dots; it flowers in summer.

Paphiopedilum concolor. From Thailand; it has flowers of white with purple dots during spring and summer.

Paphiopedilum niveum. From Thailand and Borneo; it flowers in spring and has white flowers dotted with purple. There are also some new hybrids created in recent years that, although having large flowers, are dwarfs in their growth habits and are known as the "pigmy paths."

Phalaenopsis lindenii. Has pink flowers with purple stripes in autumn.

Phalaenopsis maculata. Has white flowers with a touch of bright red on the lip.

Phalaenopsis porishii. Has white petals and brown sepals.

Phragmepedium schlimii. From Colombia. The 2-inch flowers are white and rose. It needs a cool, moist, and shady environment.

Renanthera, Tom Thumb. From Malaya. It is a spring bloomer, with orange-red flowers. The genus name refers to the kidney-shaped anthers.

Stenoglottis. A lovely terrestrial from Africa, with beautiful lavender flowers on short stems. Give it shade, a moderate temperature, and reasonable moisture while actively growing. Stenoglottis are deciduous, and after flowering the leaves dry up and fall off, at which time the plants should be rested. When new growths appear, watering can be increased.

Vanda laotica. There are two vegetative types, one of which is miniature. It is a cooler-growing orchid than most vandas and can stand temperatures as low as 45°F (7°C).

Jewel Orchids: Erythrodes

Of all the miniatures, none are lovelier than these, the *Erythrodes,* or "jewel orchids," which are found in the tropics and subtropics. They were first described by Blume in 1825. The common name refers to the reddish flowers. Nearly all are terrestrial, and most have creeping rhizomes. Their native habitat is the Philippines, New Guinea, and other Pacific Islands and the warmer areas of Southeast Asia, where they grow under trees that protect them from drying winds and direct sunlight.

Jewel orchids are noted for their beautifully variegated foliage, which is deep green with a network of gold and silver veins that makes them a welcome addition to any collection. In fact, they are more often grown for their foliage than their flowers.

Some growers consider them difficult but, if the potting material is rich and full of humus, they are grown in the shade, and the humidity is high, they are not the least bit difficult to handle. Jewel orchids must also be protected from drafts.

297 The potting material can include charcoal for drainage, screened tree-fern fiber, and an orchid mix that has been thoroughly screened. Whatever is used, it must be porous, as it should be for all terrestrial orchids. (Some growers also use a potting mix of bark, sphagnum moss, and finely shredded osmunda.) Instead of disturbing the roots by repotting each year, it is better to top-dress it, with new material replacing the top 2 inches of the old material.

A wide, shallow pan, pot, or wooden box is preferable to a standard pot, which is too tall for these plants. If the growing conditions suit them, they easily grow into specimen plants. Should a stem accidentally be broken off, it can be laid horizontally in a shallow container on top of the potting material and pinned down with a wire bent to hold the top of the stem vertically. Eventually, new shoots will grow out from this stem.

When potting, any of the old potting material that remains around the roots should be left there. The plants should be held in the center of the container in such a way that none of the leaves are buried. If the point where the stems and leaves join is buried, the chances of rot increase. In their native habitat, the rhizomes of these plants wander along the soil, giving the plant a horizontal growth pattern.

The potting material should be kept slightly moist at all times to encourage the plants to send out new roots. Old-time English growers placed their jewel orchids under bell-shaped glass jars, propping up one side to allow air to enter, but this is not necessary. Leaf growth is slow, with no more than three or four new leaves developing during each growing season.

The following are some outstanding examples of jewel orchids:

Anoectochilus. From Southeast Asia, India, and Sri Lanka (Ceylon). The leaves have a bright, shiny velvet look with a network of gold veins. The flowers are white.

Dossinia marmorata. A terrestrial plant from Borneo. It has dark velvet-green leaves with shades of brown and orange and the jewel orchid's network veins, in this case gold. Its flowers are white. The genus *Dossinia* was first found by E. Morren in 1848 and named in honor of the Belgian botonist E. P. Dossina.

Erythrodes. The leaves are yellow or brownish green, with prominently marked veins.

Erythrode nobile. Is called the "silver orchid," because its gray-green leaves have a silver veining. It has white flowers.

Goodyera. A terrestrial genus found in eastern North America, first described by Robert Brown in 1813. *Goodyera pubescens* has dark green leaves tinged with white and silver, making it a striking plant.

Haemaria. Now known as *Ludisia.* Terrestrial orchids whose native habitat is the tropical areas of Asia. As *Haemaria,* it was first described by Lindley in 1826; he gave it this name derived from the Greek word meaning "blood-red," which aptly describes the undersides of the leaves. As *Ludisia,* it was also found in 1826 and dedicated to the Spanish botanist Don Luis de Terres.

Figure 14-2. *Haemaria discolor* 'Nigrans,' ccm/aos

Ludisia discolor var. *dawsonianum* and *Ludisia discolor* var. *nigricans* are the all-time favorites among jewel orchids. They grow horizontally, making a shallow container for growing them mandatory. The same potting material suggested for other jewel orchids can be used. The plants also need a dilute solution of water-soluble fertilizer or fish emulsion once a week.

It is better not to mist these plants. The water in the axils of the leaves may cause rot. Rather, keep the surrounding atmosphere moist by damping down the floor in a greenhouse or placing small dishes of water among the plants grown indoors. Water often enough to prevent drying out.

The leaf colors are always brightest on the new growth. Remove all dead leaves promptly to keep the plants looking tidy.

In general, jewel orchids are at their best from May to November. The rest of the year they may look drab and some lose their leaves. When that happens, it does not mean that the plant is dead; it is resting. They can be prepared for their rest period by gradually reducing the amount of water and warmth starting in November, but even during rest they still must be watered and the atmosphere kept moist. They should not be completely rested (to the point of becoming absolutely dry) because all the leaves would fall off and it would be difficult for them to start into growth again in the spring.

INTERGENERIC HYBRIDS

An orchid hybrid is created when either a species or a hybrid is crossed with another species or hybrid, either by nature or by man. There are many natural hybrids throughout the world and, of course, many thousands created by man. The *bigeneric hybrids* have two distinct genera in their parentage. Some frequently grown ones are:

Ascocenda	Ascocentrum × Vanda
Brassolaelia	Brassavola × Laelia
Doritaenopsis	Doritis × Phalaenopsis
Epicattleya	Epidendrum × Cattleya
Epidrobium	Epidendrum × Dendrobium
Miltonidium	Miltonia × Oncidium
Odontioda	Odontoglossum × Cochlioda
Odontonia	Odontoglossum × Miltonia

Phaiocalanthe	Phaius × Calanthe
Sophrocattleya	Sophronitis × Cattleya
Sophrolaelia	Sophronitis × Laelia
Vandaenopsis	Vanda × Phalaenopsis

Trigeneric hybrids have three genera in their background, for example, the Brassolaeliocattleya, which was created from a Brassavola, a Laelia, and a Cattleya. Other trigeneric hybrids are:

Aliceara	Brassia × Miltonia × Oncidium
Ascovandoritis	Ascocentrum × Vanda × Doritis
Christiera	Aërides × Ascocentrum × Vanda
Colmanara	Miltonia × Odontoglossum × Oncidium
Dialaeliocattleya	Diacrium × Laelia × Cattleya
Epilaeliocattleya	Epidendrum × Laelia × Cattleya
Hagerara	Dorits × Phalaenopsis × Vanda
Phaläerianda	Phalaenopsis × Aërides × Vanda
Rhyndoropsis	Rhynchostylus × Doritis × Phalaenopsis

Quadrigeneric hybrids combine four genera, but rather than calling the plant by a name that includes each genus, a new name is generally coined. For example, Potinara contains a Brassavola, a Cattleya, a Laelia, and a Sophronitis. Some other examples are:

Allenara	Cattleya × Diacrium × Epidendrum × Laelia
Barbosaara	Cochloda × Gomesa × Odontoglossum × Oncidium
Beallara	Brassia × Cochlioda × Miltonia × Odontoglossum
Burrageara	Cochlioda × Miltonia × Odontoglossum × Oncidium
Onoara	Ascocentrum × Renanthera × Vanda × Vandopsis
Robinara	Aërides × Ascocentrum × Renanthera × Vanda
Vanderwegheara	Vanda × Ascocentrum × Doritis × Phalaenopsis

301   Some hybrids have as many as five genera in their

parentage; for example, the Goodlera has Brassia, Cochlioda, Miltonia, Odontoglossum, and Oncidium. The Rothara has Brassavola, Cattleya, Epidendrum, Laelia, and Sophronitis in its parentage.

Of course it is not possible to cross every orchid with every other and be certain of creating a new hybrid. Before an intergeneric or a multigeneric cross can be made, there must be a natural affinity between the genera. This also makes the culture of the resulting hybrids much simpler than it otherwise would be.

The first attempts at hybridizing by John Dominy were fraught with disappointment. Despite these failures, he was eminently successful in creating many outstanding hybrids, among which are:

Cattleya exeniensis	*Cattleya mossiae* × *Laelia crispa* (first flowered in 1863)
Cattleya devoniensis	*Cattleya guttata* × *Laelia crispa* (first flowered in 1863)
Phaius irroratus	*Phaius grandiflora* × *Calanthe vestita* (first flowered in 1866)
Paphiopedilum harrisianum	*Paphiopedilum villosium* × *Paphiopedilum barbatum* (first flowered in 1869)
Paphiopedilum vexillarium	*Paphiopedilum barbatum* × *Paphiopedilum fairieanum* (first flowered in 1870)
Laelia veitchiana	*Laelia crispa* × *Cattleya labiata* (first flowered in 1870)
Dendrobium dominianum	*Dendrobium nobile* × *Dendrobium linawianum* (first flowered in 1878)

Today, a little over 100 years later, hybridists are striving, among other things, to create plants that will flower more frequently than even the twice a year some do now and to create plants just as beautiful but more compact, allowing the grower to have many more in the same space. They are also striving to create strains of existing orchids that will grow in cooler temperatures.

It is also hoped that sometime in the future hybrids will be created that will prove disease-resistant. As we have seen, we are able to get virus-free plants of existing hybrids

through meristemming, but what is envisioned here are

hybrids that will be disease-resistant without the need of meristemming.

Orchids and orchid growing have come a long way since the early days of Dominy. Today's hybrids are sturdier and freer-flowering than their predecessors. By taking certain traits from each parent, hybridists hope to produce new shapes, new sizes, new colors, and hybrids that will be as easy or easier to grow than ordinary house plants

Newer and more vivid colors have been developed than were ever dreamed possible in the days of the first species and hybrids. Cattleyas now have handsome splotches of color on their sepals and petals, and phalaenopsis now come with peppermint stripes. There is a trend toward developing not only larger flowers in a greater variety of color, but also plants that will bear an increasing number of flowers on a stem and ones that will be more fragrant.

BOTANICALS

The word *botanical* is used to describe any orchids that are not grown commercially for their flowers. In fact, there are far more botanical orchids than the so-called commercial varieties.

Botanicals are frequently, but not always small-flowered. Most are extremely easy to grow and are hardy and vigorous. Some are small enough for growing on a windowsill. Others, somewhat larger, can be grown along with other orchids where there is more space. Many are rare enough to be collector's items.

The flowers of botanicals come in every color of the rainbow and just about any shape. Some have beautiful leaves, while others have no leaves at all. Most have an exquisite fragrance.

Although easy to grow, some botanicals may not adjust immediately to one's conditions. Give them time. Move them from place to place, from sun to shade, from warmth to coolness, until they show their liking for a particular place by suddenly making a spurt of growth.

Most botanicals can be potted in bark, particularly the epiphytes, with different grades used for different sizes of roots. They should be watered when they need it and fed a balanced fertilizer every two or three weeks.

Of the literally thousands of botanical orchids, we have room to touch upon just a few interesting ones here:

Bletia catenulata.   Found from Florida to Peru; terrestrial, with small pseudobulbs and small flowers.

Brassia.   Native to Florida, the West Indies, Mexico, Brazil, and Peru. Sometimes known as the "spider orchid." Many species are desirable and interesting.

Cyrtopodium paludiculum.   From Florida and South America; a large, terrestrial plant.

Sigmatostalex radicans.   A dwarf, with flowers less than $\frac{1}{4}$ inch in diameter.

Encyclia bracteata.   Has pseudobulbs and tiny flowers.

Leptotes bicolor and *unicolor.*   Dwarf plants, with stems only 1 inch long. The 2-to-4-inch flowers of the unicolor are purple; those of the bicolor are purple and white.

Pleurathallis.   An epiphyte that has extremely tiny flowers.

Bulbophyllum masenii.   An epiphyte, with very small flowers.

Rodriguezia secunda.   Has pseudobulbs in clusters, with from one to as many as six flower stalks on each. The white and rose flowers are $\frac{1}{2}$ inch in diameter.

Angraecum.   Native to Africa and the Indian Ocean islands. Most of the flowers are white and shaped like stars. *Angraecum sesquipedale* is known as the "Star of Bethlehem" because it flowers at Christmastime.

INTERESTING ODDITIES

It would take a book several times this size to discuss every orchid known. Many are rare species and seldom seen; others have never become popular for one reason or another. We shall consider here just a few that, although not as well known as the orchids discussed previously, have found their way into many collections, where they add beauty and interest.

Masdevallias

Masdevallias are extraordinary orchids. Some are true miniatures with leaves less than 2 or 3 inches high, while others are truly giants. It is a large genus, of over 300 species and hybrids. Most are epiphytic, although a relatively small

Figure 14-3. *Masdevallia coccinea* 'Chester Hills,' CCM/AOS

number are terrestrials. They grow wild throughout Central America, Ecuador, Peru, Brazil, and Costa Rica, with the majority in the Colombian Andes at elevations of 6000 to 12,000 feet, where they are subject to fogs, heavy dews, and frequent rain.

Masdevallias have no pseudobulbs. Their evergreen leaves grow closely together, and are covered with a papery sheathing; the flower stems develop from the bases of the leaves.

Masdevallias were established as a genus in 1794 by Ruiz and Paven and named in honor of the eighteenth-century Spanish physician and botanist Dr. José Masdevall. *Masdevallia chelsonii* was the first hybrid and was created in 1880 by Veitch, the well-known English orchidist. They were much admired during the early 1900s and then suffered a drop in popularity.

Flowers

The flowers are among the most unusual, with extremely large sepals and small petals. They range from 1 inch to over 1 foot in diameter. Some of the sepals are so long they resemble tails. The flowers of the *Masdevallis coccinea* group are the showiest, the most colorful, and the largest.

Many masdevallias are only of botanical interest, while others, with brilliantly colored flowers of white, red, and purple, along with other color combinations, have become increasingly popular during the last few years. The flowers never open all at once. There is an interval of from several weeks to months from the time the first flower opens until the last one appears.

Temperature

Masdevallias are cool-growing orchids and need temperatures of 50–60°F (10–15°C) at night. Even temperatures a few degrees cooler will not harm them. They must also have cool growing conditions during the summer, to get them not only to flower but to grow well. The day temperature should not go above 70°F (21°C), which is what they are used to when growing in their native habitats.

Light

These orchids cannot tolerate strong sunlight and therefore need to be shaded. A light intensity between 1800 and 2400 footcandles is adequate, and their leaves should remain dark green.

Humidity and Ventilation

Masdevallias require a moist atmosphere at all times. The humidity should be between 40 and 60%. During the warm weather the area around the plants should be kept damp and the plants lightly misted several times a day. They need as much fresh air as it is possible to give them without their becoming overheated or chilled.

Watering

During the summer masdevallias need to have an abundance of water at their roots, and even in winter they should have enough water to keep the potting material moist but not soggy at all times. Their growth is continuous. They have no pseudobulbs in which to store water and need no rest period.

Feeding

Masdevallias are extremely light feeders. A dilute solution of a balanced, water-soluble fertilizer is recommended. Use one-quarter the normal amount of a fertilizer such as 20–20–20 or 18–18–18. Plants growing in osmunda need no additional food, but those in bark should be fed every three weeks.

Potting

Since masdevallias need an abundance of water, adequate provision should be made for drainage. Either osmunda or fine-grade bark such as is used for seedlings, with some sphagnum moss mixed in, can be used for the epiphytes. For terrestrials, the potting material should contain some peat moss, perlite, and sand.

Clay pots should be used with osmunda, while those plants whose leaves form dense tufts are best grown in baskets. Masdevallias do not have deep roots, and hence grow better in shallow pots or containers. Since masdevallias dislike being disturbed, repot only every three years.

When dividing becomes necessary because a plant's center has died out, it is best done in the autumn or early winter, when the plant is making new growth. The roots can be gently pulled apart. Then place each new plant firmly in the smallest pot that will allow several years' growth.

Care after Potting

Although at first glance this may seem to be drastic treatment, if a plant refuses to flower, placing it in the food compartment of the refrigerator for several hours a day for about a week will invariably shock it into initiating flower buds. When one recalls that the temperature where they grow in the wild often falls to 45°F (−2°C), this treatment doesn't seem at all severe. However, continuously cold temperatures over a long period will inhibit growth.

Coelogynes   The name *Coelogyne* is derived from two Greek words, *koiles,* meaning "hollow," and *gyne,* meaning "female"—referring to the hollow stigma that is deeply recessed in most of these plants. There are over 125 species in this genus, first recognized by Lindley in 1822. At that time he used the name to describe *coelogyne cristata,* collected in Nepal, which is one of the easiest of all orchids to grow.

Although a few are terrestrial, the most popular coelogynes are epiphytes. They are found throughout Southeast Asia, including New Guinea and the Fiji and Philippine Islands, and from the Himalayas of Tibet and China down to Indonesia, Malaysia, Sri Lanka, and Thailand. Some grow at high altitudes; others grow nearer sea level.

The size of the pseudobulbs varies, with most being egg shaped. Ordinarily they are a medium to a dark green in color and slightly fluted. There are usually two leaves from each pseudobulb, although there may be as many as four. The leaves vary. Some are soft and pleated. Others are quite leathery.

Flowers

The flower spikes appear with the new growth emerging from the center. There may be one flower to a spike or many.

The flowers develop during the winter and spring. The most famous and undoubtedly the most beautiful of these

Figure 14-4. *Coelogyne cristata* 'Orchid Hill,' CCM

orchids is *coelogyne cristata,* which, since it comes from the Himalayas, grows best where the temperature is cool. Along with the basic white color, the flowers, which hang in drooping sprays, can also be brown, yellow, or green and have distinctive markings in contrasting colors.

Temperature

Depending upon their habitat, the plants require a night temperature of from 50°F (10°C), and lower during the winter, to 60–65°F (15–17°C) if they come from the warmer areas.

Light and Shading

Coelogynes need a bright but diffused light of about 2400–3600 footcandles. The amount of shading they need is determined by the intensity of the light. On clear, cloudless days they need to be shaded from the hot sun.

Humidity

Humidity should be between 40 and 70%. The lesser amount is better for the cooler-growing plants, while those that come from warmer areas need the higher humidity.

Watering

While the plants are growing actively they need an abundance of water, but after the growths have matured they should be kept moderately dry, but never allowed to dry out completely. Those plants that have hard, thick pseudobulbs, like *coelogyne nervosa,* can go a long time between waterings during the winter, sometimes as much as three weeks, while *coelogyne cristata* and others with soft pseudobulbs should have only a slight decrease in the amount of water.

Feeding

Coelogynes are not heavy feeders. If growing in osmunda, other than an occasional foliar feeding they need not be fertilized. If potted in bark or orchid mix, the plants will respond well to monthly feedings with a balanced fertilizer.

Potting

All potting should be done after the plants have finished flowering and as soon as the new roots emerge. Coelogynes dislike intensely being disturbed. So pot only when absolutely necessary—when the pseudobulbs are crowded and growing over the side of the pot. This is also the time when the plant may be divided.

Coelogynes take a long time, often several years, to reestablish themselves after potting, but by the second year the plants usually have recovered sufficiently to produce blooms.

A good potting material consists of osmunda and sphagnum moss. Straight bark can also be used. The plants can be grown in either pots or baskets, with the latter particularly useful for those that have a straggly habit of growth. All the old potting material should be shaken off and all the dead roots removed. Old pseudobulbs can also be cut off, so that if the plant is not to be grown as a specimen, the new plant will have only three or four new leads.

If a specimen plant is desired, the dead pseudobulbs in the center should be removed and the remaining sections placed in the pot in such a way that most of the new growths will be at the center.

Care after Potting

Some shading is needed for tender young growths. When watering, be sure that water does not become lodged in the young growths, for they easily rot. Newly potted plants also need to be kept warmer than established ones.

When the flower spikes appear, the amount of moisture from both watering and misting needs to be carefully watched. Too much moisture causes the young spikes to turn black and decay.

Resting

Coelogynes need a decided rest after the leaves and pseudobulbs have developed fully until the time the plant is ready to flower. The leaves are not shed, which means that the plants need some water and an occasional misting.

Cycnoches   There is no orchid whose name is more appropriate or more aptly describes its flowers than the *Cycnoche*, which is known as the "Swan Orchid." The long, narrow curving column on the flowers closely resembles the head and neck of a swan, and cycnoches in flower are indeed a memorable sight. It is also one of the most fragrant of orchids. Early in the morning the fragrance can be overpowering.

There are fewer than a dozen species, and their native habitats range from Mexico to Peru and Brazil. The plants have long pseudobulbs shaped like cylinders whose upper part is sheathed by the base of the leaves. Each pseudobulb has anywhere from a few to many leaves, which are soft and, like the coelogynes, pleated. The leaves grow up to $1\frac{1}{2}$ feet in length and 1 foot in width.

Because these plants are deciduous, there are times when they are completely leafless. It is then that the flowers develop. During the late autumn they should be kept dry.

Flowers

The flower spikes develop from the tops of the pseudobulbs and have green, yellow, or brown flowers spotted with purplish brown dots. Oddly, this genus produces male or female flowers or both on the same plant at the same time and sometimes hermaphroditic or bisexual ones as well. The female flowers have the larger lips and are, by far, the more beautiful. The male flower shows a marked difference in its lip, which is smaller and more disclike. Most plants flower during summer and fall, but there are some that blossom at various other times of the year.

Temperature

To assure the growths will be strong and sturdy, they need a warm and humid atmosphere during the summer. In winter, when the plants are somewhat dormant, the night temperature should not fall below 60°F (21°C), nor should the dry temperature rise above 85°F (29°C).

Light and Shading

Up high in a greenhouse, where they will be nearer the
311   light, is the ideal place to grow cycnoches. Between 2400

Figure 14-5 (opposite).
Cycnoches hakgii 'Heritage,
CCM

and 3600 footcandles provide adequate light. However, some shading from the hot sun is always necessary because the plants grow best when the light is diffused.

Humidity and Ventilation

The humidity should be moderate. During the summer keep the air circulating freely around the plants, with fans to help offset the high humidity that, without the fans, would tend to stagnate the air.

Watering

Watering cycnoches is a very exact procedure. Water thoroughly about once every week or 10 days. Then allow them to dry somewhat before watering again. If the potting material is not porous and does not drain easily, there is danger of the roots rotting. Also, keep the water off the plant and confined only to the pot to prevent crown rot.

Feeding

Even when the plants have been potted in osmunda they need to be fed while actively growing. A balanced fertilizer such as 18–18–18 at half the recommended strength for orchids every other week keeps them healthy.

Potting

Being epiphytes, cycnoches grow best in baskets or pans hung high, where the light is good, yet still diffused.

The potting material can be osmunda, bark, or one of the mixes, but it should always be coarse and porous, as in a paphiopedilum-cymbidium mix. Some sand can also be added.

The baskets or pans need a layer of crock at the bottom to assure adequate drainage, and potting is best done in the spring, just as the new growths are several inches high and the new roots are beginning to develop. The old, dried pseudobulbs should be removed, and when dividing a plant, pull the pseudobulbs apart gently instead of cutting them. Trim the roots back to 2 inches. Each pseudobulb should be tied to a stake so it will grow up straight.

313

Care after Potting

Cycnoche plants should *not* be placed in the shade after they have been potted, as is recommended for most other orchids. Instead, place them where the light is bright yet diffused. They should not be given too much water until the new growths begin. Then they can be watered and fed on a regular schedule until the growth is completed. At that time all feeding should stop and the amount of water be reduced. Although the flowers appear when the pseudobulbs start to lose their leaves, the plant continues to flower.

Resting

Cycnoches must rest when their leaves drop off. Some need a rest period of several months, while others always seem to be in some stage of growth. While resting, rely more upon frequent misting to keep them alive and less on pot watering. During the resting period, the plants can be left in their pots or taken out and divided.

Calanthes

Two Greek, words *kolos,* meaning "beautiful," and *anthes,* meaning "a flower," combine to give this native of Asia, Australia, and Africa its name. Robert Brown, an English botanist who among other things is credited with the discovery of the nucleus of a cell, gave this orchid its name. There are over 150 species of this "beautiful flower."

Types

Calanthes are mostly terrestrial and are divided into two groups based upon their vegetative habit. Those that are evergreen have small, cormlike pseudobulbs, and those that are deciduous have larger, more angular pseudobulbs. Each pseudobulb, in turn, has several large leaves whose surfaces appear pleated. The leaves grow from 1 to 4 feet long and from 3 to 8 inches wide.

Flowers

The flower stems develop from the bases of the bases of the pseudobulbs, and in some plants, such as *Calanthe veitchii,* the stem has a spray of three or four beautiful pink flowers.

Figure 14-6. *Calanthe vestita* 'Regnierii'

The advice below is primarily for the deciduous types. The modifications necessary for growing the evergreen types are given at the end of the section.

Temperature and Humidity

Calanthes require temperatures that are high, 75–80°F (22–26°C) during the summer. In winter they can stand night temperatures between 55-60°F (10–15°C). During their active growth, calanthes also require a moist environment, with the humidity around 60%.

Light

Between 2400 and 3600 footcandles provide the proper amount of light. Toward the end of summer, after the leaves have developed, the plants need more light in order for the pseudobulbs to mature and ripen, which is necessary if the plants are to flower. At this time, the more sunlight the plant receives without its leaves becoming burned, the better.

Feeding and Watering

Calanthes are heavy feeders. Give a dilute, balanced fertilizer, such as 18–18–18, every week during the growing period. Always water thoroughly when watering. The potting material must be kept moist during the growing period.

Potting

Potting should be done in the spring as soon as the plant ends its rest period and vegatative growths begin to show. Since straight bark or osmunda do not provide these plants with the rich potting material they need there should also be some loam, sphagnum, moss and peat moss—or loam, perlite, and sand—in the mixture. The pots also need a heavy layer of crock in the bottom for drainage, since these plants need large amounts of water.

All the old potting material should be removed from the roots, which should be trimmed back to only a few inches long. Use only pseudobulbs from the previous year's growth; these are the ones that will bear the flowers. Although as many as six can be put in one container to make a specimen plant, if space is limited, one or two pseudobulbs can be put into a small pot. In fact, the calanthe is one of the orchids that can be potted with just one pseudobulb per pot. (They produce better spikes when one bulb is grown in a pot just large enough to accommodate it.) The remaining pseudobulbs that have no new vegetative growths can be potted separately and should themselves produce new pseudobulbs, which will flower the following year.

The pseudobulbs should be placed so the new growths will be toward the center of the pot. If possible, provide some warmth beneath the pots so the new growths will develop more rapidly. Bottom heat is advisable only until the new growths have developed.

Care after Potting

Both the roots and the new leaves appear at the same time. When the plants are watered see that the centers of the plants, where the new growths are developing, do not become wet. This causes rot. Until the new roots and growths reach several inches, the atmosphere around the plants should be kept more moist, but they should not be given too much pot watering.

As the growths lengthen, they will need more water to keep the potting material moist, and this need for water makes the drainage important, since these new growths are tender. They should be shaded to prevent burning from the sun.

When the plants are fully grown, place them where the light is stronger—in full sunlight, if the plants can stand it—with shading provided when necessary.

Eventually the leaves turn yellow and drop off. This is natural with the deciduous type. The flower spike develops when the leaves have fully matured. It is then that the plants will need more water to prevent the spikes from becoming stunted.

When calanthes are in flower most of the leaves will drop off, but even without leaves the plants must still be watered for the flowers to remain in good condition. To make the flowers last, keep the plants in a cooler, less humid atmosphere. Then, when flowering is completed, the plant should be kept dry. It can remain in the same pot or be taken out and stored in a dry place during its rest period, which always follows flowering. Cut off the old flower spike at the base of the pseudobulb.

Evergreen Calanthes

Evergreen calanthes are considered more tropical than the deciduous ones. They require the same basic growing conditions with but one exception: the plants should never become completely dried out after they flower. They should merely be kept somewhat drier than while actively growing, until the new roots and growths appear in the spring. The potting material is the same as that above, as are also the temperature, humidity, light, feeding, and watering.

Phaius The phaius is often called the "Nun's Orchid," because of the hooded appearance of the petals and sepals, which resemble a nun whose face is enclosed in a white hood lined with brown. The name comes from the Greek word *phaios*, which means "swarthy" or "dusky" and refers to the yellow-brown coloring of the fragrant flowers.

These orchids grow wild throughout the warm parts of Asia, the Malayan Peninsula, Madagascar, Sri Lanka, Australia, and the islands of the Pacific. The first phaius orchid *Phaius tankervilliae,* was brought to England from China in 1778 by D. John Fothergill. This genus has only about 20 species, some of which are terrestrial and some epiphytic; it is the terrestrial plants that are most frequently seen and grown.

The pseudobulbs, which are almost hidden by the sheaths at the bases of the leaves, are short and set close together. Some grow at intervals along the rhizomes, which creep as they grow. Others are so thin they are almost like stems. Each pseudobulb has from two to eight large, thin, heavily ribbed leaves, which can grow up to 4 feet long and 10 inches wide.

Types

There are two types: the large-flowered, warm-growing kind that comes from Asia; and the small, more brightly flowered plants from Madagascar. Fortunately, both are among the easiest of orchids to grow and readily adapt themselves to conditions in a house or greenhouse or outdoors.

Flowers

The flower stalks grow from the bases of the rhizomes at the same place that the leaves do. Phaius flower from late

Figure 14-7. *Phaius grandifolius* 'Jean,' CCM

winter into summer, with numerous handsome $4\frac{1}{2}$-inch flowers on their two to four flower spikes. The flowers are quite showy.

Temperature

Phaius are tropical plants and therefore need warm temperatures. Yet they are adaptable enough to be grown where the temperatures are in the intermediate range, although during the winter the night temperature should not fall below 55°F (13°C).

Light

Phaius should be grown where the light is strong, but like most terrestrial orchids, they need to be shaded during the hottest part of the day to prevent burning. The most shading is needed during summer, and the greatest light intensity from early autumn on.

Watering

During the summer, when they can and really should be grown outdoors, phaius need an abundance of water. During the winter, when the leaves become disheveled, they still need water, but less frequently.

The water should be kept off the leaves and particularly away from the lower ones, which means that these orchids should not be misted.

Feeding

Like most orchids whose potting material contains loam, phaius are heavy feeders. They respond well when they have a balanced fertilizer every week during the growing season.

Potting

Potting should be done early in the year, just as the new growth makes its appearance. At this time the pseudobulbs can be split into small groups. The plants seem to flower better when they do not wait too long between pottings. Generally, plants need repotting every second year.

The potting material should be fibrous yet firm and should contain some loam, osmunda or finely shredded bark, sphagnum moss, and sand. The Madagascan phaius are more delicate than those from Asia, and therefore must be protected from drafts, both hot and cold.

Resting

Phaius have a rest period after flowering when they need less water and slightly lower temperatures.

Propagation

Once the plant has completed its flowering, the flower stems can be cut just below the first flower. These stems will be a foot or so long. Below each bract on the stem is a

Omnium Gatherum — bud capable of growing into a new plant. The stems can be laid horizontally in a pan of moist sphagnum moss with both ends of the stem buried in the moist moss. The pan should then be placed in the shade, and in a relatively short time new little plants will develop. When their roots are several inches long, the new plants can be snapped off the stem and put into small pots.

Lycastes — Among the showiest of orchids are the lycastes, a genus first described by Dr. Lindley in the early 1800s and named in honor of Lycasta, who myth tells us was the beautiful daughter of Priam, the last King of Troy. There are 35 known species, epiphytic and semiterrestrial. Lycastes grow wild throughout tropical America from sea level to the high mountains of Mexico, Peru, Brazil, and Guatemala.

The hard, oval pseudobulbs of lycastes have from one to three soft, thin, spear-shaped leaves, which remain on

Figure 14-8. *Lycaste imshootiana* 'Karen,' CCM

Courtesy American Orchid Society

the plant for about a year. These leaves are attractive and may reach $2\frac{1}{2}$ feet long and 6 inches wide. A few leaves drop off each year, but this is natural. The more deciduous ones have prickly spines on the tops of the pseudobulbs after the leaves fall.

Just as the native habitats of lycastes vary, so too do their cultural needs. Try growing them at first with the plain-leaf paphiopedilums. If these conditions do not prove suitable, change them to suit the plants.

Flowers

The flower stems develop from the base of the last pseudo-bulb and have large $4\frac{1}{2}$-inch flowers of pink, red, orange, brown, green, and yellow, with blotches on the lips. The sepals are larger than the petals, which gives the flowers a triangular shape. Many are long-lasting and heavily scented.

Temperature and Ventilation

The majority of lycastes grow comfortably with night temperatures between 55 and 60°F (13–15°C) during the winter. In summer thay can tolerate higher ones. When the new growths are developing, higher temperatures help the pseudobulbs to grow larger, but if possible, the temperature should not go above 85°F (30°C).

Lycastes need an abundance of fresh air, not only to keep the temperature at a reasonable level but also to ensure that the atmosphere will always be buoyant.

Light and Shade

Light is an important aspect of lycaste culture. They grow best in a light intensity of between 1500 and 2400 footcandles—in other words, moderate light. Like paphiopedilums, they must be shaded not only from too much direct sunlight but also from too bright light. If there is too much heat or sunlight, the plants drop their leaves to conserve water.

On the other hand, too much shade makes the growth weak and incapable of standing without being staked. During the autumn, when the plants have matured, they should have more light, but always with some protection during the hottest part of the day, and there should be sufficient space between the plants so that they receive both enough light and good air circulation.

Humidity and Water

Humidity should be moderate, between 40 and 60%; when the plants are actively growing they need an abundance of water. By autumn the growths will have matured and will need less water, at least for about two weeks, so the pseudobulbs can mature and harden.

When watering, take care to prevent the water from lodging in the young growths, for the emerging leaves quickly become spotted and then decay. Neither should the leaves themselves ever be wet. Misting is not necessary and can cause disease.

Feeding

A steady supply of a balanced fertilizer applied to the potting material twice a month is helpful.

Potting

Lycastes need a potting material that drains easily, provides aeration for the roots, and yet holds moisture. They can be grown in straight osmunda or bark or in a mixture of loam, sphagnum moss, osmunda, and sand, as is used for cymbidiums. The pots should have a heavy layer of crock to facilitate drainage.

The best time to repot is as soon as the plants have finished flowering. The new young growths and roots often appear at the same time as the flowers. Since they grow quickly, the potting should be done as soon as possible so the new roots and growths will not be too disturbed.

Lycastes should be repotted every other year. If a specimen plant is desired, all the pseudobulbs in good condition are placed in one pot. Otherwise, it is better to place only two or three pseudobulbs in a pot. The remaining bulbs can be put singly or in twos in small pots and placed where it is warm until the new growths and roots have had a chance to grow.

Resting

Lycastes have a definite rest period in winter, when they should only be watered enough to keep the pseudobulbs from shriveling. This sets the stage for a good production of flowers.

Spathoglottis

Spathoglottis are found over a large part of the Orient and in India, the Philippines, Australia, China, and Samoa. They are terrestrial, with some evergreen and others deciduous.

There are over 40 species in this genus, which was first described by the Dutch botanist Karl Ludwig Blume in 1825. The genus's name is derived from the Greek words *spathe*, meaning "spatula," and *glottis*, meaning "tongue," alluding to the sheath at the base of the leaves as well as to the lip on the flowers.

Figure 14-9. *Spathoglottis plicata*

These orchids are tall and have small, round, cormlike pseudobulbs unlike those of any other orchid. They grow close together and have four lance-shaped, strikingly veined leaves growing out from the top of each pseudobulb.

Flowers

The flower stems are also tall and slender and emerge from the bases of the pseudobulbs. Each stem carries clusters of up to two dozen flowers, ranging from yellow to lavender. Flowering is usually in summer and lasts into early autumn. The flower's three-lobed lip is its most distinctive feature.

Temperature and Light

Since these plants come from the warmest parts of the Orient, they should be grown in a warm, moist atmosphere where during the winter the night temperature does not fall below 60°F (15°C). At all other times they can stand heat as long as there is a good circulation of air.

They also stand full sunlight, provided they are given enough shading during the hottest hours to prevent the foliage from becoming burned. Some grow better in less light, about 2000 footcandles, but this can only be determined by moving the plants from one location to another.

Watering

Spathoglottis are large plants and need an abundance of water while growing actively. The deciduous kind do go through a rest period. Then they need less water and should have somewhat cooler temperatures.

Potting and Feeding

All potting should be done early in the spring, when the new growths first appear. Since the plants need water frequently, the pots require a heavy layer of crock at the bottom for good drainage.

The usual potting material is one that consists of loam, sphagnum moss, sand, and some osmunda. The addition of leaf mold to this mix provides some additional nutrients. However, spathoglottis are not heavy feeders, and if given a balanced fertilizer once a month, it keeps them growing vigorously.

Stanhopeas   A hanging basket of stanhopeas with an abundance of large, fragrant flowers growing out through the bottom of the basket makes a dramatic addition to any greenhouse. They are eye-catching and ever so much more graceful than the other standby, the staghorn fern.

Stanhopeas are natives of tropical America, from Mexico to Brazil and Peru. Their egg-shaped pseudobulbs are 2 to 3 inches high, each with a single deeply ribbed, broad leaf, which grows to 15 inches long and 6 inches wide.

There are about 25 species in this genus, which was named in honor of Philip Henry, the fourth Earl of Stanhope, President of the London Medico-Botanical Society at the time the orchid was discovered. In Mexico the stanhopea is known as *el toro* ("the bull") because of the hornlike projection on the flower's lip.

Figure 14-10.   *Stanhopea wardii* 'Stoney Point,' CCM

Flowers

The flowers, of which there may be as many as eight on a spike, are large, beautiful, and extremely fragrant. The sepals are somewhat larger than the petals, and the lips are both thick and waxy. Although each flower lasts only four or five days, the plant flowers freely.

Temperature, Light, and Shade

Grow stanhopeas where the temperature is always warm and never falls below 60°F (15°C) and in semishade where the light is filtered.

Watering and Humidity

While they are actively growing, stanhopeas must be kept moist at all times. The humidity will be increased and the plants will receive the additional moisture they need if the foliage is frequently misted, for the plants quickly deteriorate when the surrounding air is too dry.

Feeding

While the growths are developing, the plant should be generously fed with a balanced fertilizer such as 18–18–18 every three weeks. After the growths have matured, the amount of fertilizer should be reduced to one half and applied only once a month.

Potting

Stanhopeas should be potted in open-mesh baskets that can be suspended from the top of the greenhouse. A mixture of osmunda and sphagnum moss makes a good potting material and should be replaced each spring when the new growths first appear. It is always a temptation to want to grow these to specimen size, not only because of their unique appearance, but also because it is sometimes believed that the larger the plant, the more flowers there will be. Unfortunately, this is not always true. When the pseudobulbs become crowded together, it cuts down the production of flowers.

Pot only healthy pseudobulbs. If necessary, divide the plants so there will be enough room in each pot for the pseudobulbs and the new growths.

327

Resting

During the winter, stanhopeas go dormant. At this time the temperature should be lower, and they should be watered only enough to keep them alive. During the warm months, the plants produce great quantities of roots that tend to die off during their resting period.

Zygopetalums

The present-day classification of the genus *Zygopetalum* includes about 20 species. At one time it included a number of species that have since been assigned to other genera, such as the *Huntleya, Pescatorea, Warscewiczella, Colox,* and *Otostylis.*

These orchids grow wild throughout Central and South America, particularly from Peru to Venezuela. The first plant came from Brazil in the early 1800s and was established as a genus by Sir William Hooker, the first director of the Royal Botanic Garden at Kew.

The name *Zygopetalum* is derived from the Greek words *zygos,* meaning "yoke," and *petalon,* meaning "petal." The true zygopetalums, such as *Zygopetalums mackayi, intermedium,* and *crinitum* and the hybrids made from them, have medium to large egg-shaped pseudobulbs about 4 inches tall with prominent sheaths. As the pseudobulbs mature they become wrinkled, and the sheaths turn brown and become fibrous. The leaves are handsomely veined and attractive and grow to about 18 inches.

Zygopetalums are both monopodial and sympodial. The semiterrestrial plants should be grown in a potting material that contains loam, while those that are epiphytic prefer osmunda or bark.

Flowers

The flower stalks develop from the bases of the pseudobulbs and have anywhere from three to a dozen fragrant flowers of green or greenish white with blotches of purple or brown. The lip is white and heavily veined in lavender.

Temperature, Light, and Shade

At night the temperature should not go below 50°F (15°C), and during the day it should only rise 5–10°F. Zygopetalums require a lot of light, somewhere between 2400 and 3600

Figure 14-11. *Zygopetalum* Arthur Elle 'Elmhurst,' AM/AOS

footcandles, and seem to grow best in a western or south-western exposure. They should also be shaded from the hot sun to prevent burning and dehydration.

Humidity and Ventilation

Zygopetalums should be grown where the humidity is, preferably, 70% and never lower than 40%. They also need good air circulation.

Watering, Feeding, and Potting

Zygopetalums must be kept moist all year, receiving the most moisture during the summer, but water must not remain at the bases of the leaves, for the young growths are susceptible to rot. A balanced fertilizer applied to the potting material once a month will keep them well fed. Some zygopetalums can be wired to tree-fern slabs and benefit from foliar feeding. Others can be grown in pots, shallow pans, or baskets.

The flower spikes, young growths, and new roots all appear at the same time. Since this is also the time they should be repotted, extra care is necessary to prevent damage to the roots. If it is impossible to pot without breaking the roots, it is better to wait until the plant has flowered and the spike has been removed.

Pot in bark, osmunda, or tree fern. In the case of those that can be grown as terrestrial plants, add loam.

Promenaeas

There is also a group of dwarf orchids known as *promenaeas* that are related to the zygopetalums. The promenaeas were so named by Dr. Lindley in honor of a priestess in the ancient Greek town of Dodona. These are little plants and are handsome with their grayish green pseudobulbs and leaves and small, yellow flowers. Although their culture is basically the same, the potting material should contain loam.

Rhynchostylis

The genus *Rhynchostylis*, known as the "FoxTail Orchid," is closely related to the vandas. It was first described by Karl Blume in 1825, when he discovered it on a trip to Japan. It is an extremely small genus of stout, epiphytic

Figure 14-12. *Rhynchostylis gigantea* 'Dolly,' ccm

orchids with monopodial growth. The only four known
species are distributed through Burma, Indochina, Malaysia,
Java, and the Philippines.

These orchids have no pseudobulbs and range in height
from 8 inches to 4 feet. The leaves, which grow close together
on stout stems, are thick and leathery. Some are small, while
others grow to be a foot long.

Flowers

The name *foxtail* was given to the plant because its 1-inch,
sweetly scented and brightly colored white, red, and blue
331   flowers—which emerge from the axils of the leaves—cascade

down from the stem in the manner of a fox's bushy tail. Although summer is the usual time for them to flower, some plants regularly flower twice a year.

Temperature and Light

Rhynchostylis are tropical orchids and require warm growing conditions. The night temperature during the winter should not go below 60–65°F (15–18°C). During the day, the temperature can rise to 70–80°F (21–27°C).

The plants need between 2400 and 3600 footcandles of light and should always be shaded from the hot mid-day sun.

Humidity, Watering, and Misting

Since they are tropical orchids, rhynchostylis revel in high humidity, around 70%.

Although the potting material should not become soggy, the plants should be kept moist and well watered throughout the year. When not flowering, they can be misted both to increase the humidity and to help to cool the leaves on warm summer days.

Potting and Feeding

Rhynchostylis should be potted in baskets of cypress or redwood rather than in pots. They need plenty of room so that the roots can grow out into the air, and the baskets make this possible. Another advantage of baskets is that the potting material can easily be removed or replenished when necessary without disturbing the plants. Since the roots intertwine between the mesh of the baskets, the plants should be taken out as infrequently as possible. In February, the potting material can be checked and if necessary replaced with some fresh material.

A balanced fertilizer such as 18–18–18 once a month provides them with enough food, although when actively growing they also benefit from foliar feeding.

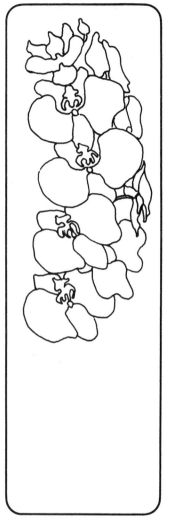

If You Want to Exhibit

In practically every country where orchids are grown there are orchid societies, most of which hold monthly meetings at which guest speakers bring to the attention of the members new and interesting facets of culture and growing techniques. Most of these societies also feature exhibitions to which the members are encouraged to bring their plants for judging and commendation. Orchid growers who do not reside near London, where the Royal Horticultural Society's Orchid Committee meets, or near one of the American Orchid Society's Regional Judging Centers are thus given an opportunity to receive the benefit of the judges' appraisal of their plants and flowers.

CHAPTER 15

The AOS Regional Judging Centers are located in Philadelphia; New York City; Washington, D.C.; St. Louis; Ann Arbor; Atlanta; Seattle; Oakland; San Francisco; Los Angeles; Costa Mesa, Calif.; Tampa, Fla.; San Antonio, Texas; and Honolulu, Maui, and Hilo, Hawaii.

Awards in the form of certificates and ribbons reward growers' cultural achievements and provide them with much appreciated accolades. When the monthly meetings are expanded into orchid shows and a certified American Orchid Society or other national orchid society judge is the evaluator, the awards become even more meaningful.

JUDGING CRITERIA AND SYSTEM

Just as England was where the growing of orchids as a hobby first began in the 1800s, so, too, it was in England that a system of evaluating orchid species and hybrids first came into being. Robert A. Rolfe, founder and first editor of England's prestigious *Orchid Review,* along with Frederick K. Sander, who later became known as the "Orchid King," began a systematic compilation in 1920 of the species and hybrids known up to that time along with the names of their antecedents. This list was later published as *Sander's List of Orchid Hybrids.* Well over a century ago the Orchid Committee of the Royal Horticultural Society took over the judging and evaluation of orchids. Out of a myriad of plants its judges selected the finest of the species and the most outstanding of the hybrids and awarded them Awards of Merit or First Class Certificates.

At the very beginning of this monumental endeavor it was decided by the judges that no plant would receive an award unless its flowers were superior to that of the plant first receiving the award for that particular species or hybrid. As each award took its place in the *Awards Register,* a painting was made of the plant so that subsequent flowers could be compared with it. Many of the paintings, mostly in watercolor, are still in existence and are treasured by those fortunate enough to possess them.

In 1956 the rules of the Royal Horticultural Society were changed so that today in order to receive an award a plant does not have to be superior to the original recipient.

An Award of Merit (A.O.M.) is bestowed on plants

that are deemed to be meritorious. A First Class Certificate (F.C.C.) is bestowed upon plants of great excellence. A Preliminary Commendation (P.C.) is given to new plants that show promise.

The American Orchid Society was founded in Boston in 1922, yet many American-bred hybrids continued to be registered in *Sander's List of Orchid Hybrids.* As the number of orchid growers in the United States increased, it became desirable to initiate a system of judging in this country not only for amateur growers who grow orchids as a hobby, but also for commercial growers whose energy and time is directed toward creating finer hybrids that, if judged to be superior plants by receiving an award, would be the parents of crosses resulting in even better orchids for the future.

The first judging in the United States took place in New York City. Since many growers were not able to send their flowers or plants from the far reaches of the country with any assurance that they would arrive in suitable condition, the Trustees of the Society chose to establish Regional Judging Centers throughout the country so that such persons might compete for the Society's awards.

The Orchid Digest Corporation, which publishes *Orchid Digest,* an outstanding monthly informational orchid journal, was formed in southern California, and it, too, set up centers where judging might take place, particularly in the western part of the United States. As the American Orchid Society expanded its Regional Judging Centers, the Orchid Digest Corporation integrated its judging with that of the society, and only one judging system now operates throughout the country.

Training New Judges

From the beginning the American Orchid Society realized that the original judges, who had acquired a vast amount of knowledge through countless years of growing orchids, would one day have to give way to others. Therefore, a system of standards for judging orchid plants and flowers was established as well as guidelines for conducting the various exhibitions and shows at which the society's awards would be made. A program was also instituted for the training of judges.

The American Orchid Society, through its officers and trustees, evaluates a prospective judge on his knowledge of orchids; his ability to judge fairly, objectively, and without personal prejudice; his willingness to travel and participate in the judging activities of areas other than that in which he resides; and his ability at all times to conduct himself with unquestioned integrity.

A program designed to train student judges through a rigorous training and probationary period was also put into effect. So before a judge is accredited, he has accumulated years of experience and undergone rigorous training. One can, accordingly, accept with confidence the judgments of those who bestow the society's awards.

A prodigious amount of work also went into the *Handbook of Judging and Exhibitions,* first published by the American Orchid Society in 1949, which has had several subsequent revisions. It serves as a valuable guide for all who wish to exhibit orchids.

THE AWARDS

The society grants its awards to individuals, to plants, to groups of plants, and to cut flowers. A point scale based upon a total of 100 has been devised by which an orchid is evaluated with regard to the form of the flower, its color, and other characteristics such as size, substance, texture, arrangement of the flowers, and the plant's floriferousness (degree of flower bearing in relation to the normal).

These awards, in the form of certificates, are granted only by the American Orchid Society's judges at show tables of the society or at shows given by the society, at regional and international orchid congresses and conferences, at regional and supplemental regional monthly judgings, at recognized shows of affiliated societies, and at established major public flower and orchid shows.

Two medals are also currently awarded: the Gold Medal of Achievement (GMA), bestowed upon individuals in recognition of distinguished work in orchid culture or scientific research on orchids and for outstanding services to the society; and the Silver Medal of Merit (SMM), which is

awarded to individuals in recognition of outstanding service to the society or for some major contribution to the orchid world. Currently, there are also fourteen certificates awarded:

Gold Medal Certificate. For a score of 91 points or over

Silver Medal Certificate. For a score of 86 to 90 points

Bronze Medal Certificate. For a score of 80 to 85 points

Bronze Medal Certificate for a Meritorious Educational Exhibit (B.M.C.). Awarded for outstanding excellence based upon a score of 90 points or over

Bronze Medal Certificate for a Meritorious Flower Arrangement (B.M.C.). Awarded in the Flower Arrangement Class

Bronze Medal Certificate for a Meritorious Display of Orchids in in Use (B.M.C.). Awarded to an exhibition—either amateur, commercial, or by a professional florist—not less than 25 square feet and judged outstanding

First Class Certificate (F.C.C.). Awarded to an orchid species or hybrid of outstanding excellence that scores 90 points or over

Award of Merit (A.M.). Awarded to an orchid species or hybrid of outstanding excellence that scores at least 80 points but less than 90

Highly Commended Certificate (H.C.C.). Awarded to an orchid species or hybrid of unusual distinctiveness that scores less than 80 points but not less than 75

Judges' Commendation (J.C.). Awarded to orchid plants or flowers, either individually or in groups, that have some notable quality the judges are unable to score

Award of Distinction (A.D.). Given just once to a cross that represents a new direction in breeding—granted without scoring and by the unanimous decision of the judges

Award of Quality (A.Q.). Given once to a cross, exhibited as a group of not less than 12 plants or their flowers, of a raised species or hybrid that may or may not have been made before, when the result shows sufficient improvement over the former type

337   *Certificate of Cultural Merit (C.C.M.).* Awarded to a

specimen plant of robust health that has an unusually large number of flowers and that has scored 80 points or over

Certificate of Botanical Merit (C.B.M.). Awarded only to well-grown plants of uncommon species that, by possessing one or more outstanding characteristics or one or more characteristics in outstanding degree, represent a worthy new concept of horticultural desirability. (This award may be granted more than once to the same species, provided different clones have significantly different characteristics.)

Show Trophy for the Most Outstanding Orchid Exhibit. Awarded with the intention of encouraging the improvement of the standards of exhibits at annual shows of domestic affiliated societies.

Show Trophy Certificate for the Most Outstanding Orchid Exhibit. Awarded with the intention of encouraging the improvement of the standards of exhibits; made available to the annual shows of affiliated societies outside the United States upon request.

Award-winning plants proudly display after their names their awards and the names of the societies that bestowed the awards. Thus the Award of Merit by the Royal Horticultural Society is indicated by the initials AM/RHS, and the Award of Merit of the American Orchid Society, by AM/AOS.

Officially Recognized Awarding Societies

The following is a list (courtesy of the American Orchid Society) of the leading orchid societies that bestow awards and whose initials may appear after a designated award:

AOC	Australian Orchid Council
AOS	American Orchid Society
CFOS	Central Florida Orchid Society
CSA	Cymbidium Society of America
DOG	Deutsche Orchideen Gesellschaft (German Orchid Society)
HOS	Honolulu Orchid Society
JOS	Japan Orchid Society
KOS	Kenya Orchid Society

MNEOS	Manchester and North of England Orchid Society
MOS	Malayan Orchid Society—now the Orchid Society of Southeast Asia (OSSEA)
NOOS	New Orleans Orchid Society
NSW	Orchid Society of New South Wales [Australia]
NZOS	New Zealand Orchid Society
OCNZ	Orchid Council of New Zealand
OCSA	Orchid Council of South Australia
ODC	Orchid Digest Corporation
OOG	Osterreichischen Orchideen Gesellschaft (Austrian Orchid Society)
OSGB	Orchid Society of Great Britain
OSSA	Orchid Society of South Africa
OSSC	Orchid Society of Southern California
OSSEA	Orchid Society of Southeast Asia (formerly the Malayan Orchid Society)
OST	Orchid Society of Thailand
OSWA	Orchid Society of Western Australia
QOS	Queensland Orchid Society [Australia]
RHS	Royal Horticultural Society [Great Britain]
RHT	Royal Horticultural Society of Thailand
SAOC	South African Orchid Council
SFO	Société Française d'Orchidophile (French Orchid Society)
SFOS	South Florida Orchid Society
SOG	Schweizerischen Orchideen Gesellschaft (Swiss Orchid Society)
STOCQ	Sub-Tropical Orchid Society of Queensland [Australia]
TASM	Tasmanian Orchid Society [Australia]
TOS	Taiwan Orchid Society
VIC	Victorian Orchid Club [Australia]

339   The system of awards contributes to excellence in the

If You Want to Exhibit   growing and culture of orchids, gives a standard by which other orchids can be judged, helps the average grower assess his own plants, provides the opportunity for invaluable contact with knowledgable orchidists who prove eager and willing to share their experiences, and, above all, maintains or, if possible, improves the high standards toward which all orchid growers strive.

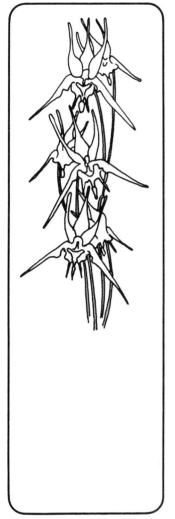

A Calendar of Seasonal Activities

Growing orchids should be a leisurely undertaking, with plenty of time for enjoyment of the plants. If some time is spent with them each day, so far as possible, and the activities appropriate to the season are attended to as needed, the plants will prosper and the grower need never experience the nerve-wracking attempts to cope with the vagaries of nature that those who grow garden flowers outdoors constantly experience. Serenity is an integral part of growing orchids and serendipity is a beneficial result.

To simplify orchid culture, this résumé of orchid activities is presented for quick seasonal reference. (For more detailed culture, refer to the earlier chapters.) It begins with the spring months, since this is the time when the days

CHAPTER 16

lengthen, the sun becomes warmer, and plant growth quickens. It is the beginning of the plant year.

Heat is still needed in the greenhouse well into May, and sometimes into June. However, even in March, if the greenhouse is closed and the blinds are raised by three o'clock in the afternoon, the sun's heat can continue to warm the interior and delay the start of the heating system until early evening.

MARCH

With the sun's rays increasing in intensity, resulting in greater warmth and longer days, the orchids will become dry much more quickly now than during the winter. Thus, there is a need for more frequent watering and misting. Root action increases, and to avoid burning the foliage some shading is necessary. Without automatic blinds a greenhouse in full sun may need frequent raising and lowering of the shades as the sun and the clouds plan an in-and-out game.

Slugs and snails now come out of hiding. Check each plant carefully to keep scale insects and mealybugs under control. Open greenhouse ventilators will mean you should give some thought to visits by bees and wasps. To prevent their fertilizing the flowers, which results in the flowers' collapse shortly thereafter, place swabs of cotton on the flowers' lips to discourage the pests.

Repotting is the main activity of this and the next few months.

Cattleyas

These begin to show signs of benefiting from the longer hours of sunlight and higher temperatures, for they love the warmth and bright light of spring. Many of the plants that flowered during the winter and then rested are now developing new roots from last year's pseudobulbs.

Plants that are still flowering should be placed where they will be out of the sun to keep the flowers in good condition longer, and those that are still forming buds will need more water than the others. In all cases, though, the potting material should still dry out between waterings so that the new roots can work their way into the potting material and thus grow both longer and stronger.

If any of the plants need repotting, do so now when the new growths and roots are just beginning. If potting

342

is done at this time of year, the plants suffer little or no setback.

Paphiopedilums

March brings to an end the flowering of many of the lady's slippers, making this the time to repot and divide them before the roots grow too long. But keep in mind that well-established plants in good condition always produce the best flowers. At the same time, carefully check for signs of basal decay.

Light that is too strong always causes some deterioration of these plants, necessitating an increasing amount of shade as the days become brighter and longer. They also need more frequent watering, perhaps as often as every three or four days—or seven to eight days during periods of cloudy, damp weather.

Cymbidiums

March could easily be called cymbidium month. This is when the majority of the plants flower. As the flower spikes fade, remove them promptly.

Keep the temperature low at night to assure the continued good growth and lasting qualities of the flowers. If the temperature rises too high at night, it will contribute to a softening of the foliage, which makes it more susceptible to disease. Bud drop may also occur on those plants whose buds have not opened.

Plants still developing spikes need an abundance of light, but never hot sunlight, and those in full bloom need more water to sustain their flower spikes and to prevent the pseudobulbs from shriveling. Never let cymbidiums dry out.

Odontoglossums

As indicated earlier, these orchids must never be allowed to become dry. They continue to need frequent watering along with cool, moist growing conditions. Sufficient shade goes a long way toward keeping them healthy and growing well.

Early morning sunlight is best. Bright sun bleaches the foliage and may cause the leaves to fall prematurely. Keep odontoglossums medium green.

April is a fickle month with regard to weather, with great fluctuations in both temperature and sunshine. With April somewhat warmer than March, the plants show an even greater increase in growth, for growing conditions are approaching their best.

Any repotting needed should be done promptly, and shading should be increased. In fact, some shade will always be necessary during the hours when the sun is brightest, for new growths are soft and easily damaged. Ventilation should also be increased.

Cattleyas

These now need shade from ten to two o'clock each sunny day, for cattleyas are now entering their peak growing period, which will last for the next six months.

Leaves and pseudobulbs need misting once a day, more often on warm ones.

Paphiopedilums

Growing conditions for these should remain as nearly constant as possible throughout the year. Keep them moist but not soggy, never allowing them to dry out. Grow in semishade with filtered sunlight.

Cymbidiums

Many have finished flowering and are now beginning active growth. Those in need of repotting should be attended to as soon as possible. Some may only need to be top-dressed with fresh potting material. Keep them well watered and do not allow them to dry out.

Try to keep the temperature as near 60°F (15°C) as possible. From now to the end of August feed with a fertilizer high in nitrogen, such as 30–10–10, as often as once a week. Some growers like to feed their cymbidiums with a dilute solution of a water soluble fertilizer every time they water during the summer. Water them copiously and give each plant enough room so that the leaves do not touch.

Phalaenopsis

Many are now in full bloom, some are about to bloom, and others have finished. It is quite possible to have these lovely flowers all through the year if they are given ample food, sufficient water, and enough filtered light. When old flower spikes are cut off, a new spike often develops from one of the remaining nodes on the stems.

After this second spike flowers, however, the plant should not be allowed to develop a third. Too much flowering weakens the plants. Instead, concentrate upon building the plants' strength for the next flowering season.

Phalaenopsis need a short rest after flowering. Repotting should be delayed until new growths develop.

Dendrobiums

Dendrobiums now begin to show signs of new growth. If any need repotting, do it now. Repotted plants should be kept somewhat dry until new roots appear, then kept well watered. Shade only during the hottest part of the day.

Odontoglossums

Repotting must be completed this month if the plants are to be established before the arrival of the hot summer.

Species and Botanicals

All such plants should be checked over carefully. If any need repotting, get it done before the warm weather arrives, for they, too, like a long period in which to grow and store up energy for the winter.

MAY

Spring is now well advanced, and all orchids will show an increase in growth activity. Plants repotted earlier will now be rooting freely and need more water. During May the sun's rays are sometimes brighter than at any other time of the year. Scorching of the leaves may occur if plants are not shaded, yet the days should not be shortened by shading for too long a time. The purpose of shading is merely to filter out the hot, burning rays of the sun.

Cattleyas

Those recently repotted are now sending up new growths and roots. Some may even be developing sheaths or beginning to show buds. All will dry out faster now and need more frequent watering and misting.

345

Paphiopedilums

Continue to keep lady's slippers both moist and cool. When the days are warm, they will need to be watered more often. Their new roots are really growing now. From now on they also need more shade. Remember, these are terrestrial orchids. In their native habitat they grow on the ground, beneath tall trees and seldom see direct sunlight.

Cymbidiums

Before the end of the month older plants that need repotting should be taken care of. Those recently repotted should now be well rooted and need to be kept moist. When you water, do it thoroughly. Misting the foliage several times a day during bright, sunny spells keeps it healthy.

At this time cymbidiums need shade and cool, moist growing conditions.

Dendrobiums

Finish potting all dendrobiums that are through flowering.

Vandas

This group can now be repotted or topped with new growing material and grown outdoors for the summer.

Oncidiums

While flowering, oncidiums need no extra care beyond careful watering. One way to keep the pseudobulbs from shriveling is to cut off the flower spikes on plants not strong enough to bear flowers. After the new growths develop, any plants that need it can be repotted.

JUNE

June brings the beginning of summer in the Northern Hemisphere. The weather is usually mild. At times it can be quite warm, and there is generally none of the haze that often cuts down the glare of the sun later on in July.

The days also reach their maximum length this month, and the combination of longer hours of light and the clear atmosphere calls for special attention to shading, ventilation, watering, and misting. This month brings ideal growing conditions for all warm-growing orchids.

June nights are often warm and humid. So plants in greenhouses benefit from having both doors and ventilators open all night, and these cool, moist night conditions do much toward keeping the plants in good health.

Early morning and late afternoon sunlight, with some shade during the middle of the day, give the plants the light they need without burning. They also need to be fed more frequently than during the winter and require more water. Greenhouses should be damped down early in the morning, at noon, and again at midafternoon to maintain humidity. Frequent misting may also be needed to keep the plants cool and fans should be set in place for use when necessary.

June is also the month when orchids are put outside for the summer and it is the time to give the greenhouse a thorough cleaning. Check the heater, wash the pots, clean the tools, and order any supplies that will be needed.

If you are fortunate enough to have an air-conditioned greenhouse or evaporative coolers, there will be no problem maintaining ideal growing conditions throughout the summer.

Cattleyas

Although cattleyas are sun-loving orchids, they will need more shade this month and the next than at any other time of the year. The plants should never be misted any later than the middle of the afternoon. If necessary, use fans to keep good circulation of air in the greenhouse.

Paphiopedilums

Their roots are now growing well. The plants must be kept both moist and cool.

Cymbidiums

They grow vigorously from now until about the middle of August. Since they need plenty of fresh air, they prefer growing outdoors during the summer. Give them as much sunlight as they can stand without burning their foliage. The more water they receive, either from rain or pot watering, the more food they need.

Dendrobiums

Shade, warmth, and a moist atmosphere are needed until their pseudobulbs are fully formed later on in the summer.

Odontoglossums

Unless air conditioning is available, they are not going to enjoy the warm weather at all. Keep them as shaded and as cool as possible, using fans, if necessary, to cool and circulate the air around them. Whether grown as house plants indoors or in a greenhouse, opening the windows or ventilators wide on hot days just lets in warm air. Close the windows during the day and open them at night. In the greenhouse, keep odontoglossums where it is coolest and where they can get the full benefit of any fans used for cooling.

JULY

In most areas July is the warmest month of the year as well as the sunniest. Summer heat necessitates more frequent misting, watering, ventilating, and shading. In fact, on bright days three or four mistings are not excessive, as long as the leaves have a chance to dry off before nightfall.

Warm weather also encourages insects, and a regular schedule of spraying with an appropriate insecticide should be maintained.

Shading continues to be needed, as rapid growth still is being made and growths have not yet hardened. Of course, location governs the amount of shading needed. Plants in a northern or eastern exposure need less shade than those growing in a southern or western one.

Orchids need all the air they can get this month, and it may take a little ingenuity to provide the cool, moist conditions some of the plants need.

Cattleyas

July is a great growing month for cattleyas. If their flower buds are developing, the plants will need even more water. Even though cattleyas like more light than most orchids, they must be shaded when the sun is hot, and they need frequent mistings to keep the pseudobulbs plump.

In a greenhouse the night temperature should still always be lower than the day temperature. However, the combination of shading and abundant water can cause rotting of both the roots and growths or, at the least, cause soft growths that will be too lush and soft to bear flowers. So be careful.

Paphiopedilums

These continue making new growths and should be kept both moist and shaded. Although lady's slippers can be misted on hot days, they have a tendency to retain water in the axils of their leaves, which causes basal rot. If this happens, use a cotton swab to remove any excess water.

Cymbidiums

They still will require shade and copious amounts of water, as well as misting on warm, sunny days. The undersides of the leaves should be misted as well. Notice that they are always fresher and greener in the morning after a night of cool, moist air.

Phalaenopsis

Because these orchids come from the hot areas of Asia, they like warm weather and tolerate summer warmth very well. However, they neither like nor need strong light. They do love humidity and should be watered often enough so that the potting material never becomes dry.

Dendrobiums

Growth is rapid this month. They need only enough shade to prevent their leaves from becoming scorched. When the terminal leaf appears, decrease the amount of water they are receiving but give them enough water to keep their pseudobulbs from shriveling. Misting helps to keep them fresh.

Miltonias

Miltonias can safely be repotted if necessary. They do not seem to mind being disturbed in warm weather. But they should be kept shaded and moist and be given as much fresh air as possible. The Colombian group will need more shade than the Brazilians, but to be safe keep both kinds shaded from the hot sun.

Odontoglossums

Keep them as cool and moist as possible and mist the leaves frequently. Leafless pseudobulbs are the result of their being too dry during the summer.

Shade early in the morning to counteract the rise in temperature. If repotting has not been completed, hold off until cooler weather. They then will have a better opportunity to develop new roots and growths.

Phaius

These orchids make great garden plants, if grown in a shady place. They need plenty of water and should be fed once a month.

AUGUST

With the arrival of August you begin to realize that summer is passing. There are still many days of heat and humidity, but the days themselves are shorter and the nights longer and cooler. The majority of plants are now maturing at a fast rate. Although they still need shading, let them gradually have more sunlight so that the pseudobulbs and foliage can harden before winter. There are still times when the sun can be hot enough to cause leaf burning.

Misting and watering should be done less frequently so that the plants can become somewhat drier between waterings. Plants that have flowered during the past few months should be repotted now so that they will still have some warm weather in which to make new growths.

Cattleyas

The time for repotting cattleyas is fast coming to an end. Cattleyas now need somewhat less water than during the previous months, because the sun is nowhere near as bright or as hot. Give them longer hours of direct sun.

Paphiopedilums

Most of these have completed their growing cycle, and the flower buds are beginning to form on the earlier varieties. As buds begin to form, the plants need a little more water. Continue to keep them shaded, except for some filtered early morning sunlight. They will continue to need cool, moist, shady growing conditions to protect the still-tender new foliage.

Cymbidiums

Many of the earlier-flowering varieties have completed their growth and will shortly develop flower spikes. On the later varieties, the bases of the new growths are beginning to fill out and will soon be followed by the firming and hardening of the pseudobulbs.

Give them more light from now on to ripen the growths. Without this ripening process there would be no flowers. Watch the color of the leaves closely. If they become too yellow, the plants are getting too much light.

Cymbidiums continue to need plenty of moisture at their roots and on their leaves until near the end of the month. From the middle of August on, they should be fed with a high-phosphorus fertilizer, such as 10–30–20, to put a brake on vegetative growth and to initiate flower buds.

Now the night temperatures are a good 20°F cooler than during the day. This temperature differential is important for good flowering later on.

Phalaenopsis

An abundance of water, filtered light, and fresh air continue to be needed. Any time the plants become dry they tend to lose their basal leaves, and since these leaves are their only means of storing water, the loss can be disastrous.

Dendrobiums

A brisk, warm atmosphere helps them continue making rapid growth. The amount of light should be increased gradually so that by the end of the month they are shaded only during the hottest part of the day. Continue to water thoroughly and mist frequently.

SEPTEMBER

With the passing of August we are now moving toward autumnal conditions. September is the halfway mark between the longest days of June and the shortest days of December. Even though there may still be periods of warm weather during the day, the nights are longer and cooler. This means that the culture the orchids have been receiving during the past few months needs to be modified. With fewer hours of sunlight, the plants do not dry out as quickly and therefore do not need to be watered as frequently, nor do they need as much misting or shade.

The process of hardening or ripening of the mature growths is begun this month by gradually increasing the amount of light the plants are given. This increase must be gradual, for a sudden flood of light would retard the growths instead of hardening them. On dull days, misting should be dispensed with.

Some though should also be given to bringing the plants now outdoors back inside before any signs of frost.

Check over each plant carefully, wash the pots, sponge off the leaves, remove weeds from the potting material, and give the plants a good spraying with an insecticide such as malathion before they are brought in.

Cattleyas

Now is the time that the new growths made during the summer should be ripened, for it is the well-ripened growths that produce the best flowers.

Once the plants are back indoors, they will need plenty of fresh air until they adjust to the new growing conditions.

Cattleyas flowering at this time still need shade to help the flowers last.

Water all cattleyas whenever the potting material becomes almost dry. Pseudobulbs and leaves should be misted on bright, sunny days to keep them plump and healthy.

The importance of light this month cannot be overstressed. The strongest growth is always attained with the greatest amount of light the plants can safely tolerate. Too much strong light too suddenly will cause the leaves on the pseudobulbs that are farthest back on the plant to become shriveled and even to fall off. All potting should be finished. Late potting never is good for cattleyas.

Paphiopedilums

From now until well into the spring, these should flower profusely. They should be kept moist, for any dryness at the roots leads to short stems and small, hard flowers. The flowers should also be staked.

Cymbidiums

The amount of light should be increased gradually to make the bulbs firm before winter. This is one of the best ways to get good flower spikes. Some shading is still needed on hot, bright days, but as the month moves along, even that can be eliminated.

They should be kept drier but never allowed to become completely dry. This is the *one* time of the year that—for a few weeks—cymbidiums should not be given copious watering.

Dendrobiums

By now most of their growth should be nearly complete, although not always completely developed. But just because the terminal leaf appears it does not mean the resting period for the deciduous kinds must begin. Some plants still have a lot of growing to do. If they are moved to a cooler place and dried off too quickly the newly formed pseudobulbs will never have a chance to develop properly.

High temperatures and high humidity are needed to develop strong pseudobulbs. At no time during their active growing should they become dry, and plants that have not yet formed their terminal leaves should continue to be watered freely.

The deciduous dendrobiums—not the evergreen kinds—have their resting period in the fall. For this the night temperatures should be somewhat lower and watering reduced to one-half the usual amount.

To avoid confusion, water all dendrobiums as they begin to show their terminal leaves. When the pseudobulbs have matured, the amount of water can then be reduced even further for a while.

Odontoglossums

Since summer heat is now a thing of the past and the days are shorter, these plants can now be repotted if necessary. They respond rapidly to the cool, crisp days of autumn.

Odontoglossums should always be kept as cool as possible and the pseudobulbs misted as often as necessary to keep them from shriveling. They need only filtered light.

OCTOBER

Autumn is now in full swing, good growing conditions are fast drawing to a close, and we now have several months when there may be quick changes from warm, sunny days to prolonged periods of cool, cloudy days.

The frequency with which the plants are watered is reduced this month as are also temperatures and humidity.

Plants need just enough shade to prevent the foliage from burning. The leaves on wholly or partly deciduous plants may turn yellow and fall off. It is only when new growth turns yellow and drops off that we should become concerned.

Cattleyas

Toward the end of the month cattleyas should be getting all the sun they can tolerate. Overwatering at this time kills more cattleyas than anything else.

Very little, if any, repotting should be done after the middle of the month. Try to maintain a fresh and buoyant atmosphere.

Paphiopedilums

While these plants are flowering, they must always be kept moist. The atmosphere around them should be kept cool, yet comfortable. Dead leaves should be cut off promptly to prevent rot from getting a start, and the leaves should be wiped gently once in a while if dust accumulates on them. Plants cannot breathe if the pores on their leaves are clogged.

Cymbidiums

Most now have completed their growth. On some the flower spikes are beginning to emerge. From now on stop misting the foliage except on bright, sunny days. Once the flower spikes develop, the plants should have an abundance of water at the roots but be allowed to dry out somewhat before being watered again.

By the end of the month cymbidiums should be able to receive full sunlight without shading, and the plants should now be placed where you expect to keep them through the winter. The flower stems will develop much better this way, for they will always be facing the light from the same direction.

Dendrobiums

Their growth should be completed by now, and they can be moved to a cooler location where they will have an abundance of light and air. Give them just enough water to keep the newest pseudobulbs from shriveling until the flower nodules appear.

NOVEMBER

There are those who consider November the dullest month of the year. Yet it does not have to be—with a greenhouse full of orchids. Shading should be removed from most plants and will not be needed again until February. For the next three or four months the plants should receive all the sunlight possible.

At this time they need less water and should only be watered on bright, sunny days between ten in the morning and two in the afternoon. This allows the foliage to dry off before night.

There should be no further potting now until the spring.

Cattleyas

Growth is at a standstill, making it doubly important that plants dry out before being watered again. Misting on sunny days will help keep the pseudobulbs from shriveling.

If the pseudobulbs do begin to shrivel, it is not a sign they need more water, just a moister atmosphere. The one exception is that plants that are flowering will need more water, but when they have finished flowering, watering should again be reduced.

Paphiopedilums

As their buds open, the flower stems should be held erect with stakes. While the flower buds are developing and the plants are flowering, they should never become dry. The flowers should last for several months and provide a welcome display during the holidays.

Cymbidiums

From now until the spring, cymbidiums are at their best. Some are flowering, while others are still developing their spikes to bloom during winter's dullest days.

Those flowering must never dry out. Be sure to stake the spikes so they do not break from the weight of the flowers.

Keep the atmosphere moist and well ventilated.

Dendrobiums

The nobile type should have as much air as possible. To ripen their pseudobulbs, watering should now be gradually reduced.

DECEMBER

For almost everyone, poinsettias, holly, and mistletoe symbolize Christmas. To the orchid grower it is these—plus cattleyas, paphiopedilums, cymbidiums, and early-flowering odontoglossums.

Days are short and sunlight less than at any other time of the year. Most orchids need all the light they can get at this time. Thus, shading can for the most part be dispensed with. The growths will continue to harden and the plants to become sturdy and better able to get through the next few months.

Be sure that on cold nights the plants are not too close to the window glass. Continue to guard against overwatering. Look over the plants carefully before you water.

A word of caution about humidity: at this time, artificial heat tends to dry the atmosphere; and sunny days do the same thing. If necessary, damp down the greenhouse floor early in the day or place dishes of water among those plants growing indoors.

The temperature the day should not rise too high before you let in some air.

This is a season to sit back and enjoy your flowers. For the orchid grower this season brings the culmination of the work done during the spring, summer, and fall.

Cattleyas

As far as root action is concerned many cattleyas are now in a holding or resting period. They should not be rushed into making premature growth by being kept too warm. Before watering, pick up the pots to see whether they need water, but do not go to the other extreme and give them so little that the dormant eye becomes dry and perhaps dies off. Keep pseudobulbs and leaves as plump as possible by misting on sunny days or raising the humidity.

Paphiopedilums

The mottled-leaved varieties need slightly higher temperatures during the day than the plain ones.

Even at this time of year, lady's slippers should be shaded from the sun, and the atmosphere around them should be kept always moist and comfortable.

Cymbidiums

Stake the flower spikes as they develop. Give as much air as possible during the middle of the day, but continue to keep them cool and moist. Keep them well watered so that the pseudobulbs do not shrivel. From mid-December to March switch to a balanced fertilizer such as 18–18–18 or 20–20–20.

Phalaenopsis

These are now in full growth. Many are showing their flower spikes and should be staked. Soon they, too, will be in flower and should provide a display well into the summer.

Dendrobiums

The leaves should be kept free of dust. They need very little water this month, and the temperature should be lower. For the deciduous types, dormancy will gradually set in, and then they will need to be kept cool and dry.

Miltonias

The new growth should now be showing good root activity. Do not let them dry out.

Odontoglossums

By now these cool-loving orchids have had a chance to regain their strength and vigor. Keep them moist and do *357* not let them become dry.

JANUARY

Cattleyas

This month there is little root activity among the mature plants. Those that are flowering should be kept moist and out of the direct sunlight so that the flowers last longer.

Cattleyas that have completed their flowering should be kept on the dry side until their normal growing period begins in spring. They should not be overwatered. Go over each plant and remove the dried skin on the pseudobulbs, which is a favorite haven for scale, but be careful that you do not injure the eye at the base of the pseudobulb.

The night temperature should always be 10°F or so lower than during the day.

Paphiopedilums

Many are still flowering. Always keep them moist, for they should not dry out between waterings, as do cattleyas. Avoid misting; they do not need it now. Do not let the temperature get too warm.

If any early-flowering varieties have finished blooming and the potting material is in poor condition or the plant overcrowded, repot.

Cymbidiums

These revel in the cool, moist temperatures so easy to provide at this time. They are still flowering and should continue to do so for several more months. However, the early-flowering varieties, which end their flowering this month, should be allowed to rest. They need less water. A daily misting of the pseudobulbs and foliage to prevent dehydration is enough.

FEBRUARY

For the orchid grower the year comes to a close with February. The days are beginning to lengthen, and the heat of the sun is gradually becoming stronger. Yet we are still in the middle of winter.

The foliage is still soft after the dull days, and the increase in sunlight should help to strengthen it.

Shading should, once again, be gradually increased toward the middle of the month and always during the middle of the day. Remember that orchids can be burned by the sun when there is not enough fresh air to temper the atmosphere and the humidity is dangerously low.

Cattleyas

These are beginning to show signs of benefiting from the greater sunlight and warmer conditions. Keep the atmosphere buoyant by ventilating on warm days, at least for a short time during the middle of the day.

Root action is becoming more noticeable, and the plants therefore need more frequent watering. Also, keep the plants misted.

Paphiopedilums

We have been enjoying their flowers since December, and although many are still blooming and a few are yet to flower, do not get into the habit of taking them for granted. They never tolerate neglect.

Keep them shaded, moist, and comfortable. After they have been repotted, they should be shaded a little more and given less water until their new growths start.

Cymbidiums

Since these are still flowering, they need an increased amount of water to sustain the flower spikes and prevent their shriveling.

Those that are flowering—and this means the majority of the plants—need some shade to protect the flowers from bright sunlight. Continue keeping them cool and comfortable, and increase the amount of fresh air.

Dendrobiums

The deciduous types, which have been resting, will now begin to show their flower nodes. Therefore, they will now need more water and fresh air.

Root action is also starting and by the end of the month will be quite noticeable.

In many areas of the country flower showtime is at hand, and sometimes Nature does not cooperate by providing flowers when they are needed. By lowering the temperature somewhat both during the day and at night you can delay the opening of the buds. Once the buds have opened, the temperature should never be kept too low as this will reduce the size of the flowers and even cause their crippling. Once the flowers have fully opened, their life can be prolonged by keeping the plants at a temperature of 52°F (11°C).

It has often been said that orchid growers never grow old. Perhaps this is because in growing orchids each day brings so much pleasure. There is always something to look forward to to make each day one of adventure, joy, and fulfillment.

Happy orchid growing for many years to come.

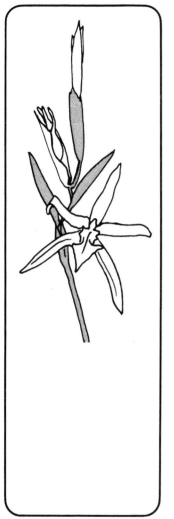

APPENDIX

Rod McLellan Co.
    1450 El Camino Real
    South San Francisco, Calif. 94080

Sea God Nurseries
    Box 6
    Hollywood, Calif. 90028

DeRosa Orchids
    212 West Central St.
    Natick, Mass. 01760

**SOURCES OF
PLANTS AND
SUPPLIES**

Fennell Orchid Co.
    26715 S.W. 157th Ave.
    Homestead, Fla. 33031

Alberts & Merkel Bros., Inc.
          2210 South Federal Highway
          Boynton Beach, Fla. 33435

          Black River Orchids, Inc.
          P.O. Box 110, 77th St.
          South Haven, Mich. 49090

          Fred A. Stewart Orchids, Inc.
          1212 East Las Tunas Drive
          San Gabriel, Calif. 91778

          The Quiedan Co.
          Box 4873
          Carmel, Calif. 93921

          Adelaide Orchids
          Box 1, O'Halloran Hall
          South Australia 5158

          Brighton Farms
          Poplar and Shore Roads
          Linwood, N.J. 08221

          Westinghouse Electric Corp.
          Lamps Division, 1 Westinghouse Plaza
          Bloomfield, N.J. 07003

          GTE Sylvania
          100 Endicott St.
          Danvers, Mass. 01923

          Lord and Burnham
          2 Main St.
          Irvington, N.Y. 10533

          Homasassa Springs Orchids
          P.O. Box 8
          Homasassa Springs, Fla. 32647

          G&S Laboratories
          645 Stoddard Lane
          Santa Barbara, Calif. 93103

          Faire Harbour Boats
          44 Captain Pierce Rd.
          Scituate, Mass. 02066

          Armacost and Royston of Santa Barbara, Inc.
          3376 Foothill Rd.
Carpinteria, Calif. 93013

Everglade Orchids
$75\frac{1}{2}$ Southeast Ave. F
Belle Glade, Fla. 33430

Automatic Sunblind Installations
98 Rushes Rd.
Petersfield, Hants., England

Finck Floral Co.
9849 A Kimber Lane
St. Louis, Mo. 63127

Jones and Scully, Inc.
2200 N.W. 33rd Ave.
Miami, Fla. 33142

Vacherot & Lecoufle
"La Tuilerie"
30, Rue de Valenton, B.P. No. 8
94470 Boissy St. Leger, France

Shaffer's Tropical Gardens, Inc.
1220 41st Ave.
Capitola, Calif. 95010

Standard Engineering
281 Roosevelt Avenue
Pawtucket, R.I. 02860

S and G Exotic Plant Co.
22 Goldsmith Ave.
Beverly, Mass. 01915

ORCHID PERIODICALS

American Orchid Society Bulletin
Botanic Museum
Harvard University
Cambridge, Mass. 02138

Orchid Review
462 Chaldon Common Road
Caterham, Surrey C R 35 DD England

Orchid Digest
Mrs. Forrest A. Slack, Secretary
25 Ash Ave.
Corte Madera, Calif. 94925

APPENDIX   *Australian Orchid Review*
P.O. Box M 60, Sydney Mail Exchange
N.S.W. Australia 2012

In almost every state in the United States as well as in most other countries there are orchid societies, many of which are affiliated with the American Orchid Society and that publish interesting and informative newsletters and magazines that are a welcome addition to the library of every orchid grower.

INDEX

365

367

369

370